FOUCAULT AND HIS INTERLOCUTORS

FOUCAULT

AND HIS INTERLOCUTORS

edited and introduced by
Arnold I. Davidson

THE UNIVERSITY OF CHICAGO PRESS
Chicago & London

The University of Chicago Press, Chicago 60637
The University of Chicago Press, Ltd., London

01 00 99 98 97   5 4 3 2 1

"Report from Mr. Canguilhem on the Manuscript Filed by Mr. Michel Foucault, Director of the Institute Français of Hamburg, in Order to Obtain Permission to print His Principal Thesis for the Doctor of Letters" is reprinted with kind permission from Georges Canguilhem. English translation © 1995 by The University of Chicago.

"On *Histoire de la folie* as an Event" is © *Le Débat,* 1992. Used with kind permission from Pierre Nora, Éditions Gallimard. English translation © 1995 by The University of Chicago.

"Introduction to *Penser la folie: Essais sur Michel Foucault*" is © 1992 by Éditions Galilée. Used with permission. English translation © 1995 by The University of Chicago.

"The Geometry of the Incommunicable: Madness" is © 1968 by Les Éditions De Minuit, from *Hermes ou la communication.* Used with permission. English translation © 1996 by The University of Chicago.

"'To Do Justice to Freud': The History of Madness in the Age of Psychoanalysis" is © 1994 by Éditions Galilée. Reprinted with permission.

"Madness, the Absence of Work" is used with permission from The New Press, New York. English translation © 1994 by The University of Chicago.

"Human Nature: Justice versus Power" originally appeared in *Reflexive Water,* edited by Fons Elders, © 1974 by Fons Elders. Reprinted with permission from Fons Elders and Souvenir Press, Ltd.

"Foucault Revolutionizes History" is © 1971 by Éditions du Seuil, from *Writing History* by Paul Veyne, English translation © 1984 by Wesleyan University Press. Appendix translated from the original French edition and © by The University of Chicago. Permission granted by the University Press of New England.

"Desire and Pleasure" first appeared in *Magazine litteraire,* no. 325 (October 1994) as "Désir et plaisir." Used with permission from Gilles Deleuze. English translation © 1997 by The University of Chicago.

"Forms of Life and Forms of Discourse in Ancient Philosophy" is used with permission from Pierre Hadot. English translation © 1990 by The University of Chicago.

"The Final Foucault and His Ethics" is used with kind permission from Paul Veyne. English translation © 1993 by The University of Chicago Press.

"Writing the Self" originally appeared in *Corps écrit,* no. 5 (1983), and is © 1983 by Presses Universitaires de France. Used with permission. English translation © 1997 by The University of Chicago.

Library of Congress Cataloging in Publication Data
Foucault and his interlocutors / edited by Arnold I. Davidson.
      p.   cm.
   Includes bibliographical references and index.
   ISBN 0-226-13713-9 (cloth).—ISBN 0-226-13714-7 (pbk)
   1. Foucault, Michel.   2. Chomsky, Noam.   3. Philosophy.
I. Davidson, Arnold Ira.
B2430.F72F68   1997
194—dc21   97-50315
                                             CIP

To Stanley and Cathleen Cavell

and

To Pierre and Ilsetraut Hadot

Contents

III. FOUCAULT AND THE ANCIENTS

Structures and Strategies of Discourse: Remarks Towards a History of Foucault's Philosophy of Language

Arnold I. Davidson

With the publication of Michel Foucault's *Dits et écrits* in 1994, we are in a new position to begin to assess the significance of his work. We have still not yet reached a firm and stable position, since his courses from the Collège de France, still unpublished, go well beyond anything that can be found in his books or in *Dits et écrits*.[1] But with more than three thousand pages of essays, interviews, lectures, prefaces, and reviews—many of them virtually inaccessible as originally published—in Japanese, Portuguese, Italian, German, English, and French, *Dits et écrits* requires us to rethink the place of Foucault in twentieth-century intellectual life, allows us to rediscover the scope and importance of his work, and, above all, to recognize his continued philosophical force. We should not underestimate the power of the chronological ordering of these writings, for we can now put together dimensions of Foucault's work that had far too long remained separated in the dispersal of his writing. Ten years after his death, reading through these four volumes, one can almost be seized by the illusion that Foucault has never left us, so pertinent and singular are these texts.

It is in light of the publication of *Dits et écrits* that I want to begin to reconstitute the voices of some of Foucault's most privileged interlocutors. With one exception, which involves the participation of Foucault himself, I have chosen to publish essays by Foucault's French interlocutors, not because they possess, as if by nature, some intrinsic superiority, but because all of these French interlocutors were part of a genuine dia-

1. Two of Michel Foucault's courses have been published in unauthorized Italian translations, his 1975–76 course at the Collège de France, *Difendere la società* (Florence, 1990) and his 1983 course at the University of California, Berkeley, *Discorso e verità nella Grecia antica* (Rome, 1996).

logue with Foucault. He was as affected by their interventions as they were by his texts. They constitute another missing context for his work and help us to understand his appropriations of and struggles with his own philosophical culture. In my opinion, no English-speaking audience could possibly come to grips with Foucault's intellectual specificity in the absence of the context provided by these philosophical surroundings. Of course, as *Dits et écrits* makes equally clear, it was not as if Foucault was enclosed within the parameters of French intellectual life. His engagement with political, cultural, and intellectual problems outside of France, formed through his encounters in, among other places, Sweden, Poland, Tunisia, Japan, Brazil, and the United States permeates his work from beginning to end.

I am going to focus on what one might call Foucault's philosophy of language or, put otherwise, on some of the ways in which analyses of discourse animated Foucault's work. To begin with, and to give an example of a very un-French philosophical engagement, let me turn to a lecture Foucault delivered in Japan in April 1978, published in *Dits et écrits* as "La Philosophie analytique de la politique." Despite what one may be tempted to think, the phrase "analytic philosophy" is not used by Foucault as a generic rubric but rather to refer specifically to contemporary Anglo-American philosophy. Discussing the relation between philosophy and power, Foucault suggests that philosophy might "cease posing the question of power in terms of good and evil, but pose it in terms of existence," no longer asking, "is power good or is it bad, legitimate or illegitimate, a question of law or of morality?" but rather asking "this naive question . . . : at bottom, relations of power, in what do they consist?" Foucault proceeds, in a tone reminiscent of Wittgenstein, but without mentioning his name:

> For a long time one has known that the role of philosophy is not to discover what is hidden, but to make visible precisely what is visible, that is to say, to make evident what is so close, so immediate, so intimately linked to us, that because of that we do not perceive it. Whereas the role of science is to reveal what we do not see, the role of philosophy is to let us see what we see.[2]

(One cannot help but invoke for comparison, among other passages, the following from *Philosophical Investigations:* "It was true to say that our considerations could not be scientific ones. . . . We must do away with all *explanation*, and description alone must take its place" [§109]; "Philosophy simply puts everything before us, and neither explains nor deduces anything.—Since everything lies open to view there is nothing to explain.

2. Foucault, "La Philosophie analytique de la politique" (1978), *Dits et écrits, 1954–1988,* ed. Daniel Defert and François Ewald with Jacques Lagrange, 4 vols. (Paris, 1994), 3:540–41; hereafter abbreviated "PA."

For what is hidden, for example, is of no interest to us" [§126]; "The aspects of things that are most important for us are hidden because of their simplicity and familiarity. [One is unable to notice something—because it is always before one's eyes]" [§129].)³ And so Foucault goes on to indicate that to this extent "the task of philosophy today could well be, What are these relations of power in which we are caught and in which philosophy itself, for at least one hundred and fifty years, has been entangled?" ("PA," 3:541).

Finally, in a remarkable and unexpected passage, which I will give in full, Foucault, in effect, justifies his title "La Philosophie analytique de la politique" with an *explicit* reference to Anglo-American analytic philosophy:

> You will tell me that this is a quite modest, quite empirical, quite limited task, but we have nearby a certain model of a similar use of philosophy in the analytic philosophy of the Anglo-Americans. After all, Anglo-Saxon analytic philosophy does not give itself the task of considering the being of language or the deep structures of language; it considers the everyday use that one makes of language in different types of discourse. For Anglo-Saxon analytic philosophy it is a question of making a critical analysis of thought on the basis of the way in which one says things. I think one could imagine, in the same way, a philosophy that would have as its task to analyze what happens every day in relations of power, a philosophy that would try to show what they are about, what are the forms, the stakes, the objectives of these relations of power. A philosophy, accordingly, that would bear rather on relations of power than on language games, a philosophy that would bear on all these relations that traverse the social body rather than on the effects of language that traverse and underlie thought. One could imagine, one should imagine something like an analytico-political philosophy. Then one should remember that Anglo-Saxon analytic philosophy of language truly refrains from those kinds of massive qualifications—disqualifications of language such as one finds in Humboldt or in Bergson—Humboldt for whom language was the creator of every possible relation between man and the world, the creator itself, therefore, of the world as of human beings, or the Bergsonian devalorization that never stops repeating that language is impotent, that language is frozen, that language is dead, that language is spatial, that it can therefore only betray the experience of consciousness and duration *[la durée]*. Rather than these massive disqualifications or qualifications, Anglo-Saxon philosophy tries to say that language never either deceives or

---

3. Ludwig Wittgenstein, *Philosophical Investigations*, trans. G. E. M. Anscombe (Oxford, 1953). On the role of description in Foucault and Wittgenstein, see my "Foucault and the Analysis of Concepts," *The Emergence of Sexuality: Historical Epistemology and the Formation of Concepts* (forthcoming).

reveals. Language, it is played. The importance, therefore, of the notion of game.

One could say, in a way that is a bit analogous, that in order to analyze or to criticize relations of power it is not a question of affecting them with a pejorative or laudatory qualification, massive, global, definitive, absolute, unilateral; it is not a question of saying that relations of power can do only one thing, which is that of constraining and compelling. One should not imagine either that one can escape from relations of power all at once, globally, massively, by a sort of radical rupture or by a flight without return. Relations of power, also, they are played; it is these games of power *[jeux de pouvoir]* that one must study in terms of tactics and strategy, in terms of order and of chance, in terms of stakes and objective. It is a little bit in this direction that I have tried to indicate to you some of the lines of analysis that one could follow. ["PA," 3:541–42]

This Anglo-American model of philosophy provides a basis of analogy for two of Foucault's central claims: first, we should not assume that relations of power have only one function; we should describe power, in all of its diversity and specificity, as it actually works; second, we should take seriously the notion of game, employing the ideas of tactics, strategies, stakes, and so on as tools for the analysis of power relations. Thus, Foucault calls for a descriptive analytic of our *jeux de pouvoir* rather than a global theory, a fixed picture, of how power must work. I do not know how Foucault's Japanese audience reacted to his no doubt unanticipated analogy, but I suspect that both American and French audiences will be unprepared to find Foucault supporting his task, "quite modest, quite empirical, quite limited," with the model of analytic philosophy of language, more specifically with the analysis of our everyday language games.

Foucault's use of the notion of strategy, his analysis of relations of power as strategic games, certainly had other, also unexpected, sources, since we know, for example, that when he read the texts of the Black Panthers in 1968 he discovered that "they develop a strategic analysis freed of the marxist theory of society."[4] But Foucault wanted to apply the notions of strategy and tactics not only to relations of power but also to discourse, proclaiming, in a one-page text from 1976, the need for a new "political analysis of discourse" that would show discourse to operate as a strategic field, discourse as a field of battle, and not simply as a reflection of something already constituted and preexistent:

Discourse—the mere fact of speaking, of employing words, of using the words of others (even if it means returning them), words that the others understand and accept (and, possibly, return from their side)—this fact is in itself a force. Discourse is, with respect to the relation of forces, not merely a surface of inscription, but something

4. Foucault, letter to Defert, Oct. 1968; quoted in "Chronologie," in *Dits et écrits*, 1:33.

that brings about effects *[non pas seulement une surface d'inscription, mais un opérateur].*[5]

For this very idea of considering discourse as "strategic games of action and reaction, of question and response, of domination and evasion, as well as of battle," where does Foucault draw his inspiration?—"from the investigations carried out by the Anglo-Americans," as he puts-it at the beginning of his extraordinary set of lectures delivered in May 1973 at the Pontifical Catholic University of Rio de Janeiro.[6] While criticizing certain Anglo-American analyses for their concern with "strategic games that are interesting, but that seem to me profoundly limited," Foucault goes on to remark that

> the problem would be to know if one couldn't study the strategy of discourse in a more genuine historical context, or within practices that are of a different kind than those of common-room conversations. For example, in the history of judicial practices it seems to me that one can find again, one can apply the hypothesis, one can delineate a strategic analysis of discourse within genuine and important historical processes. ["V," 2:631–32]

And a few pages later, he redescribes the problem as that of introducing

> rhetoric, the orator, the struggle of discourse within the field of analysis; not to do, as linguists do, a systematic analysis of rhetorical procedures, but to study discourse, even the discourse of truth, as rhetorical procedures, as ways of conquering, of producing events, of producing decisions, of producing battles, of producing victories. In order to "rhetoricize" philosophy *[Pour "rhétoriser" la philosophie].* ["V," 2:634]

Foucault frames his discussion anew with references to the Greek sophists and to the analyses of Georges Dumézil, but there is every reason to see here the effects of his reading of analytic philosophers, which, as early as 1967, he said allowed him to see how "to treat statements in their functioning."[7]

As Foucault himself recognized in these 1973 lectures, this way of treating language was placed at a different level than those earlier analyses that concerned the laws and internal regularities of language (see "V," 2:539). With the invocation of these latter analyses, Foucault was refer-

---

5. Foucault, "Le Discours ne doit pas être pris comme . . ." (1976), *Dits et écrits,* 3:123–24.
    6. Foucault, "La Vérité et les formes juridiques" (1974), *Dits et écrits,* 2:539; hereafter abbreviated "V."
    7. Foucault, letter to Defert, May 1967; quoted in "Chronologie," *Dits et écrits,* 1:31.

ring, most generally, to the type of structural analysis that itself bore a dense relation to his own archaeological investigations, a relation that is not clarified or illuminated simply by claiming that Foucault was a structuralist. If one looks, from an overall perspective, at this dimension of Foucault's work, one sees a surprising set of French and non-French references interacting in the background. Foucault links together, in what might seem to be an almost Borgesian brew, Russell, Wittgenstein, Lévi-Strauss, Lacan, Dumézil, Althusser, New Criticism, and linguistics as exemplifications of what he calls "analytic reason," and which he opposes to humanism, anthropology, and dialectical thought.[8] The latter triad, including existentialism and humanist Marxism, and represented by Sartre's *Critique de la raison dialectique,* cannot take account of "everything that depends on analytic reason and that is deeply a part of contemporary culture: logic, theory of information, linguistics, formalism."[9]

The existentialist rejection of the unconscious is related, according to Foucault, to the rejection of the logic of analytic reason. For the philosophical anthropology of existentialism, the unconscious and this logic both represent the same kind of obstacle to be overcome, a threat to the existentialist ideal of transparency:

> existentialism tried to describe experiences in such a way that they could be understood in psychological forms, or, if you wish, in forms of consciousness, that you could not, however, analyze and describe in logical terms. To put consciousness everywhere and to release consciousness from the web of logic were, on the whole, the great concerns of existentialism, and it is to these two tendencies that structuralism is opposed.[10]

This is perhaps one reason why the concept of the unconscious, with its logical structures, plays such an important role in Foucault's early descriptions of both structuralism and his own work.

According to Foucault, it is not only that structuralism "calls into question the importance of the human subject, of human consciousness, of human existence" through its analysis of the internal laws of autonomous structures ("I," 1:653):

> In a positive manner, we can say that structuralism investigates above all an unconscious. It is the unconscious structures of language, of the literary work, and of knowledge that one is trying at this moment

8. See especially Foucault, "L'Homme est-il mort?" (1966), *Dits et écrits,* 1:540–45. Foucault was repeating these claims as late as 1973 in a non-French context; see "Foucault, le philosophe, est en train de parler. Pensez" (1973), *Dits et écrits,* 2:423–25. These remarks are taken from a lecture given on 29 May 1973, in Belo Horizonte.

9. Foucault, "L'Homme est-il mort?" 1:541.

10. Foucault, "Interview avec Michel Foucault" (1968), *Dits et écrits,* 1:654; hereafter abbreviated "I."

to illuminate. In the second place, I think that one can say that what
one is essentially looking for are the forms, the system, that is to say
that one tries to bring out the logical correlations that can exist
among a great number of elements belonging to a language, to an
ideology (as in the analyses of Althusser), to a society (as in Lévi-
Strauss), or to different fields of knowledge; which is what I myself
have studied. One could describe structuralism roughly as the search
for logical structures everywhere that they could occur. ["I," 1:653]

And then in another interview, given in the same month of 1968, Foucault gives a characterization of his own work that echoes his characterization of structuralism, in that we find again the key terms of the
unconscious and logical correlations or structures, here described in
terms of rules.

> My work? You know, it is a work that is very limited. Very schemati-
> cally, it is this: to try to recover in the history of science, of knowl-
> edges *[connaissances]* and of human knowledge *[savoir humain]*
> something that would be like the unconscious of it. If you wish, the
> working hypothesis is roughly this: the history of science, the history
> of knowledges does not obey simply the general law of the progress
> of reason, it is not human consciousness, it is not human reason that
> is in some way the keeper of the laws of its history. There is beneath
> that which science knows of itself something that it does not know;
> and its history, its development, its episodes, its accidents obey a cer-
> tain number of laws and of determinations. These laws and these
> determinations, it is these that I have tried to bring to light. I have
> tried to extricate an autonomous domain which would be that of
> the unconscious of knowledge, that would have its own rules, as the
> unconscious of the individual human being also has its rules and its
> determinations.[11]

This description already anticipates the famous remark of Foucault, in
his 1970 preface to the English edition of *The Order of Things*, that his
work is intended to "bring to light a *positive unconscious* of knowledge," an
unconscious that is precisely the site of those rules of formation that make
possible the objects, concepts, and theories of scientific discourse, a site
that Foucault now also calls the archaeological level.[12]

Everywhere that humanism, existentialism, and dialectical reason
hoped to find the nature, essence, or freedom of man, analytic reason
found unconscious structures and systems of logical correlations.[13] And

11. Foucault, "Foucault répond à Sartre" (1968), *Dits et écrits*, 1:665–66.

12. Foucault, "Préface à l'édition anglaise" (1970), *Dits et écrits*, 2:9–10; hereafter abbreviated "P." In this text, Foucault also denies quite vigorously that he is a structuralist. The
reasons for this denial and the differences between Foucault and structuralism could be the
subject of a separate essay.

13. Here, I am reading together the two interviews from March 1969. See especially
"I," 1:659 and Foucault, "Foucault répond à Sartre," 1:663–64.

for Foucault, in the mid and late 1960s, it was precisely the task of analytic reason to "bring to light this thought prior to thought, this system prior to every system"[14] with the consequence that "man no longer holds onto anything, neither his language, nor his consciousness, nor even his knowledge" ("I," 1:659), the first divestment due to linguistic analysis, the second due to psychoanalysis, and the third to the archaeology of knowledge. Foucault well knew that the long-standing prestige of dialectical reason in France had functioned as a source of resistance to these new methods of analysis. And he could be biting in his assessment of a certain kind of French intellectual narcissism.

> But whereas the *New Criticism* has existed in the United States for a good forty years, and all the great works of logic were done there and in Great Britain, a few years ago one could still count on one's fingers the French linguists . . . We have a hexagonal consciousness of culture which sees to it that, paradoxically, De Gaulle can be considered an intellectual.[15]

Foucault's reference to linguistics here is far from occasional or superficial; he was deeply interested in the role that linguistic models played with respect to the other *sciences humaines*. In 1969 he published a remarkable essay, which has gone unnoticed, in the *Revue tunisienne de sciences sociales*, entitled "Linguistique et sciences sociales." In this article Foucault discusses various epistemological problems centered around the relationship between linguistics and the social sciences, without *ever* speaking directly of his own work. Indeed, one would not have been able to discern, on the basis of this essay, that one was dealing with the author of *Les Mots et les choses* and *L'Archéologie du savoir*. What makes his discussion so significant is that one can find, in this context, the description of problems that Foucault had himself transposed to the history of knowledge.

Foucault tells us that structural linguistics is concerned with "the systematic sets of relations among elements" and that these relations are independent in their form from the elements on which they bear; that is, the form of relations is not determined by the nature of the elements involved, and thus these relations are generalizable and can possibly be "transposed to something quite different than elements that would be of a linguistic nature." Given this type of analysis, the important empirical question arises, "Up to what point can relations of a linguistic type be applied to other domains and what are these other domains to which they can be transposed?" But Foucault turns directly to a second question, a question that raises important philosophical and epistemological issues, namely, "What are the relationships that exist between these relations that one can discover in language or in societies in general and what one

---

14. Foucault, "Entretien avec Madeleine Chapsal" (1966), *Dits et écrits*, 1:515.
15. Ibid., 1:517.

calls 'logical relations'?"[16] That is, are these kinds of relations, discovered by structural linguistics and perhaps extendable (this is the first empirical question) to myths, narratives, kinship, and society in general, capable of being completely formalized? If the answer to this question is yes, and Foucault, no doubt having in mind work that had already been done by 1969, proceeds as if it were, then a fundamental epistemological problem emerges. Foucault calls this problem that of "the insertion of logic into the very heart of reality" ("L," 1:824). It is this discovery of the logical structure of reality, of logical relations that, of course, are not transparent to consciousness, that is the work of analytic reason, and that elsewhere Foucault says cannot be taken account of by humanism with its dialectical reason. Thus we find a central locus of Foucault's early philosophical battles in the epistemological possibilities and consequences drawn from linguistics.

These battles are closely connected to the problem of how to characterize the rationality of analytic reason:

> Formerly, the rationalization of the empirical was done through and thanks to the discovery of a certain relation, the relation of causality. One thought that one had rationalized an empirical domain when one could establish a relation of causality between one phenomenon and another. And now, thanks to linguistics, one discovers that the rationalization of an empirical field does not consist only in discovering and being able to ascribe this precise relation of causality, but in bringing to light a whole field of relations that are probably of the type that are logical relations. Now these latter do not deal with the relation of causality. Therefore one finds oneself in the presence of a formidable instrument of rationalization of reality, that of the analysis of relations, an analysis that is probably formalizable, and one has realized that this rationalization of reality, so fruitful, no longer passes through the ascription of determinism and of causality. I believe that this problem of the presence of a logic that is not the logic of causal determination is currently at the heart of philosophical and theoretical debates. ["L," 1:824]

In light of the passages I have previously cited, where Foucault does discuss his own work, no one can doubt the significance he attributed to the discovery of this kind of rationalization of reality. To look for logical relations where they had not been previously thought to exist, where one had searched only for causal relations, is to provide a new means of understanding certain domains of reality, of articulating their previously invisible determinations. As if to reemphasize the philosophical significance of this kind of logical rationalization, Foucault goes on to remark that the most important research being done on Marx is not bound by a "primary

16. Foucault, "Linguistique et sciences sociales" (1969), *Dits et écrits*, 1:823–24; hereafter abbreviated "L."

causalism" *[un causalisme primaire]*, and at the same time frees Marxist analysis from dialectical logic, a logic that "has nothing to do with all these logical relations that one is discovering empirically in the sciences of which we are speaking."[17] Thus, "what one is trying to recover in Marx is something that is neither the determinist ascription of causality nor the logic of a Hegelian type, but a logical analysis of reality" ("L," 1:824–25).

It is no accident that Foucault focuses on what we might call the logical rationalization of reality and the causal rationalization of reality, since these dimensions are the locus of another major issue in his own work. The status of causal explanations is connected to the problem of how to account for change and to the issue of whether structural analysis is ahistorical or even antihistorical. And if we want to understand the absence of causal analysis in *Les Mots et les choses* we would do well to attend closely to what Foucault says about this problem in "Linguistique et sciences sociales."[18] As Foucault first points out, we should not identify history with the dimension of the successive since "the simultaneity of two events is no less a historical fact than their succession." Moreover, according to Foucault, the synchronic analysis done by linguists is in reality an analysis "of the conditions of change," where the dimension of change must not be confused with that of cause ("L," 1:826). Foucault always insisted that causal relations represented only one kind of change and that one should not collapse the different types of changes into a single level.[19] Foucault claimed that it was humanist Marxists, like Sartre and Roger Garaudy, who insisted that one speak exclusively of causality and who therefore wanted to impose a reduction of "the field of exploration" ("I," 1:656). Furthermore, in practice the search for causality always risked losing itself in "a more or less magic fog" ("L," 1:827); notions like the spirit of the times, influence, social change, crisis, interest, all of which were supposed to have some causal force, seemed to Foucault to provide explanations "for the most part, more magic than real" ("P," 2:11).[20] As Foucault indicated, causal explanations aside, "change can be an object of analysis in terms of structure."[21]

The outlines of this latter kind of analysis of change are to be found in Foucault's discussion of linguistic models. He tells us that linguists ask, What are the modifications, the necessary and sufficient correlations, required in the language in order for a single element of the language to undergo change? This kind of analysis of the conditions for change is

17. Foucault is thinking here of the Althusserian analyses of Marx.
18. On the problem of causality in *Les Mots et les choses*, see "P," 2:11–12.
19. See Foucault, "Sur les façons d'écrire l'histoire" (1967), *Dits et écrits*, 1:586–87 and "P," 2:10–11.
20. See also Foucault, "Sur les façons d'écrire l'histoire," 1:588.
21. Ibid., 1:586.

explicitly contrasted with causal analysis:

> Whereas the old successive analysis asked the question: given a change, what could have caused it? synchronic analysis asks the question: in order for a change to be able to be obtained, what are the other changes that must also be present in the field of contemporaneïty? ["L," 1:827]

This latter question, we shall see, is precisely the question that Foucault posed for his archaeology of knowledge.

To describe the problem in more detail, imagine that we begin with a state of affairs consisting of a certain number of features, say a set of elements $(a \ldots n)$. The task is then to try to describe the logical relations between these elements in the form of rules that govern the structure of which they are a part. On the basis of the description of these relations, we will then see that a change of a to a' requires a change of b to b', c to c', etc. The transformation of the structure $(a \ldots n)$ to the structure $(a' \ldots n')$ will be rationalized by an understanding of the rule-governed relations that characterize the structures. With respect to this kind of analysis, it is important to emphasize that, for example, the change of a to a' should not be described as causally bringing about the change of b to b', c to c', etc. Rather, what one shows is that one will not find the change from a to a' without there being correlative changes, all of which are governed by a structure of relations or rules.[22] This kind of analysis is characterized, first, by an anti-atomism, by the idea that one should not analyze single or individual elements in isolation but that one must look at the systematic relations among elements; second, it is characterized by the idea that the relations between elements are coherent and transformable, that is, that the elements form a structure.

How did Foucault transpose this kind of analysis to the study of the history of thought? Foucault was concerned not with the formal possibilities of a linguistic system but with the accumulated existence of discourses, with the archive of statements that have been uttered, and especially with those statements that, at a given time, claim the status of knowledge.[23] His aim was to do nothing less than attempt to describe the rule-governed structures whose elements were knowledge-statements and then to describe the transformations that had to take place in order for new structures of knowledge to have emerged. Foucault's descriptions of epistemic changes are to be located at this level of transformation and have no more to do with causality than do the transformations described in structural linguistics. Thus, in *Les Mots et les choses* Foucault wanted to describe the transformations that made possible, for instance, the birth of natural history, economics, and grammar, that gave rise to a new struc-

---

22. On the anti-atomism of structural linguistics, see "L," 1:823.
23. See Foucault, "Sur les façons d'écrire l'histoire," 1:595.

ture of thought, a new epistemological space.[24] By examining the systematic relations among elements, describing the rule-governed structures of
which they are part, Foucault was able to show how possibilities of knowledge that concerned very different kinds of objects were related, as well
as to identify and describe the changes or transformations that made possible new structures of knowledge.

When explicitly describing his own project in *Les Mots et les choses,* a
year after its publication, Foucault uses the same terminology found in
"Linguistique et sciences sociales." After criticizing the "magical" concepts
that often appear in causal analyses employed in the history of ideas,
Foucault adds that in the history of ideas, as traditionally practiced, when
one is confronted with a difficulty, for example a change that consists in
the emergence of new kinds of statements, one searches for an explanation by moving from the level of analysis of the statements themselves to
another level that is external to them. That is, one looks for an explanation of the change drawn from "the social conditions, the mentality, the
vision of the world, and so on." Foucault says that, "for the sake of a methodological game," he has wanted to do without these kinds of explanations and that he has therefore tried "to describe statements, entire
groups of statements, while making the relations of implication, of opposition, of exclusion appear that could link them." And then comes a
characterization of the problem of change that exactly parallels the characterization, for an entirely different domain, given in "Linguistique et
sciences sociales":

> For example, one tells me that I have allowed or invented an absolute
> break between the end of the eighteenth century and the beginning
> of the nineteenth century. In fact, when one looks at the scientific
> discourses from the end of the eighteenth century, one finds a very
> rapid change and, to tell the truth, very enigmatic to the most atten-
> tive look. I wanted to describe precisely this change, in other words
> to establish the set of necessary and sufficient transformations in or-
> der to pass from the initial form of scientific discourse, that of the
> eighteenth century, to its final form, that of the nineteenth century.
> The set of transformations that I defined preserves a certain number
> of theoretical elements, displaces certain others, one sees old ones
> disappear and new ones appear; all of this allows one to define the
> rule of passage in the domains that I have considered.[25]

Just as linguistic analysis is concerned with "the necessary and sufficient
conditions in order that a local change occur" ("L," 1:827), so Foucault
is concerned with "the set of necessary and sufficient transformations"

24. See "P," 2:9–11. I have discussed some of these issues at greater length in my "On
Epistemology and Archaeology," *The Emergence of Sexuality.*
25. Foucault, "Sur les façons d'écrire l'histoire," 1:588–89.

required to pass from an initial state of affairs, eighteenth-century scientific discourse, to a second state of affairs, nineteenth-century scientific discourse. Although this change is global rather than local, the conceptualization and the epistemological status of the analysis are astonishingly similar to that employed by Foucault when, without mentioning his own work, he is attempting to describe the type of rationalization carried out in linguistics.

Moreover, just as Foucault thinks that his description of these kinds of transformations constitutes "an indispensable stage if a theory of scientific change and epistemological causality should one day take shape" ("P," 2:11–12), so he believes, more generally, that this kind of analysis "allows one to define the precise domain in which a causal relation will be able to be located" ("L," 1:827). I take it that Foucault's basic idea is that a condition of adequacy for any possible causal explanation of the phenomena he is describing is that it give an account of the types of transformations that his analysis has allowed one to isolate. His analysis describes the structures that need to be explained, the parameters and relations of transformation that a causal explanation needs to be an explanation *of.* Without this type of systematic description, which allows the previously unconscious structures of thought to appear, causal analysis will not have the appropriate object of explanation. It is in this sense that a structural analysis allows one to define the field within which a causal explanation has to operate (see "L," 1:839). One could say, recurring explicitly to the terminology of "Linguistique et sciences sociales," that for Foucault, in both the archaeology of knowledge and the structural analysis of language, the logical rationalization of an empirical domain articulates the logical space within which a causal explanation is to be assigned.[26]

From this early engagement with linguistics and analytic reason to his later engagement with Wittgenstein and the strategic analysis of discourse, we find that Foucault's interlocutors comprise a background that makes it pointless, *merely* ideological, to describe him as a continental philosopher, as if the category of continental philosophy could give any genuine content to the specificity of his concerns. Developments outside of philosophy and outside of France were as crucial to his intellectual formation as were his constant exchanges inside of French philosophy. Without understanding the latter, we will certainly not know who he was; but without acknowledging the former we will make of him something he wasn't. Foucault still remains to be discovered and appropriated. I have been told, especially in France, that Foucault no longer represents a live philo-

---

26. I leave aside the important issue of the relation between structural analysis and political action, on which this whole discussion also bears. See Foucault, "La Philosophie structuraliste permet de diagnostiquer ce qu'est 'aujourd'hui'" (1967), *Dits et écrits,* 1:581–83; "I," 1:655–56; and "L," 1:827.

sophical option. Let the dead bury the dead. The essays in this book are meant to keep him amongst us.

I shall not here undertake to provide the historical and philosophical setting for each of the essays in this volume, although, in my opinion, each of them represents a decisive encounter with Foucault, and each could be the subject of its own lengthy discussion. A few of these essays were first published in *Critical Inquiry* with brief separate introductions, which I have reprinted in this book in order to give at least a hint of the essays' contexts.

In the first section of this collection of essays, I have put together a series of interventions that begins from Foucault's *Histoire de la folie*, but whose implications go far beyond that single work. Georges Canguilhem's importance for Michel Foucault is too well known to need repeating again; his decades-long interaction with Foucault's writings, which has only begun to be carefully examined, will, one can only hope, be the topic of many future studies. Michel Serres's critical review of *Histoire de la folie* was justly considered, at the time of the publication of that book, the single most important study of this work. Foucault and Serres often had discussions when they were colleagues at Clermont-Ferrand, and Serres's review sets out a complex of issues that no contemporary reader of *Histoire de la folie* can afford to ignore. Jacques Derrida's contribution to this volume begins from the site of his famous exchange with Foucault over a text of Descartes but moves far beyond that initial debate to consider in depth the tangled issue of Foucault's relation to Freud. If that early debate concerned a detailed and meticulous interpretation of a text of Descartes, it also represented another decisive moment (beyond that of Foucault and Sartre) for the history of twentieth-century French philosophy. The person sitting next to Foucault during Derrida's lecture of March 1963, "Cogito et histoire de la folie," told me that Foucault was so excited during that lecture that he could literally not sit still, continually bouncing up and down in his seat. I think that Foucault recognized, even then, the stakes that would be at issue in their exchange. In an initial version of his response to Derrida, published in Japanese in 1972 and only now available in French in *Dits et écrits,* we can see very clearly that Foucault found in this debate about Descartes nothing less than the question and status of the profound "interiority of philosophy" and of the singular events that are external to it. Foucault wrote that he wanted to show, no doubt without having been at all clear about it when he wrote *Histoire de la folie,* that "philosophy is neither historically nor logically the founder of knowledge; but that conditions and rules of formation of knowledge exist to which philosophical discourse finds itself subjected in every period, like any other form of discourse with a rational claim." And he was not simply being ironic when he accused himself of not being sufficiently free from the postulates of the philosophical tradition since he had "the weakness to place at the head of a chapter, and consequently in a privileged manner, the analysis of a text of Descartes," something that he "should have renounced" if he had wanted to be consistent in his "offhandedness *[désinvolture]* with respect to philosophy."[27] Against these remarks, Derrida's own writings, with their radical challenges to the traditions of philosophy, should require us to re-ask what is internal and what is external to philosophy. If Canguilhem's and Serres's essays can serve to mark out Foucault's relation to the history and philosophy of science, Derrida's represents a crucial moment of Foucault's encounter with philosophy. This first section concludes with a short text by Foucault that I hope can serve as a gesture towards the barely explored domain of Foucault's engagement with literature.[28]

The second section of this volume begins with Foucault's debate with Chomsky, an event that took place in 1971, broadcast on Dutch national television and moderated by Fons Elders.[29] Divided roughly into two parts, on epistemology and politics, it is remarkable for both the agreements and divergences that it registers. In the end, and no doubt unexpectedly, the most profound disagreements concern the theory of politics. In 1971 Foucault had not yet worked out his strategic analysis of power and still employs a Marxist terminology that he will later forcefully criticize. But he cannot accept Chomsky's use of the idea of human nature in political theory as a basis for the justification of political actions. As Jules Vuillemin recognized when presenting Foucault's candidacy to the Collège de France, Foucault wanted to "construct a history without human nature," and one should likewise say that he wanted to construct a politics without human nature.[30] He could not but see Chomsky's invocation of human nature here as an instance of that "anthropological slumber," "absolutely inevitable and absolutely fateful," from which he thought we had to awake.[31] The longest essay in this volume is Paul Veyne's "Foucault Revolutionizes History." Here we have another decisive encounter— of Foucault and history. This legendary essay, which strangely has never previously appeared in English, is an extraordinary guide that charts for us the explosive effects of Foucault's work on the writing of history. And for what it is worth, Foucault himself once told me that he found it the single most penetrating essay on his work. This section concludes with a

27. Foucault, "Réponse à Derrida" (1972), *Dits et écrits*, 2:295, 284.

28. Judith Revel has written some of the most significant texts about Foucault's relation to literature. See, for example, her "Foucault e la letteratura: Storia di una scomparsa," in vol. 1 of *Archivio Foucault: Interventi, colloqui, interviste* (Milan, 1996).

29. The broadcast version of the debate sometimes differs importantly from this transcript, but I have been informed by Fons Elders that both Foucault and Chomsky approved this written version.

30. Jules Vuillemin, "Rapport de M. Jules Vuillemin pour la création d'une chaire d'*Histoire des systèmes de pensée*," in Didier Eribon, *Michel Foucault (1926–1984)* (Paris, 1991), p. 371.

31. Foucault, "Philosophie et psychologie" (1965), *Dits et écrits*, 1:448.

text by Gilles Deleuze, written in 1977 as a series of notes on *Surveiller et punir* and *La Volonté de savoir.* Since Deleuze was the French philosopher to whom Foucault felt most sympathetic, this record of Deleuze's assessment of their agreements and disagreements is an invaluable document, to which we can now also add Foucault's brief discussion of Deleuze in the question period following his 1973 Brazilian lectures.

The final section of this volume turns around Foucault's encounter with ancient thought and the significance of this encounter for the conception of ethics he developed in his last writings. Pierre Hadot's inaugural lecture to the Collège de France does not directly discuss Foucault, but it gives an overview of Hadot's work that was so decisive for Foucault's understanding of ancient thought.[32] That Foucault once announced to Hadot his intention "to devote all of his future teaching to ancient philosophy" is remarkable, but no less remarkable is the role that Hadot's interpretation of ancient philosophy played in Foucault's reconception of philosophy in his final works.[33] Only after Foucault's courses on ancient philosophy at the Collège de France are made available will we be able to fully assess this influence. Paul Veyne's brief but rich essay on Foucault's ethics testifies to the intense discussions between Veyne and Foucault on the topics of ancient thought and to the use that we might still make of ancient philosophy. Finally, this volume closes with a previously untranslated essay by Foucault in which he discusses, with passion and depth, a series of texts from Greco-Roman antiquity that fascinated him and that only his death prevented him from returning to and pursuing even further.

Of all the possible lacunae in this book, the one I most regret is the absence of an essay by Georges Dumézil. Both personally and intellectually, Dumézil accompanied Foucault from the beginning until the end of his career, and I do not think Foucault was exaggerating when, in his inaugural lecture to the Collège de France, he wrote that it was Dumézil

> who taught me to analyze the internal economy of a discourse in a quite different manner than by the methods of traditional exegesis or by those of linguistic formalism; it was he who taught me to register, by the play of comparisons, the system of functional correlations from one discourse to another; it was he who taught me how to describe the transformations of a discourse and its relations to institutions.[34]

32. Pierre Hadot's assessment of some of the aspects of Foucault's last works can be found in his "Reflections on the Idea of the 'Cultivation of the Self,'" *Philosophy as a Way of Life: Spiritual Exercises from Socrates to Foucault,* trans. Michael Chase, ed. Arnold I. Davidson (Oxford, 1995), pp. 206–13.

33. Hadot, "Pierre Hadot: Histoire du souci," *Magazine littéraire,* no. 345 (July–Aug. 1996): 23.

34. Foucault, *L'Ordre du discours* (Paris, 1971), p. 73. On the relation between Foucault and Dumézil, see Eribon, *Michel Foucault et ses contemporains* (Paris, 1994), esp. chaps. 1–4.

This absence will have to serve to represent the work that remains to be done if we wish to grasp fully all of the layers of Foucault's thought and to understand the connections that linked his work to that of a diverse, and often surprising, set of figures in the history of twentieth-century thought.

I am profoundly indebted to all of the translators for producing such excellent English translations of these essays. The contributors to this volume unfailingly offered help when called upon, and Georges Canguilhem and Gilles Deleuze, no longer here to see this volume, responded generously and enthusiastically when I first approached them about contributing.

I am grateful to the Wissenschaftskolleg in Berlin for a fellowship during which the work on this volume was begun. As always I am indebted to my coeditors at *Critical Inquiry,* and especially to Tom Mitchell, for their continuous support of this project. David Grubbs, Aeron Hunt, and Jennifer Peterson provided valuable research assistance, Tess Mullen devoted extraordinary attention to all of the many details of the book's production, and Mari Schindele provided her usual superb manuscript editing. Most of all I am indebted to Jay Williams, whose intelligence, consummate editorial skill, and persistence were crucial to bringing this book into existence.

MADNESS

Introductory Remarks to Georges Canguilhem

Arnold I. Davidson

In putting together these three short essays by Georges Canguilhem, I hope to be able to give some indication of the remarkable intellectual fruitfulness of the exchanges between Canguilhem and Michel Foucault. Canguilhem's own work in the history and philosophy of science, which Foucault always recognized as an important source for some of his own books, contains a specific orientation and kind of analysis that has perhaps not yet been sufficiently exploited in the Anglo-American disciplines of science studies. More specifically, these essays by Canguilhem allow us to see the continuing importance and extraordinary density of Foucault's *Histoire de la folie*, which, it is still hard to believe, has never been fully translated into English.

The first essay published here is Canguilhem's report on Foucault's thesis, *Folie et déraison: Histoire de la folie à l'époque classique,* submitted in 1960. In a few short pages of summary, Canguilhem makes it possible to understand the originality and significance of what will become Foucault's first major book. In emphasizing the historical development "of a medicine of the mind and of a psychiatric practice" on the basis of the social experience and constitution of madness, Canguilhem's reading of Foucault permits him to see that "calling into question the origins and 'scientific' status of psychology will not be the least of the grounds for surprise provoked by this study," a prediction whose truth we now know very well. The second essay, published after Foucault's death, both places *Histoire de la folie* in its historical context and raises a series of important issues about the relation between this work and Foucault's later works. From the power of internment in *Histoire de la folie* to the power of normalization in *Surveiller et punir* and *La Volonté de savoir,* Canguilhem sees Foucault presenting himself, from the beginning, as "a denouncer of the normality of anonymous norms." Thus, in the suggestive last two paragraphs of this essay, Canguilhem points out that rather than taking Foucault's elaboration of an ethics in *Le Souci de soi* as a rupture with his previous work, it can be seen as produced "in the face of normalization and against it." Foucault's writings about ethics must be seen in the light of and as a form of response to his previous analysis of "the power of normalization and the formation of knowledge in modern society." The third essay, written on the thirtieth anniversary of the publication of *Histoire de la folie,* despite its brevity, centrally raises the still-unresolved problem of Foucault's relation to Freud. Canguilhem's nuanced questions here can serve as an index of how much remains to be said about Foucault's analysis of and attitude toward psychoanalysis.

In a lecture given at the University of Bahia in 1976, to be published in French in his *Dits et écrits,* Foucault writes: "A society is not a unitary body in which one and only one power would exert itself, but it is in reality a juxtaposition, a conjunction, a coordination, a hierarchy, also, of different powers, which nevertheless remain in their specificity." Foucault's corpus is obviously itself not a unitary body, but, as Canguilhem shows, his books should be read with their juxtapositions, conjunctions, and coordinations, even while maintaining their specificity. Foucault gave so many provocative reinterpretations of his own thought by seeing his earlier work in the wake of work that came later. Canguilhem gives us the opportunity to reapproach Foucault's *Histoire de la folie,* to allow it to illuminate Foucault's subsequent work while at the same time allowing his later writings to clarify and rearticulate it.

I am grateful to Georges Canguilhem for his permission to allow us to publish his report on Foucault's thesis.

Report from Mr. Canguilhem on the Manuscript Filed by Mr. Michel Foucault, Director of the Institut Français of Hamburg, in Order to Obtain Permission to Print His Principal Thesis for the Doctor of Letters

Georges Canguilhem

Translated by Ann Hobart

Folie et déraison: Histoire de la folie à l'époque classique, such is the subject that Mr. Foucault treats throughout a work whose density vies with its scope (943 typewritten pages, plus 40 pages of documenting appendices and bibliography).[1] Despite the extent of the documentation brought into play (archival documents, personal testimony, works of doctrine), the guiding ideas of this work are always rigorously set out. The style is incisive: never searching for a turn of phrase for itself but neither, on occasion, retreating from one. We are truly in the presence of a *thesis,* which renews not only the ideas but also the techniques for understanding and presenting the facts regarding the history of psychiatry.

Mr. Foucault designates as the classical age in the history of Europe the seventeenth and eighteenth centuries or, more exactly, the period that extends from the end of the sixteenth century to the constitution, in the first third of the nineteenth century, of a medicine of the mind and of a psychiatric practice, the one claiming the dignity of science and the other the efficacy of an application of theory. Because Mr. Foucault goes back beyond and comes down on the other side of the furthest limits of the period studied, with a view toward grasping the significance of institutions, attitudes, and concepts by means of differences or contrasts, his picture of social structures and his analysis of mental structures finally extends from the Renaissance to the birth of psychoanalysis.

The French text of this report appears in Didier Eribon, *Michel Foucault,* 2d ed. (Paris, 1989), pp. 358–61.

1. See Michel Foucault, *Folie et déraison: Histoire de la folie à l'âge classique* (Paris, 1961).

Mr. Foucault essentially endeavors to show that madness is an object of perception in a "social space" structured in diverse ways throughout the course of history, an object of perception created by social practices rather than grasped by a collective sensibility, rather, above all, than broken down analytically by speculative understanding. Madness at first occupied the social space left vacant by a plague that was progressively diminishing. The perception of madness at first participated in the terror inspired by the evil that had been penned up in leper colonies when these were turned over to the hospitalization of the insane. The real "invention" of the classical age was internment (in 1657 in France), in which the mad, because incapable of work, joined the beggar, the indigent, and the unemployed, whom an attempt was made to recuperate for compulsory labor when economic crises deprived them of paid labor. This administrative and police practice was also an ethical managing. Internment threw together in the same spacial limits of reprobation the idle, the prodigal, the libertine. Madness here loses its individuality in the indistinction of what classical reason (a value indiscriminately logical and social) opposes to itself under the collective noun *unreason* [*déraison*]. The internment of the "insane" for a long time only aimed at their neutralization or their "amendment," but not their cure. However, from the middle of the eighteenth century and well before the reforms of Tuke in England, Pinel in France, and Reil in Germany, madness regained a certain specificity. Nevertheless, the appearance of houses of internment reserved for the mad must not be considered a prescientific insight about madness as a fact of psychopathology. It seems rather that it was the protests of certain categories of inmates that resulted in a new division of the space of internment. The previous epoch had confused madness with unreason. It is in the space of this first division, brought about by reason, that unreason fragments in delimiting the specific space of madness. To the extent that new economic structures and new demands of a demographic order (the peopling of colonies) led to the revision of concepts of poverty and assistance, the massive and illusorily unconditioned evidence of internment disintegrates; and in the undifferentiated space of imprisonment, madness emerges as a specific social problem among many others. In short, police and juridical practices and the historical constitution of *a social experience of internment* were necessary in order for categories of abnormality to emerge from that point as realities offered to knowledge. Medical knowledge of madness that benefits science rests without any doubt on an active experiment in social segregation based on anathema.

The entire history of the beginnings of modern psychiatry prove to be falsified by an illusion of retroactivity according to which madness was already *given*—although unnoticed—in human nature. The truth, according to Mr. Foucault, is that madness had to be *constituted* at first as a form of unreason held at a distance by reason as a necessary condition for it to come into view as an object of study. This look [*regard*] of reason—

cold, impartial, objective, or so it believes—is thus in fact secretly oriented by a distancing reaction. This reaction, which appears unreasonable in the eyes of nascent psychiatry, a positivist discipline and philanthropic attitude, is the underlying reason for the scientific interest in madness. In the history of civilization, fear has traced out the object of observation. Between the madness of the Renaissance—a symptom of ontological scission, of the appearance of nothingness at the very core of existence (and no longer at its end, as in death)—and the madness of the positive state—an empirical phenomenon of mental illness—comes the historical process of moralization. It is the social ethic that enables the transition between the magical concept and the scientific concept of madness.

But the entire Enlightenment experience of madness cannot be summarized nor even symbolized by the practice of internment. Mr. Foucault cannot ignore that madness had always been, to some extent, an object of medical care. However, this medical care never enjoyed autonomy. If internment resulted from an administrative decision that hardly ever relied on medical expertise, it remained that *juridical* problems of interdiction, which did not cover those of internment, required the medical definition of criteria whose elaboration anticipated the subsequent analysis of psychopathology. In the prehistory of psychiatry, the subject of law is more important than the mentally deficient or sick man. It is by way of juridical alienation that medicine is brought to the aspects and forms of alienation as madness. In this way, until the nineteenth century medical knowledge concerning madness could not be an autonomous knowledge to the exact extent that it accepted its modes of classification from the domain of law. Mental nosology is thus at first hampered and lost in an enterprise of classification whose framework imitated some of the classifications of the naturalists but whose content proceeded in the final analysis from social experience. Madness was always divided between nature and society. It is thus not surprising that at the moment of the "liberation of the interned" at the time of the French Revolution, when the purely asylumlike institutions and techniques of internment were finally consolidated, madness, becoming a theoretical object of medical judgment, remained an object of ethical behavior and that the doctor-patient couple continued to be more a matter of an existential "situation" than of a relation of knowledge.

The reforms and the teaching of Tuke and Pinel express more an evolution in the practical attitude of reason regarding madness than a conceptual revolution that finally would have made appear, in the truth of nature, what the seventeenth and eighteenth centuries obscured beneath the customs of society. And the three fundamental forms of madness in the first half of the nineteenth century—general paralysis, moral insanity, and monomania—conceal still more than they recover of the structure of an experience of madness that the positivist age inherits, without realizing it, from the eighteenth century.

It is thus the significance of the early stages of positivist psychiatry—before the Freudian revolution—that is in question in the work of Mr. Foucault. And via psychiatry, the significance of the advent of positive psychology is revised. Calling into question the origins and "scientific" status of psychology will not be the least of the grounds for surprise provoked by this study.

One can already see what the importance of this work will be. Because Mr. Foucault never lost sight of the many faces that, from the Renaissance to our time, madness offers to modern man in the mirrors of the plastic arts, of literature, and of philosophy, because it sometimes disentangled and sometimes entangled a multiplicity of vital leads, his thesis is presented simultaneously as a work of analysis and of synthesis whose rigor does not always make reading easy but that always rewards intelligent effort.

As for documentation, Mr. Foucault on the one hand reread and reviewed but on the other hand read and made use for the first time of a considerable quantity of documents from the archives. A professional historian could not help but be sympathetic with the effort made by a young philosopher to access primary sources. On the other hand, no philosopher will be able to reproach Mr. Foucault for having alienated the autonomy of philosophical judgment in submission to sources of historical knowledge. While putting its considerable documentation into play, the thought of Mr. Foucault maintained from beginning to end a dialectical vigor that comes in part from his sympathy with the Hegelian vision of history and from his familiarity with the *Phenomenology of Mind*.

The originality of this work inheres essentially in its revision at the superior level of philosophical reflection of a matter until now abandoned by the philosophers and the historians of psychology to the sole discretion of those among psychiatrists whom—most often in keeping with fashion or convention—the history or the prehistory of their "specialty" interested.

Having enriched his training as a professor of philosophy with subsequent studies in psychology and by teaching psychology (he was an assistant in psychology at the faculty of letters in Lille and instructor at the École Normale Supérieure), Mr. Foucault has always taken an independent interest in psychology and its history.

I do not know whether Mr. Foucault in writing his thesis had the least intention or the least consciousness of contributing to the history of what one would call today "the social psychology of the abnormal." It seems to me that he has done so nevertheless. It seems to me as well that, doing this, he has helped to revive a fruitful dialogue between psychology and philosophy at a time when many psychologists are willing to separate their techniques from an interrogation of the origins and the meaning of these techniques.

I thus believe myself able to conclude, convinced as I am of the importance of Mr. Foucault's research, that his work merits coming to a defense before a jury of the faculty of letters and the human sciences, and, as far as I am concerned, I recommend that the dean authorize its publication.

On *Histoire de la folie* as an Event

Georges Canguilhem

Translated by Ann Hobart

The introduction to *L'Usage des plaisirs* as well as Michel Foucault's interview with François Ewald were judged by certain commentators at the
time of the philosopher's death to be a kind of admission of his conversion
to a new historical problematic.[1] Reading the end of that introduction
closely, however, it in fact appears that Foucault had not ceased to propose as the object of his historical research the "conditions in which human beings 'problematize' what they are, what they do, and the world in
which they live."[2] In 1977, in "Vérité et pouvoir," Foucault confided that
his personal problem since *Histoire de la folie* had been to seek, from the
side of power, the explanation of certain practices for which the guaran-
tee had formerly been sought from the side of specific scientific values.[3]

With the death of Foucault, how could one not ask oneself the question: What could he have thought when, revived from his coma on the
hospital bed where he had been rushed, he learned that he was at the

Unless otherwise noted, all translations are my own.—TRANS.

1. See Michel Foucault, *L'Usage des plaisirs*, vol. 2 of *Histoire de la sexualité* (Paris, 1984),
pp. 9–39; trans. Robert Hurley, under the title *The Use of Pleasure*, vol. 2 of *The History of
Sexuality* (New York, 1985), pp. 3–32. See also François Ewald, "Le Souci de la vérité: Propos
recueillis par François Ewald," *Magazine littéraire*, no. 207 (May 1984): 18–24; trans. Alan
Sheridan, under the title "The Concern for Truth," in *Michel Foucault: Politics, Philosophy,
Culture: Interviews and Other Writings 1977–1984*, ed. Lawrence D. Kritzman (New York,
1988).

2. Foucault, *L'Usage des plaisirs*, p. 16; *The Use of Pleasure*, p. 10.

3. See Foucault, "Vérité et pouvoir: Entretien avec M. Fontana," in *La Crise dans la tête*,
L'Arc, no. 70 (1977): 16–26; trans. Colin Gordon, under the title "Truth and Power," *Power/
Knowledge: Selected Interviews and Other Writings 1972–1977*, trans. Gordon et al., ed. Gordon
(New York, 1980), pp. 109–33.

Salpêtrière? The work in which he had taken a path that was supposed to lead him to others—but not elsewhere—*Histoire de la folie à l'âge classique,* retraced the history of the successive functions of the Salpêtrière: arsenal, hospital, in fact a house of correction and of alms, directed by Pinel from 1795, made famous by Charcot from 1872 to 1889, frequented by Freud in 1885—Freud named by Charcot in an 1889 lecture on *syringomyélie*— and henceforth mentioned in every account of Foucault's death on 25 June 1984.[4] It is quite moving to note the insistence with which Foucault cites Freud in order to show how the psychiatry of the nineteenth century begun at the Salpêtrière had encountered on its historic course, at the Salpêtrière itself, the person who was supposed to demystify the struc- tures of the asylum, with the exception of the medical practitioner. "The good genius of Freud had placed it at one of the critical points marked out for it since the eighteenth century by the strategies of knowledge and power."[5] Freud, inventor and model of antinormalization, who had con- ferred on psychoanalysis "the political credit . . . of having been in theoretical and practical opposition to fascism" (*VS,* pp. 197–98; *HS,* p. 150).

If the concepts of norm and normalization, destined to render intelli- gible the strategies of different powers (political, juridical, and medical) in modern societies, were only systematically used at the end of *Surveiller et punir,*[6] *Histoire de la folie* showed from the beginning of its analysis that what the supposedly scientific psychology of the nineteenth century had attempted to establish as truth, the delimitation of the "normal," is in fact only the discursive consecration of practices for establishing the juridical incapacity of an individual. It is possible that initially Foucault was more sensitive in his analysis of the functions of power to the repressive aspect of internment than to patient research on the means of normalization and control. It remains nevertheless that from the beginning of his "gene- alogical" investigations regarding cultural behaviors he presents himself and defines himself as a denouncer of the normality of anonymous norms. Hence his attitude of complicity with Freud before the time when, in *Histoire de la sexualité,* he begins to pursue the analysis of the rules of individual conduct, the elaboration of an ethics.

If I believe it necessary to return to and insist on the confirmed im- portance of *Histoire de la folie* in the constitution of Foucault's oeuvre, it is

    4. See Foucault, *Folie et déraison: Histoire de la folie à l'âge classique* (Paris, 1961). A much-abridged version of *Histoire de la folie* was published in 1964 and was translated into English by Richard Howard under the title *Madness and Civilization: A History of Insanity in the Age of Reason* (New York, 1965).
    5. Foucault, *La Volonté de savoir,* vol. 1 of *Histoire de la sexualité* (Paris, 1976), p. 210, hereafter abbreviated *VS;* trans. Robert Hurley, under the title *The History of Sexuality: An Introduction* (New York, 1978), p. 159, hereafter abbreviated *HS.*
    6. See Foucault, *Surveiller et punir: Naissance de la prison* (Paris, 1975); trans. Sheridan, under the title *Discipline and Punish: The Birth of the Prison* (New York, 1977).

because of the theoretical interest that he accorded to "the concept of the event" one day when he appeared annoyed at the label of structuralist generally attributed to him.[7] He returned to the question in 1980 in *L'Impossible prison*, vaunting the method of "eventialization" [*"événementia-lisation"*] the bringing to light of "ruptures of evidence," and regretting that historians no longer care for events.[8] But it seems to me incontestable that *Histoire de la folie* must be judged initially in relation to the event. I cannot avoid, in order to do this, evoking some memories.

When, having taken advantage of his stay at Uppsala to work a lot, that is, first of all to read, which is only a way of casting about, Michel Foucault, then at the Institut Français of Hamburg, submitted to Jean Hyppolite, director of the École Normale Supérieure, a big manuscript of 943 pages, he received from his admiring reader the advice to give his work to me. As it happened, I had previously reflected and written on the normal and the pathological. Reading Foucault fascinated me while revealing to me my limits. I proposed in May 1960 that this work be accepted for defense as a thesis at the Sorbonne and be printed before-hand. I foresaw in my very favorable report that calling into question the origins of the "scientific" status of psychology would not be the least of the grounds for surprise provoked by this study.

The defense of the thesis brought to light the appearance of a differ-ence and a fissure in academic knowledge. A history of psychiatry had been less disconcerting than a history of madness. Although the history of medicine had never previously had in France the prestige it had long had in Germany, it was not far from being considered a history with aca-demic status. The jury for Foucault's thesis obviously could not but in-clude the holder of the chair of pathological psychology, a doctor of medicine and of philosophy, and, what is more, a psychoanalyst. In this way, at the moment when the history of psychopathology could lay claim to academic sanction, one of those whom it most concerned was able to appear sincerely nonplussed. In Foucault's thesis, it is madness that is primarily at issue, not mental illness; it is exclusion, internment, and dis-cipline that is primarily at issue, not asylum, assistance, and care. It is from a power of relegation and not from a knowledge of identification that medicopsychological practice proceeds by way of a practice of intern-ment-assistance. "Isn't it important for our culture that unreason could only become an object of knowledge to the extent that it had previously been an object of excommunication?"[9] Foucault accorded to the madman a truth of being that did not cancel his freedom to be mad. He refused the nineteenth-century specialist in mental health credit for truth for a conception of madness that amounts to denying the freedom to be mad.

7. Foucault, "Vérité et pouvoir," p. 19; "Truth and Power," p. 114.

8. Foucault et al., *L'Impossible prison: Recherches sur le système pénitentiare au dix-neuvième siècle*, ed. Michelle Perrot (Paris, 1980), pp. 43, 45, 52.

9. Foucault, *Folie et déraison*, p. 129.

He took the census of the mental health specialist's antinomies of knowledge.

It was difficult in 1961 for an expert in pathological psychology to recognize with Foucault that psychology "never exhausts what it is at the level of true knowledge."[10] It was even more difficult for him to discern in this work the explosive charge that would detonate in *Naissance de la clinique* for revealing that if the nineteenth-century asylum brought about the advent of an epistemologically fragile psychopathology, the nineteenth-century hospital brought about the advent of a pathological anatomy and an epistemologically solid clinical anatomy: "medical gestures, words, and gazes took on a philosophical density that had formerly belonged only to mathematical thought."[11] Finally, perhaps he suspected, without being able to prognosticate, that to reduce the power of the psychologist to a technique for the control of normality, that is to say, of precariously tolerable deviations, was to open the door to the critics of contemporary medicine. It was clearly difficult to foresee that between the years 1968 and 1975 the text of Foucault would be called upon, rightly or wrongly, to support antipsychiatric protests about ten years—the usual interval in France—after the first works of Laing and Cooper. On this subject, one can read the article by A. F. Zoïla, "Michel Foucault, anti-psychiatre?"[12]

To sum up, one must not be too hard on those academics whom *Histoire de la folie* disconcerted in 1961. This recalls to men of my age the astonishment provoked in the same milieu in 1938 by the doctoral thesis of Raymond Aron, *Introduction à la philosophie de l'histoire*. Bringing to light the limits of scientificity in psychology scandalized as much as bringing to light the limits of objectivity in history ever could have done.

It is undeniable, however, that in tearing open the envelope by which a technique of normalization presented itself as knowledge with his first magisterial work Foucault comforted, if he did not sustain or lead, movements of cultural and political indiscipline that were still looking for justification. The most explicit manifesto of his undertaking the epistemological desacralization of the powers of psychological, medical, and judicial correction is presented in the last pages of *Surveiller et punir*, where the reflexive redoubling "the normalization of the power of normalization" appeared to characterize a technique for the control of norms still in use today.[13] The last note of that work, published ten years ago, is worth recalling: "At this point I end a book that must serve as a historical

10. Ibid., p. 634.

11. Foucault, *Naissance de la clinique: Une archéologie du regard médical* (Paris, 1963), p. 200; trans. A. M. Sheridan Smith, under the title *The Birth of the Clinic: An Archaeology of Medical Perception* (New York, 1973), p. 198.

12. See A. F. Zoïla, "Michel Foucault, anti-psychiatre?" *Revue internationale de philosophie* 32 (June 1978): 59–74.

13. Foucault, *Surveiller et punir*, p. 303; *Discipline and Punish*, p. 296.

background to diverse studies of the power of normalization and the formation of knowledge in modern society."[14] This project persisted at least until *La Volonté de savoir,* where Michel Foucault sought to discern the "strategic intention" of the discourses of presentation of the juridical, economic, medical, and pedagogical practices concerning sex in familial and extrafamilial relations, practices by which an administrative technology for the management and regulation of the life of a population was constituted without premeditation in the nineteenth century. After the normalization of behaviors, here is the normalization of life processes by "the modern technologies of power that take life as their objective" (*VS,* p. 200; *HS,* p. 152).

It seems in fact that the effort sustained in order to track down every surreptitious enterprise of normalization under the appearance of the sole "authority" of knowledge is the sign, in the work of Foucault, of a profound personal refusal to offer himself as a model, to produce himself as a master. In this relation, the short preface that he composed for the new edition of *Histoire de la folie,* while confirming this book's character as an event, exposes the reasons for his new refusal to write a real preface, that is, to direct the reader, to consent to a "declaration of tyranny."[15] The role of an author is not to insinuate how a reader ought to read. "The role of an intellectual is not to tell others what they have to do."[16]

Is it understandable from this why what could be taken as a rupture in the last works of Michel Foucault would only be at its core a completion precipitated, perhaps, by a premonitory anxiety? It was normal, in the properly axiological sense, that Foucault would undertake the elaboration of an ethics. In the face of normalization and against it, *Le Souci de soi.*

---

14. Ibid., p. 315 n. 1; p. 308.
15. Foucault, preface to *Histoire de la folie à l'âge classique* (1961; Paris, 1972), p. 8.
16. Ewald, "Le Souci de la vérité," p. 22; "The Concern for Truth," p. 265.

Introduction to *Penser la folie: Essais sur Michel Foucault*

Georges Canguilhem

Translated by Ann Hobart

Why have I agreed to be the first to say a few words on a work published thirty years ago? It is because, as the third reader of Michel Foucault's manuscript, I delight in having helped to make it famous. To be more precise: third reader after Georges Dumézil and Jean Hyppolite, in an institutional space where the manuscript could pretend to be taken for a doctoral thesis. I make this qualification out of respect for Maurice Blanchot, who claims to have been made aware of it first through the mediation of Roger Caillois. It has happened, in the course of my career as teacher, that I have been taken as capable and culpable of self-satisfaction. Naturally I am no judge of these judgments. But if there is a moment in my work as academic about which I am happy, even today, to be able to flatter myself, it is to have been the reporter on the doctoral thesis of Michel Foucault. Allow me to forget for an instant that it is thirty years later and to resituate myself thirty years ago. I was at that time rather controversial for not holding in high esteem certain schools of psychology. I was not, however, totally uneducated on the subject. In 1925–26, when a classmate of Daniel Lagache at the École Normale, I attended with him some courses and lectures by Georges Dumas. Later, when a colleague of Lagache at the Faculté des Lettres at Strasbourg, removed at that time to Clermont-Ferrand, I attended a number of his lectures. If my doctoral thesis in medicine, in 1943, principally concerned problems of physiology, to interrogate the normal and the pathological invited reference to such authors as Karl Jaspers, Eugène Minkowski, and Henri Ey as well. In the summer of 1944, when doctor to the *maquis* of Auvergne, I hid and cared for their wounded for several weeks in the psychiatric hospital at Saint-Alban in Lozère and in the surrounding areas. I had known previously, at Toulouse, the director of the hospital, Lucien Bon-

33

nafé. He welcomed into his home the doctor François Tosquelles; the position he has since held in the debates on institutional psychotherapy is well known. I witnessed some of their work. We debated a good deal. The memory of their cordiality is still alive in me.

Here, no doubt, are some of the reasons for the trust my friend Jean Hyppolite saw fit to put in me when he advised Michel Foucault to come to present his work to me. I never concealed that I was immediately won over. I learned to know, better than I had ever done before, another figure of the abnormal than organic pathology. And Foucault obliged me to recognize the historical existence of a medical power that was equivocal.

On the misinterpretations and deviant usages that Foucault's thesis on power has incited, there is a closely argued study by Robert Castel, entitled "Les Aventures de la pratique," published in a special issue of the journal *Le Débat* in 1986, after Foucault's death.[1] For my part, I believe that it is at the end of *Histoire de la folie* that one learns when and how psychiatry ceases to be in reality, under cover of philanthropy, a policing of madmen. It is with and through Freud. Foucault said of him: "Freud demystified all the other structures of asylums. . . . He transferred to himself . . . all the powers that had been dispersed throughout the collective existence of the asylum."[2] And fifteen years later, in *La Volonté de savoir*, Freud and psychoanalysis are praised once again for having, in rejecting the neuropsychiatry of degeneracy, broken with "the mechanisms of power" that pretended to control and manage the daily practice of sexuality. This stand immediately follows the pages in which Foucault has described the ways and means of what he has called "biopower."[3] A quick reminder of these pages does not seem to me superfluous at a time when the French are discovering in their own country what biopower is capable of.

But a question remains for which my reading of Foucault does not yet permit me to sketch the beginning of a response. I cannot believe that he was seduced by psychoanalysis, even as he celebrated the *rupture* that Freud's work represented. Could the victory that the analysand, listened to by the analyst, wins over censure seem to him to be pure of all resemblance to confession? Is the refusal of any attempt at corrective recuperation, which is the self-justification of psychoanalysis, always totally transparent? If the recognition of sexuality is to be credited to psycho-

1. See Robert Castel, "Les Aventures de la pratique," *Le Débat*, no. 41 (Sept.–Nov. 1986): 41–51.

2. Michel Foucault, *Folie et déraison: Histoire de la folie à l'âge classique* (Paris, 1961), p. 611. A much-abridged version of *Histoire de la folie* was published in 1964 and was translated into English by Richard Howard under the title *Madness and Civilization: A History of Insanity in the Age of Reason* (New York, 1965), pp. 277–78.

3. Foucault, *La Volonté de savoir*, vol. 1 of *Histoire de la sexualité* (Paris, 1976), p. 185; trans. Robert Hurley, under the title *The History of Sexuality: An Introduction* (New York, 1978), p. 140.

analysis, is this the same for Foucault as the recognition of the unconscious?

Thirty years afterwards, would Foucault maintain what he said of Freud, that he had "expanded the miracle-working powers" of the medical practitioner?[4] I have not found the elements of a response to these questions in the work of Hubert L. Dreyfus and Paul Rabinow, *Michel Foucault, un parcours philosophique,*[5] nor in Jacques-Alain Miller's important presentation on Foucault and psychoanalysis during the 1988 international conference "Michel Foucault, philosophe."[6] Perhaps the lectures at the Collège de France in 1973–74 on "Le Pouvoir psychiatrique," which dealt extensively with antipsychiatry, would supply some new information concerning his opinion of psychoanalysis.[7]

It has been thirty years! Since 1961, other works by Foucault—*Naissance de la clinique, Les Mots et les choses, Histoire de la sexualité*—have in part eclipsed the initial influence of *Histoire de la folie.* I admire the first two. In *Le Normal et le pathologique,* I said how much I had been moved by the first.[8] I wrote an article on behalf of the second for which I had nothing but praise. But for me, 1961 remains and will remain the year that a truly great philosopher was discovered. I had already known at least two, who had been my classmates: Raymond Aron and Jean-Paul Sartre. They did not get along with one another. Nor did they get along with Michel Foucault. One day, however, all three were seen united. That was to sustain, against death, an undertaking without limits.

---

4. Foucault, *Folie et déraison*, p. 611; *Madness and Civilization*, p. 277.

5. See Hubert L. Dreyfus and Paul Rabinow, *Michel Foucault: Beyond Structuralism and Hermeneutics* (Chicago, 1983); trans. Fabienne Durand-Bogaert, under the title *Michel Foucault, un parcours philosophique: Au-delà de l'objectivité et de la subjectivité* (Paris, 1984).

6. See Jacques-Alain Miller, "Michel Foucault et la psychanalyse," in *Michel Foucault, philosophe: Rencontre internationale, Paris 9, 10, 11 janvier 1988* (Paris, 1989), pp. 77–84.

7. See Foucault, *Résumé des cours 1970–1982* (Paris, 1989).

8. See Georges Canguilhem, *Essai sur quelques problèmes concernant le normal et le pathologique* (Strasbourg, 1943); trans. Carolyn R. Fawcett, under the title *On the Normal and the Pathological,* ed. Robert S. Cohen (Boston, 1978).

The Geometry of the Incommunicable: Madness

Michel Serres

Translated by Felicia McCarren

If Michel Foucault approached his *Maladie mentale et personnalité* as a clinician, he approaches *Folie et déraison: Histoire de la folie à l'âge classique* as a historian.[1] It is, however, and in many ways, an unusual kind of history, a re-creation. This book marks an important moment; its methodology, its construction, the technique of its development of a "historical ensemble" are too complex for a critical analysis of this length to allow them the space they require. First of all, then, it is important to give all due credit to the erudition that will not be discussed at length here but that is evident in the mass of facts explored in the terrain of madness. Three centuries of experience—from the end of the Middle Ages and the Renaissance, through the seventeenth and eighteenth centuries, up to the so-called liberation of the inmates of Bicêtre—are minutely studied on the European scale. The scope of the study is broad, not only chronologically and geographically, but above all culturally. Far from being satisfied with monuments having some relation to "psychiatry" (we should say to the archeology of psychiatry, giving the term its most philosophical sense), the author instead surveys all imaginable horizons where the shadow of unreason might have left some trace. Curiosity is awakened wherever an allusion, a cry, an image, a supplication, a caricature is found, and lucid and profound analysis follows. This magnificent odyssey leads the reader from the old lazar houses in ruin to the shores where the Ship of Fools sets sail; from medieval iconography to the popular images of Samuel Tuke's asylum; from the tragic furors of Orestes to the

---

All translations are my own.—TRANS.
1. See Michel Foucault, *Maladie mentale et personnalité* (Paris, 1954) and *Folie et déraison: Histoire de la folie à l'âge classique* (Paris, 1961); hereafter abbreviated *F*.

strange dialogue of *Rameau's Nephew;* from Jean-Baptiste Colbert's decrees to the revolutionary proclamations. Widely diverse kinds of general cultural activity are considered worthy of study, which explains the density of the historical ensemble brought to light.

Next, the problem is entirely one of organization, architecture, structure. To the merits of erudition are joined the clarity of a philosophical mind, of historical synthesis, and of the attentive and ardent approach toward the latent realities of unreason. Rather than trying to size up this work through the multiplicity of its concrete analyses, we are going to try to follow the movement by which its author masters this multiplicity, which will give us some idea of the level of this mastery.

We begin with language, the writing style and linguistic technique of Michel Foucault. His style itself seems to have created the structures—both the most immediate and the most profound—that organize the work and its object. These structures are clearly of a "geometric" nature; they cover the historical ensemble under consideration with a highly developed network of dualities. It is necessary to deploy these "binary" structures across every possible level of experience (whose number we have just suggested) to get a picture of the rigorous organon guiding the organization of this book.

It is clear that such an analysis can only give the reader a vague idea of a work that, even beyond its subject and its organization, locates itself consciously at the juncture of the richest inspirations, bringing together the Jules Michelet of *La Sorcière,* the Nietzsche of *The Birth of Tragedy,* Sade's underground intuition, the poetic and linguistic illuminations of René Char and Antonin Artaud, to name only a few—all inspirations coming together in a logic whose construction the reader will have to pardon us for only sketching in outline.

1

In order to discuss madness, one has to find a language. This decision envelops all the other problems. One can speak about unreason, or let unreason itself speak.

In the first case, one uses the idioms of rejection and covering up, as if one were talking about a foreign land, a voyage to Erewhon, an animal with bizarre habits, a dangerous thought, or a naturalized object. The object thus finds itself imprisoned behind the facade of a linguistic perspective where truth is at the center, in the mouth of the speaking subject. It is he who is understood, and not that of which he speaks. The reasonable one is understood, the one who describes the madman according to his own norms; the madman is rejected, excluded from the very norms of language of which he is the object.

On the other hand, it is possible to borrow the autochthonous language of the object in question. He who listens must then turn to the necessary translations and decipherings. This presupposes their possibility, the possibility that every human language has ciphers that transpose it into another language, which is generally true. But, at the limit, this cipher seems to vanish if the language spoken exists outside of the rules of this rational game that makes translations possible; no one could understand someone who speaks to the birds if he really expressed himself in their own song. The chosen idiom thus comes as close as it can to expressing its subject, but when it comes to delirium may seem to have no more sense than nonsense. Ultimately, the madman speaks of himself, but he cries his madness in a desert. For example, this is the case with dreams.

At this first stage of choice, facing this first dilemma, Foucault has the courage to choose the other path and its difficulties. He seeks—and finds—the keys to the language of madness, as Freud found those to the language of dreams, and in the same way: by allowing it to speak. Thus the languages of rejection and covering up are themselves rejected; positivism's definitions and classifications, its genealogical trees and its garden of species, the entire linguistic system projected onto the reality of madness are all rejected. The rationalist attitude toward the problem of unreason arises as a repudiation of its profound truth: it translates unreason into the norms of reason and thus loses its autochthonous meaning. Reading a book of spells for syntax could only lead to misinterpretation; it identifies only mirages. From now on we have to allow those whom we have not heard previously to speak, even if the substance of their words is madness. That this choice implies major difficulties, we shall see; but already one part of the history of madness is understood. During three centuries of misery, we have spoken of a mute; and here he recovers his abolished language and begins to speak by himself, of himself.

Thus speech is given—no doubt for the first time—to those who had always been refused it before. (The conditions of this gift will make apparent, through a remarkable symmetry, the cruel motivations of this refusal; this idea of mirror symmetry is one of the keys to this work.) But how do we allow a man to speak who has been immured in muteness from the beginning of history, a man who does not know how to express himself except in an incommunicable language? How does the nonlanguage of unreason develop? How is the most transparent of mirrors discovered in such a way that every screen is removed from in front of the madman? But, on the other hand, supposing that the author succeeds in his enterprise, such transparency would allow only delirium and nonsense to be seen or brought into focus. Thus we have to go to the extreme limit of two qualities of language, to the limit of transparency and the limit of opacity, to explain the truth of unreason with structures that are appropriate to it and yet expressive and communicable. We have to put up a screen and remove it, make it both translucent and dense. We have to decipher, we might say, the equations of black light.

That is why Foucault's book was an impossible work to write, without a miraculous way of untangling these two necessary conditions. Yet here it is written. We must explore what made it possible, the miracle of its writing, if we wish to enter into the world, literally unheard, that it opens for us.

This is one of the secrets of its writing: Foucault has chosen to write this book in the language of geometry—geometry understood in what we might call its earliest form, at the precise moment when it is still aesthetic and already formalized, when its form of expression is still concrete but already highly rigorous, when its density is presented in a conceptual quasi-emptiness. In fact, if we consider the terms and vocabulary, the style, the logic, the organon of the work, we will see clearly that they are drawn from a meditation on the primary qualities of space, on the immediate phenomena of *situation*. If we analyze its contents, reading attentively for repeated vocabulary, we will notice the weight of words like *space, emptiness, limit, situation, division [partage], separation, closure*. . . . In the same way, his arguments (we will look at some examples) frequently reproduce pure descriptions of *position*. And, in fact, the problems of unreason are perfectly explicable following such a schema of language and logic. Because the most substantial experience of unreason—and historically the most frequent—the *loi d'airain*, is precisely that of the segregation of dementia in a contained, isolated, closed, and distinct space.[2] Closure and segregation are actual experiences, historical laws resulting in an excommunication that soon proscribes all exchange or dialogue. Consequently, the form of language used here very quickly approaches an explication of the silence of the mad. The spatial style that expresses the fundamental experience of quarantine becomes the style of the conditions of possibility of this silence. The exclusion of all language is here recounted in the language of an abstract theory of pure exclusion. It was difficult to resolve in a sufficiently rigorous manner such a tightly tied knot of contradictory exigencies. We shall see, as a result, that these languages of rejection and covering up find themselves explained by this same theory.

But, before pursing this, it is important to insist again on these "geometrical" structures, because the history of madness, with a singular fidelity, will follow along these spatial lines. One might say that at the origin there is a single space, structured in a *chaotic* manner, as undefinable as the space of the sea where the *Stultifera Navis* sails. The madman is there, everywhere, always as proximate, as imminent, as one might imagine,

2. *La loi d'airain* (literally, "the law of bronze") is identified in the *Petit Robert dictionnaire de la langue française* as the name given by Lassalle to the law of capitalism that reduces workers' salaries to the minimum necessary for survival.—TRANS.

representing—with the poor, the downtrodden, and the disinherited—
the Kingdom of all hope, that is to say, a world—a special enclave—as
near or as far from this world as one might imagine. The experience of
madness is thus connected to the experience of the immediate proximity
of all possible points of space, and also to the experience of the fusion of
the world and such special enclaves. There are even, in some sense, two
spaces, but they are made one by virtue of the ubiquity of the immanent
representation of Christ's agony and of the Cross. The border, boundary,
division, the tain of the mirror are all dissolved and yet present in every
point; they form the system of all possible proximities. And then, suddenly, the space of madness will be structured in a new way. For the complexity of this infinite system of proximities and recognitions will be
substituted the gross division of space into two terms: on one side, the
region of all reason and all victories; on the other, the country where I
am sure never to go, that my courage and spiritual energy will keep me
from, however tempted I may be. And, as Descartes would say, because
the other is there, and I am certain to be different from him, I think
rightly. From this moment on, the structuration of space is inherited for
more than two centuries, more or less. Just as one cages wild beasts and
imprisons criminals, just as there is a separate domain where the damned
expiate their sins, so the insane begin to suffer quarantine and disgrace.
Beginning here, the author's and reader's attention will be focused—ver-
tiginously—on the nature, the function, and the orientation of this un-
crossable border between the two domains thus divided. The entire
history of madness will be contained in the varying responses to these
few questions:

What is the nature of the division between these two spaces?

What is the nature of the boundary that separates them?

What is the particular structure of each one of these spaces, and,
more precisely, the structure of the space of "rejection"? Is there some
relation, some kind of symmetry between these two domains? Does the
style of the space of "liberty" influence the manner in which the subject
of this space structures the space of "rejection"? In other words, does this
repudiation reveal any kind of liberty? any kind of reason? Is it, ultimately, possible to discover if the space of "rejection" is structured by the
"rejected" themselves? In other words, to make of the kingdom of slaves
a land of liberty?

We understand, then, how the problems of language and logic are
reflected in the understanding of history in Foucault's work, and why, at
the beginning of the book, he salutes the method of Georges Dumézil. In
fact, the history of madness will never be interpreted here as the genesis
of psychiatric categories, as a search for the premonition of positive ideas
in the classical age; it will not follow the recurrent curve of an evolution
stabilized in contemporary medical thought. Rather, it describes the vari-

ations of structures that it is possible to locate in this kind of double space and that in fact have been located there: structures of separation, of relation, of fusion, of opening up, of foundation, of rejection, of reciprocity, of exclusion, or even of "nourishment"—in short, all the structures imaginable and imagined, more or less unconsciously, in history, in this double unity, including the unending circle that allows moving from one domain into the other without interruption. Far from being a chronicle, the history of madness is a history of the variation of dual structures ("binary structure[s]" [*F,* p. 625]) located in the two spaces of reason and nonsense.

The necessity of this "geometric" language and of this problematics of *situation* is revealed to the reader as the history, in unfolding, specifies its elements. And, suddenly, we understand that the only essence of madness is situation itself: "[Madness] necessarily becomes embodied in this closed world that is at once its *truth* and its *condition*. Through a recurrence, which is strange only if madness is taken to exist prior to the practices that define and concern it, its situation becomes its nature" (*F,* p. 528). The closed space of internment is the concrete support for a pure theory of situation that will summarily express the profound nature of unreason: alienated because it is disgraced. A bit further on we see how the perception of situation becomes the essential vision.

Foucault's goal is also to make us understand how the lines are drawn that open, close, or connect these two envisioned spaces. Certainly, he who holds the pen inhabits, in all good conscience and security, the space of reason; he reinforces, with all possible resolution—even cruelty—the borderline that separates him from the "other," that maintains the *alienus* in the caged space. Some moments of illumination in history, however, permit us sometimes to see a shadow in the immediate vicinity of the dividing line (as in the old days when the madman was close by), or even a mouth speaking from the domain of silence. This is how *Rameau's Nephew*'s dialogue is understood; the interlocutors are both close to the line: the madman is not so mad and the reasonable one doesn't take refuge from and doesn't exclude him. The history of madness is from then on this broken line, rarely a line of approach, most often a line of aversion, defining the border, the boundary, the division.

It is important to add that one naturally finds these formal or linguistic structures on the most visible level of the author's style, in his images and in the images that he analyzes—for example, the great descriptions, austerely rich, of such double domains as land and sea, day and night, of their limits at dawn and dusk. We will see further on with what felicity the Racinian dream and dawn, for example, are explained through this first method.

In addressing the primary problems of language, Foucault addresses the fundamental problems, makes his critical structures clear, designs his architectonics, brings his program into view. From the book's formal construction to its stylistic nuance, the word and its images, the word and its meanings lead us without discontinuity. In a remarkable reversal, the most rational word can become expressive of the unenunciable because it is neutral language par excellence, both rigorous and drained of meaning or content in itself. It is consequently a transparent structure, never one that covers up.

Let us look at some examples; they bring to light the concrete significance of these formal structures. What is a border or boundary? It is, first of all, the line that is drawn, let us call it its "ridge"; its significance is one of definition. This boundary, this line, always has two sides. If I trace around me a closed contour, I keep myself in and defend myself against. One side of the line protects me and the other side excludes others. Consequently, it is convenient to distinguish the "forms of liberation" and the "structures of protection" that are the left and right sides of the dividing line (*F,* p. 553). Example: the eighteenth century prided itself on its practice of dividing madmen from criminals in the space of internment. But do we believe these to be humanitarian concerns for the insane? Let us then consider how the line of division is situated, in which direction it is drawn. In fact, everything converges to show that its guarding side is situated in the space of the mad (see *F,* pp. 427–35, where we get the expression "the space of internment is badly closed"). This is one of the particular cases of a law, a constant in the general history of madness: in all its divisions, the side of exclusion of the line of separation is always directed at the space of unreason. This is true even of the more detailed studies of this space, which, naively, might be taken as attempts at liberating the insane. The pseudoliberation always hides a more obscure and more real enclosure. Thus the hagiography of the miracle cures of Bicêtre, when, in fact, we are constantly liberating Barrabas.

This general law has a consequence of the first importance. It is evident that the line of division, given the characteristics of its edges, never determines an approach toward madness but always the most considerable distancing from it, the most perfect exclusion, in short, the purest misjudgment. Consequently, the domain of the insane is more and more closed off, and with continuous enclosures and isolations its *peau de chagrin* shrinks. Then, through a necessary reversal, madness finds there its account. In becoming purified, bit by bit (it was what other domains were purified of), it gets determined, defined, individualized. We should take the words *define* and *determine* in their etymological sense. By force of being excluded from all possible proximities—and its history, sometimes, is reduced to the enumeration of the proximities it is separated from—it thus finds itself, at the limit, alone excluded, that is to say, finally recognized in the purity of its nature, in the unity of its difference. Madness is identical with the excluded, the distinct, what is closed off in confines, terminals, ends, limits. So many divisions in the course of history converge at an *epistemological clarification*. The repeated enclosures and alienations lead to the discovery of what we might call the body in its pure state: the successive *eliminations* become *analyses*. The most spectacular and the most significant of the laws of this strange history, almost its teleology, can now be identified: madness is, in essence, the ultimate exclusion. This is how the perception of situation becomes an essential vision. It would have been difficult for the author to discover it without the constant support of the structure posited at the very beginning of this meditation. Only what we called the pure theory of exclusion can define madness— define, or discriminate, or delimit an essence, nature, or situation.

We cannot help but point out two themes that are *analoga* of this law on completely different levels: on the level of image, we move from the *marine* wandering of the Ship of Fools to the fortress, cell, cellar, convent, chateau, island (see *F,* pp. 437, 485); on the level of conscience, the historic movement whose epistemological translation we have just obtained becomes here a movement of continuous *internalization*. Chapter two of the third part must be read with this in mind, as expressly indicated by the author. There we see articulated, with all desirable precision, the set of spatial structures and the results of the idea of limit: how, in particular, a singular space gets developed in the former communal space (see *F,* p. 467); how this singular space is covered with a network of distinctions and varieties (see *F,* p. 469), in other words, how the limits of defense become the very limits of a closed space of internment itself; how this space inside the former communal space is structured by a precise relationship with the space of reason (see *F,* p. 475). This meditation culminates at the moment when the limit that closes off the space of madmen is transformed and becomes the filter that itself decides on entrances and exits (see *F,* p. 332). It is really the end of this movement of structuration. It is the limit that judges and defines the madman; it is at the foot of this wall that he is differentiated as such. Self-definition is accomplished: what pure theory anticipates.

It would be useful to apply these last themes more broadly. To use in this way the most elementary structures of space—that is to say, the rigorous structures closest to the aesthetic—is to institute, through this example, a remarkable methodology of pure description. No doubt we recognized, in the preceding lines, some elements of a geometry that freed itself from quantity and measure, a geometry fairly close to perceived quality. This methodology has a philosophical significance that is difficult to underestimate; in fact, this is a formal, rigorous organon of the purely qualitative. Consequently, when we wish to describe phenomena escaping by their nature from all preliminary measurement, when we wish to grasp the rigor of a pure form, of a continuous, unquantifiable variation, we can only use the organon that responds in a precise way to these requirements. If we were to consider it in its purity—that is to say, outside of the historical example of madness discussed here—if we were to consider in itself this structural apparatus applied by Foucault, we might easily obtain the general organon of the sciences that are as yet only at the stage of description (or that will never go beyond this stage), and to which we attempt, via various procedures, to apply falsely qualitative structures. If this enterprise were to succeed, it would take every effort of contemporary thought, but no doubt a new family of exact sciences would come to light that it would be possible to call morphological sciences.[3] There is no doubt that Foucault has had the clearest understanding that only this language of geometry, taken at its nascent state, is capable of furnishing this set of structures consciously or unconsciously sought by so many of the thinkers of our time. In this way, this history of a prescientific experience (anterior in all possible senses) can in fact be considered one of the first acts of a scientific research that is imminent and necessary.

The rigor of this architecture would be pointless if, beyond this structural understanding, there were not a more personal insight, a more passionate investigation; the work would be precise without being quite true. That is why, at the very heart of the logical argument, at the heart of the impressive erudition of the historical study, circulates a deep-seated love—not vaguely humanitarian but really almost pious—for these obscure people in whom is recognized the infinitely proximate, the other himself. Responding to the clear structures of division is their pathetic pain of separation.

Thus this book, striving ceaselessly to master an impossible language, structuring the unstructurable with the greatest rationality, is also an outcry. Rejecting the pathos of the rationalism that is snobbery and scorn, rejecting the point of view of a separate, outside observer, it is the refusal of the medical gaze. With the tearing apart accomplished and painfully endured, this cry comes from the heart of the thousand concentric circles, hurled at and against those who, slowly, inexorably, trace them with the bitter point of their compass.

Thus, this transparent geometry is the moving language of those who undergo the major suffering of suppression, disgrace, exile, quarantine, ostracism, excommunication. This is a book of all forms of solitude. And amidst such suffering appears the attraction toward all limits—the vertigo of proximity, the hope of new connections.

---

3. "The geometry without measurement that is called topology, . . . refusing all quantification, suggests the possibility of treating things in their quality or in their form" (Michel Serres, communication with translator, June 1996).

2

The first linguistic and logical theme of the work is thus the structure of this divided space, of the duality of separated domains. We find it everywhere in the historical interval under consideration, with a thousand visages and aspects, in the filigree of sociopolitical, economic, and moral practices of internment; in the obscure presuppositions of medical theory; in the cruel arbitrariness of a therapy as crazy as the patient it pretends to cure. The total independence of these three levels among themselves is, on the other hand, an element of the experience of madness at least as important as the way in which this structure varies analogously across each of them.

But, before getting at this, we have to draw from the meditation on space a major consequence, without which one of the book's important discoveries would be overlooked. Let us again consider the figuration of two separate domains as if we understood their relation only through the idea of their common border. In fact, we must, in a certain sense, consider them as inverse or complementary. It goes without saying that one of these two subsets of the global space is understood to figure the set of rationalism's immediate attitudes, attitudes of exclusion and defense, the cultural, moral, and religious "norm," in short, the sum of experiences that constitute the classical world of action and thought familiar to the *honnête homme*. The second subset represents the world of unreason itself, the projection into a form of what internment is *in vivo*. It follows from this arrangement that the descriptions of complex organizations of this second space will function as the system of all inverses, of all opposites, or all complements of the cultural world constituted by classical reason. This second domain is appropriated by what we could call the negative sign; it is itself the negative of the classical values of thought and culture. "Our" seventeenth and eighteenth centuries are discovered and read as in a mirror, on the other side of the silver.

However, we must not believe, from this analysis, that the themes thus brought to light are only images, identified inside a formal space; rather, they are conditions. Uncovering the obverse of classical reason, while the hallucinations of unreason repudiated by reason surface, Foucault unveils the double of that which we thought we knew, and this double is not a repetition of the classical order in the image of delirium but a necessary condition of the establishment of this very order. So much so that the work of Foucault is, precisely, to classical tragedy (and, more generally, to classical culture, as we shall see) what the thought of Nietzsche is to Hellenic tragedy and culture: it reveals latent Dionysianisms under an Apollonian light. If the reader follows the author's noble effort, in the first three hundred pages, to penetrate into the correctional world, into the insane space of internment, he has only to turn around to perceive suddenly, under a new light and as if multiplied a thousand times by the virtue of this mirror, that this is what the classical world is built on, both in relation to it and against it: its social, political, and economic organization and, ultimately, Descartes's *Meditations,* Racinian tragedy, the Malebranchian edifice, and the axiomatics of Spinoza are built both on and against it. To say that this rationalism is pure is to say what it has purified itself of, through exclusion, rejection, scorn. What appeared before to be only an image, a double, a reciprocity, thus becomes foundational. The most marvelous reward of the first part of this work is precisely this retrospective understanding of reason's effort to bring to light all its purity, which madness seemed to it to sully. If Aeschylus and Sophocles, like Socrates, can be better understood after Nietzsche, Descartes and above all Racine can be better explained after Foucault, and for parallel reasons. We finally know what nights surround these days, what errors surround our truths, and what nonexistences surround our realities. This formal spatial border that from the point of view of pathos was a tearing apart is, from reason's point of view, dawn or dusk. Thus, from the tragic point of view one sees delirium pierce the indistinct barrier of dawn, to bathe daylight with shadow, to tear night apart with the sun's dazzling glare. Error and reason, dreams and lucidity, day and night, suffering and tyranny—these dualities correspond as do good sense and madness. The second space contains mimics, caricatures, the very conditions of existence of the themes of the first space, the domain of victories that can only incorporate and consolidate them through acts of protection, rejection, and covering over. Such mirror relations, symmetries, and conditions are not the only possible relations, because the boundary that separates the two domains, changeable in its nature, pluralizes them to infinity.

For the author, these transformations, affecting the precise nature of the border and consequently the reciprocal forms that are exchanged between the two spaces, constitute the history of madness. If we look at the spatial structures of the medieval experience, we can in fact see the beaten path. We have called its organization chaotic, to follow as closely as possible the language of geometry: all the points are in proximity to one another; the madman is nearby, as are the beggar and the pauper. Superimposed on this chaos is a transcendent partition of space, and the neighbor is the sign (the image) and the revelation of the city of God, that is to say the form of his mystical recognition. So much so that the two spaces (or rather the two times two spaces) have almost no boundary, other than a constantly disappearing one. The madman is right here, as is Christ. This structuration of space is profoundly Christian, responding to the distinction and fusion of immanence and transcendence and to the reading of symbols. There are clearly two Kingdoms, but the "other" one is always infinitely close and signified everywhere. But this indistinct boundary will suddenly become clear and defined; it will materialize in the walls of internment. In place of the thousand dazzling lights of a shattered mirror infinitely reflecting all the lights of meaning is now the inflexibility of an absolute limit and the permanently established differentiation of two separates spaces. What God could not accomplish, Colbert and Descartes, and St. Vincent de Paul, did. The madman no longer represents the proximity of an absent Kingdom but is thrown away into the deepest, darkest dungeon, where he has also lost his value as a sign. But the chaos of global space where the lucid, the poor, the insane, and the sick are not differentiated will be rediscovered in the separate space of all wretchedness. If, on the one hand, the reasonable one is saved by this partition and from now on reigns in his purified kingdom, the madman remains in the chaotic space, in proximity to the poor, the sick, and the asocial. After the division, then, we have to consider the removal of the chaotic structure. The madman is removed both from material proximity and from signification; the boundary that rejects him is defined but madness is not at all; it is, vaguely, evil, error, misery, nonexistence—in short, everything that one has purified reason of. Thus we encounter again the "binary" structure of the classical age, and, with this example, see how this history is constituted from a simple structural variation.

Consequently, the analysis lets us see the space of madness, following the great classical dualities, as the space of all possible negatives, all purifications. The earlier explication then takes on all the richness of its meaning. We understand how it is possible to get to the root of all the *positivities* of the age of reason. For example, traditional economy has as its object wealth and prosperity, and Foucault writes the history of all forms of poverty; morality is the system of good, and Foucault puts himself at the root of all evils. The philosophy of these centuries of understanding and enlightenment is that of the rule of reason, and here we find described the chaos of unreason. . . . And, each time, with our backs turned to the classical positivities, we smell the flowering of this family of negatives, of which madness is the limit: antinature, antireason. History then only appears to us as the history of successes and fortunes, in the familiar sense. Yet it appears so only through this uninterrupted movement of putting under quarantine anything that is not the good fortune of enterprise or argument. It slowly covers up, in its inexorable movement forward, the failures and false starts of this triumph. (We will want to connect these ideas to the ultimate definition of madness, according to Foucault, as the absence of work.) At this level, the central project of the book is simply to uncover these mutilated ensembles, these whisperings of thought and language, and to make of them the most profound reagents in the history of ideas.

The very detail of this system of complementarities is impossible to describe. It is ordered by the principle, specifically announced, according to which "'the history of madness is the counterpart of the history of reason'" (*F,* p. 456). Behind the tain of internment's mirror takes place an obscure history that is the inverse of the one our culture knows, in a reversal that needs explaining. Everything happens as if the history of ideas had its counterfeit in the closed space of the asylum.

Already we saw Descartes reject without reasoning or demonstration one possibility of madness that absolutely could not concern him: a high-minded rejection in a virtual image, in a wild hallucination. In the same way we saw the crystal dawn reflect the terrors of the night in the rational light of classical tragedy. Thus we see—and, for lack of space, will simply have to enumerate—in the eighteenth century no longer the image of a philosophy of reason but the negative of a philosophy of nature (see *F,* pp. 428–29, 568–69), of a philosophy of enlightenment, and of its projects of future organization. In the same way, we see the negative of the theme of the noble savage (see *F,* pp. 451–52); opposing the theory of progress, as its concave side, is the theory of degeneration. And for what concerns the notion of the "milieu" in Montesquieu: just as climate, and so on, are thought to explain the Constitution of England, so, in contemporary authors, the same kind of reasons are charged with justifying those English maladies, melancholy and suicide (see *F,* p. 442). This overlapping is quite remarkable; the same family of reasons is valid for the positive of institutions and for the negative of history's failures. As for the asylum, here is it presented as the inverted image of society itself, with an exact replica of bourgeois morality reigning there. With a new replica, that of *The Social Contract,* Sade will become, further on, the anti-Rousseau. But here, little by little, positive psychology is born in this terrain of negativities, which are its conditions of development and its original sin; it emerges fully armed from psychopathology (see *F,* pp. 555, 629, 633–34). It is the same with psychoanalysis: Tuke's asylum creates a pantomime of family relations; in it are born both the reality and the themes of the parental complexes. It is not the family situation in its positivity that is decisive, but its image in the asylum (a quasi-imaginary simulacrum, says the text [see *F,* pp. 587–90]). We read with admiration the parallel analysis of the psychoanalytic monologue (see *F,* pp. 595–97) and of the psychoanalyst as thaumaturge (see *F,* pp. 607–12). This is first-class writing, surpassed in fineness perhaps only by the important passage on Joseph Babinski's pithiatism, where, in a dazzling short circuit, the concepts of images and negatives suddenly take on the whole constellation of possible meanings (see *F,* pp. 610–11).

All the same, these mirror symmetries and complementarities have their own reason. This is that the thinking subject always finds himself on the other side of the dividing line. So much so that he transports into the space of unreason the values, language, and organization of his own rational space. There are certainly symmetry and recognition in the mirror, but there is above all transport. And this transport is, no doubt, one of the dramas of classical reason that must, in order to function, separate from its object, which is paradoxically imprisoned by this transportation. And as soon as its object becomes what it imagines to be its opposite, this transport becomes a reversal; this is the reason governing this family of symmetries and replicas. Thus is identified one of the fundamental conditions of knowledge in the classical sense. The knowing subject must be separated from his object (or his object separated from him); he must objectify his object (that is to say, be certain not to be it) and master it to the point where it is freed from all anxiety and all emotion of which it could be the source. This Apollonian serenity, the condition of knowledge and the liberation of emotion, becomes dramatic when the object is man. In this case, knowledge is misunderstanding. The reasoning of reversal becomes the reasoning behind ignorance—and exclusion.

Two concrete illustrations reveal the remarkable reversibility of these symmetrical structures. Let us suppose that, in a new "form," the madman himself speaks, questioning reason from the depths of unreason; this is how *Rameau's Nephew* delivers the converse of the classical reversal, ironically reconstructing the world in the theater of illusion (see *F,* pp. 421–22). Another example is therapeutic experimentation, always understood as an awakening to the values of positivity, to reason, to nature, to morality, as a return to the current cultural norms of the period, a return to the reality erased by dreams and hallucinations. Moving from unreason to reason, one returns to what is inalienable, moving from the reversed image to the object set aright. Therapy is consequently the concrete transporting that takes on the meaning opposite to that of theoretical knowledge.

If on occasion Foucault's writing sounds somewhat Hegelian, it is rare that his thought moves toward the dialectic. No "historical ensemble" examined this closely could put us under the spell of that magical methodology. Foucault's is, in fact, the system of negatives and the odyssey of alterities. But what we have to examine with attention is the variability of these negations, their fine analysis; without a doubt, the explanation would have fixed in a univocal signification a function that is never the same, all along this odyssey and across this system.

Sometimes the negative is, very precisely, an image, a representation, part of an elsewhere, or another world, transporting here an unknown presence; sometimes it is what is rejected, what surely I am not, an other, absolutely a stranger and someone with whom I have no relation. Thus even the relation of alterity is excluded: the other is isolated, foreclosed in his insularity; or else he is the morally bad, the sinner of the Scripture; sometimes he is the asocial or unintelligible, he who speaks a language that has nothing human left to it; ultimately the one whose work runs between his hands without his being able to stop and accomplish it. . . . It is thus very much a question of the system of all possible variations of the negative, and this structural variation of the negation constitutes history itself, the odyssey of alienation. In a sense, we get the structural genesis of every possible alienation. We will no longer be surprised to find, from this point on, as if at their foundation, all the meanings of alterity, at the different moments and in the diverse efforts that compose the experience of madness. To grasp this experience amounts to finding *in vivo* all the formal models of the treatment of the other. It is thus possible to describe this experience using the structures in question. But so rich is the immediate perception of madness that it would surpass, by far, the formal and comprehensive possibilities of these structures if they were taken univocally, one to one. Thus we see why we need an extremely general, transparent, and analytic language. It is consequently most obvious that the "geometric" language we have just described—presupposing a space bordering the rational and separated from it by boundaries whose nature varies—makes universal and applies in one step, contains in a single process, all the meanings that we have just seen were present, either together or separately. This language is thus the "geometral" of negatives. It can express, at will, the Greek and classical sense of the other, its logical, existential, ontological, moral, epistemological, and religious meanings; it can express, in a single appellation, Platonic alterity, Marxist alienation, medical alienation, and existential estrangement.

These formal domains are thus not gratuitously or abstractly general designations but foundational regions from where all the languages of alienation emerge and where all their conditions of possibility are located. It follows then that alienation in the strictly medical sense is no more than the positivist covering up of a portion of this global domain of alterities—in a sense, one particular case badly explained. From this follows the genesis of abnormal psychology, whose essential relativity it brings to light. (The greatest success of this work, in the project described here, is without doubt contained in the pages already cited that treat the emergence of psychoanalysis [see *F,* pp. 587–608] and of psychopathology in general [see *F,* pp. 555, 629–34]; this method, at once genetic and structural, constructs a sort of generalized "psychoanalysis" of psychoanalysis itself, which in spite of its pretensions to depth, suddenly seems limited and dated as a result.) Everywhere the history follows this structure: the task of two centuries has consisted in isolating the alienated in a closed space, in separating them from the nonalienated (in separating the absolute other from relative others); just as the so-called miracles only unchain the madmen in order to liberate the non-mad and more closely confine the insane, so in the same way we have not defined madness as such except to cover it up and ignore it better. It is around this point of analysis that a second epistemological reversal will be effected.

Seek a definition of madness, but above all, be conscious of the inanity of your pretension. For two centuries now supposedly essential visions have been proposed, all reducible to a pure theory of internment in general, meaning a formal theory of separated spaces where the quarantined suffer. It is important not to say simply, in a banal sense, that internment creates madness; we must say first of all that there is a correspondence between the style of an "enclosure" and an experience of unreason, and that this correspondence is never a relation of knowledge or of therapy. This relation is never one built from madness to internment but, on the contrary, from internment to madness, as if the cares and definitions of the latter merit the locks of the former. Or, if the word *definition* signifies that the mind traces a line around an unknown thing to differentiate it, in fact we have never defined anything but madness. But the style of definition is more revealing of the reason—or the society—that isolates in order to recognize than of the madness that is isolated, and it produces the relativity of alienation and the shock of return. Obviously madmen exist only in respect to some culture; this is almost trivial, except when we think that, to be established, and in the very act of being constituted, this culture makes madmen just as necessarily as a river leaves alluvial deposits. But there is more: this reversal or shock of return. For there to be clarification, analysis, and differentiation of unreason, for this differentiation to lead to an image of the rational, implies, all of a sudden, that one has to define, in their turn, both *reason* and *norm*. And, suddenly, it is they who are going to appear insulated and limited. Lock up madness behind a gate, but understand, in so doing, that you limit reason. This is how what we could call the *Copernican revolution of unreason* is set in motion: in the infinite sea of the irrational, of the indecipherable and the silent, the closed insularity of reason slowly takes shape. And this surrounding, this shadowy proximity, nourishes reason. Foucault's book is organized by this revolution, which is its finality. Everything that precedes it constitutes only the thousand rejections of this nourishment, only the thousand ways of not admitting what we owe those who are exiled and maintaining by distancing and separation a proximity necessary to the life of the mind. Very profoundly, then, the lessons of this book take up those of Nietzsche, as well as Hellenic and medieval lessons. It is a *discourse of unreason on reason* for which these stutterings of reason on madness prepare the way. Here we discover the inspiring chain that was loosed from the hands of Goya, van Gogh, Chekhov, Artaud. But we also understand at what depth is situated the initial project of finally giving speech to this people of silence, of reversing the perspective of language in finally placing a thinking subject, a cogito, a historical subject, a speaking subject, in the domain of unreason where until now only passive objects had been situated, whom we observed at leisure, as if at a fair or circus sideshow. The thinking, functioning subject of enterprise and argument was held in the space of reason; there were his domain and empire; and he defended it, protected it, fortified it. In the neighboring islands are the objects that are only objects. Thus the entire history of these structures of experience that a culture can make of madness consists in seeing how, in this no-man's-land, subjects are going to arise who can finally

speak of their own country, conceive of their own domain, divide it according to autochthonous norms, without leaving this task to anyone else
(see *F,* pp. 475–77, 534). It is profound to say that the end of the nineteenth century and the twentieth give themselves over to this new division, to this new structuration by which the family of reversals acquires
its positivity, even becomes the most dynamic set of positivities. It is true
to say that madmen only exist vis-à-vis a given society or culture; Foucault's book designates for us a perspective that is profound in a different
way, from which we see that there is no reason except by virtue of the
madness that borders it and nourishes it, the madman against which one
is always on guard while accepting it. Ultimately, the message of madness
is expressed in human works along with that of triumphant, reasoning
reason. The true madness is, in essence, the absence of this work, the
rejection of this struggle and this acceptance. There is no madman but
he in whom work sleeps, he who forgets to create it.

Thus the whole system of alterities is organized in retrospect by a
return from the other to the same, from the negative to the positive,
through which the madman solemnly opens for himself the gates of human culture.

3

At this point in the analysis, not everything has been said. There
remains the real thickness of the historical ensemble understood in and
through these structures. What we have seen is how these vary across
different levels. To characterize these levels is to acknowledge the work's
concrete content, to describe at close range the mass of facts by which the
experience of madness is constituted.

These facts are developed in the sociopolitical practice of internment, in medical theory, and in therapeutic practice. These three programs are, most often, independent of each other; this independence
makes this history a drama of ignorance. In the first, economic, sociological, and demographic exigencies condition a political decision to "en-
close" in the old walls of the lazar houses abandoned by lepers a mixed
group of the mad, the poor, and the insane; the second is marked by a
tendency toward philosophizing and alchemical daydreams; in the third,
the guardian persecutes the prisoner. The profiles of these levels are
strongly marked, and we conceive that the jailor has nothing in common
with Doctor Faustus or the minister who decrees. Or rather, yes: what
they have in common is precisely a structure, unvarying each time, that
unifies their analogous (or analogical) experience of madness. The set of
structures described above is this analogon of three detached experiences, of three different perceptions: that of the politician who invents
the closed space of internment or utilizes preexisting spaces, depending

upon his jurisdiction; that of the theoretician who dreams up this pure space without experimentation; and that of the "practitioner" who has a constant relation with the patient, in this space, but who also does not dream of making it a science. The meaning of the history of madness is precisely the norm common to these three isolated perceptions. Its meaning is the following: these three experiences come together little by little to converge in the character of the alienist, who gathers the impressive heritage of he who imprisons, who guards, and who knows, the impure heritage where the functions of father, executioner, chief, thaumaturge, theoretician, and moralizer are all mixed up. The doctor cannot avoid these weighty obligations when the galley becomes a hospice. The modern asylum is the depository of all these mixed alluvial deposits that history swept along. We see, in this last example, how analogical structures of experience arrive at the identity of a unitary perception.

It is useful, besides, to recognize how, at these three levels, the experience that a culture makes of madness is accomplished, to recognize the reasons behind these structural analogies. Certainly, the pillars of this experience are diverse; it is built on economic, judicial, and demographic givens. . . . But all the same it is built on common ground; it is, in fact, political power and its discretions, penitentiary power and its brutalities, theory and its oneiric ignorance, all forging a figure of madness not particularly valued in an economy of poverty, a religion of sin, a morality of fault, an ethics of passion, a logic of error, a metaphysics of nonexistence. All these negative values, which we know constitute the structural analogon, conspire together in a common diagram of unreason, which is less an essential vision than a *projection of this cultural world itself onto itself.* We find again the earlier themes and the domain of symmetries of the history of ideas. The historical ensemble considered is ordered exactly by the described principles; but, on the other hand, because of this, it is necessary to reject these totalizing cultural languages to avoid falling again into such projections, to avoid naturalizing the object, to reveal the cover-up for what it is. Thus, it is very much a question of a history of cultural experience, but above all this history identifies the conditions of such experience. Its object, we have seen, becomes its subject; and, in new forms, old experiences are naturalized.

If all of this is true, from the point of view of language as well as of that of its adequacy to the reality of madness, a new problem must be posed: that of a dialogue between the supporters of such a language and the practitioners of the contemporary psychiatric categories. It is at this precise point that we take up the history again.

In fact, this book is fairly far from contemporary medical reasoning. But not through ignorance or error; on the contrary, by a necessity of a historical kind—we must not forget the terminal dates of the study. Here the whole problem turns on the conception that we can make of the genesis of a particular scientific knowledge. Let's take a detour to better bring it to light. Let us suppose that the same problem comes to be posed for an objective knowledge other than psychiatry, for example physics. No one has posed the problem of its prehistory, its archeology, better than Bachelard. And everyone knows that he posed it in terms of a "psychoanalysis of objective knowledge." What is the result of this research concerning the relation between a prehistoric knowledge and a contemporary one? It is absolutely clear in this regard that the Abbé Nollet is cut off by Pierre Berthelot; there is no historical recurrence that can bind them, neither in the object they study nor in the methods they advocate.

For the object, Bachelard shows that the alchemist considers not so much a natural phenomenon as the psychological subject himself. The object of this archaic knowledge is thus none other than a projection of the cultural universe itself into the unconscious subject of the emotions and the passions. Mutatis mutandis, it is the same with Foucault: in the classical age, the object of archaic psychiatric knowledge is not so much the madman (one doesn't know who or what he is) as a projection of the classical cultural universe into the space of internment. And, just as one does not discover the object-electricity except in tapping an enormous mass of emotive reactions, in the same way one does not discover the madman until after having tapped an enormous mass of reactions (here the word takes on an intensely rigorous meaning) and of rejections. The comparison of these two "projections" reveals an eminently remarkable phenomenon: an immense crisscrossing in the structures of genetic explanations of knowledges. To discover the archaic object of physics, Bachelard is led to speak psychoanalysis; to discover the archaic object of psychoanalysis, Foucault is led to speak "geometry." Let us generalize: to understand the rupture in historical recurrences, one adopts a contemporary language, but one changes discipline. This, by the way, is not strange: it is necessary to explain, on the one hand, that one is mistaken in assigning unreason to a knowledge that will become rational; on the other, in assigning rigor (here we accept the ambiguity of the term) to unreason. A strange crisscrossing of mind and soul. In short, here are two sciences where the genetic path is ruptured; in order to find it again, to rediscover the path of the archeology, one practices an epistemological crossing. The parallel is just as revealing for methodology, with the same rupture between the language of alchemists and that of the physicists: we get lost in trying to understand the language of the former with the aid of the latter's grammar. In the same way, a nuisance is not some approximate form of one paranoia or another. Thus, the complexity of modern analyses of mental illnesses is to the simplicity of the spatial language used by Foucault what the complexity of the table of Dmitry Mendeleyev is to the simplicity of the language of the elements, water, earth, fire. We can spin out the parallel as much as we would like; it always gives the same results: historical rupture, explanatory crossing. One language is dead forever, revived by another language, imported from another region, identified by the history of sciences.

But it seems impossible, at least in our judgment, to spin it out to the end. Because although the epistemological rupture is definitive, a fait accompli, for the physical sciences, it does not seem yet quite completely so for the human sciences. The modern laboratory is done with Doctor Faustus's retorts. Can one say—and, certainly, this is not to judge the great discoveries of psychiatry—that it is the same for our understanding of dementia? Supposing that one day this rupture would be definitive, a fait accompli—for us, this is nothing less than the definition of a science arrived at its maturity—then, no doubt, the dialogue of the historian-archeologist and the psychiatrist will no longer be a controversy.[4] This latter will have acquired all the epistemological serenity needed to perceive his own history head on. Although Bachelard's works have never been invested with the function of purging electrical science of its amorous daydreams, perhaps Foucault's book will have this virtue of epistemological catharsis. To do a history of what is nowhere near finished (whereas prehistory never finishes dying) is perhaps to show the psychologist the country whence he comes and into whose prisons it is useful not to return.

The result is that the work of Foucault is in no way a history (or a chronicle) of psychiatry, inasmuch as the recurrent exploration he engages in does not bring presciences to light. It is an archeology of the subject who is sick in the most profound sense, that is to say, more than a generalized etiology, in that it reveals the conditions of knowledges indissolubly linked to conditions of sickness. The work demonstrates that the relation of classical theoreticians to madness is one of dream and of rejection, and of positive theoreticians, one of covering up. Positivism on mental illness is a particular case of all that has been said about positivity in general, as medical alienation is a narrowly defined case of what has been said of alterities. A chronicle of psychiatry at the moment could only be an incomplete history of science in the sense that we have defined it. Here instead appears the genesis of a knowledge and of its "object," the slow, complex, and plurivocal constitution of every possible relation to unreason. From the formal assessment of the terrain proper to this arche-

---

4. A science arrived at its maturity is a science that has entirely absorbed the rupture between its archaic state and its present one. The history of what are called sciences could thus be understood as the exploration of the interval that separates them from this precise point of rupture, recurrent for this genetic explanation. This point is easily assignable as soon as the language used in this interval makes earlier practices incomprehensible. Beyond this point, it is a matter of *archeology*. These definitions in no way judge the comparative value of forms of knowledge. This might seem tautological, if we did not consider the crossing considered above. A science arrived at its maturity, then, possesses the self-regulation of its autochthonous language (that is why, in a certain way, it escapes "philosophy") and no longer needs to go seeking its values in the field of another form of knowledge. On the contrary, it must do so in order to explain to itself its own prehistory.

ology to the concrete developments of the treatment of the other in general, Foucault leads us toward the transcendental domain that organizes the set of conditions of this relation.

This *Folie et déraison* is thus, in fact, a history of ideas. It is a history found in the mirror of the asylum's microcosm, disfigured certainly, silent and pathetic, but rigorously organized by virtue of the reversals that we now understand. And this hallucinatory mirror does not open a space of virtual images, but rather discovers the originary terrain of cultural processes, the forgotten latencies in human works.

There was once upon a time a country called Erewhon. In this wild country criminals are cared for, the sick are judged, and, often, condemned. It is a hell for innocence. Its name, strangely reversed, signifies, for those who refuse to understand, nowhere. Nowhere, or the other side of the mountains.

"To Do Justice to Freud": The History of Madness in the Age of Psychoanalysis

Jacques Derrida

Translated by Pascale-Anne Brault and Michael Naas

When Elisabeth Roudinesco and René Major did me the honor and kindness of inviting me to a commemoration that would also be a reflection, to one of these genuine tributes where thought is plied to fidelity and fidelity honed by thought, I did not hesitate for one moment.

First of all, because I love memory. This is nothing original, of course, and yet how else can one love? Indeed, thirty years ago, this great book of Foucault was an event whose repercussions were so intense and multiple that I will not even try to identify much less measure them deep down inside me. Next, because I love friendship, and the trusting affection that Foucault showed me thirty years ago, and that was to last for many years, was all the more precious in that, being shared, it corresponded to my professed admiration. Then, after 1972, what came to obscure this friendship, without, however, affecting my admiration, was not, in fact, alien to this book, and to a certain debate that ensued—or at least to its distant, delayed, and indirect effects. There was in all of this a sort of dramatic chain of events, a compulsive and repeated precipitation that I do not wish to describe here because I do not wish to be alone, to be the only one to speak of this after the death of Michel Foucault—except to say that this shadow that made us invisible to one another, that made us not associate with one another for close to ten years (until 1 January 1982 when I returned from a Czech prison), is still part of a story that I also love like life itself. It is part of a story or history that is related, and

On 23 November 1991, the Ninth Colloquium of the International Society for the History of Psychiatry and Psychoanalysis devoted a conference to Foucault's *Histoire de la folie* to mark the thirtieth anniversary of its publication. This essay, which was given as a talk at that conference, was published in French in *Penser la folie: Essais sur Michel Foucault* (Paris, 1992).

that thus relates me by the same token, to the book whose great event we are commemorating here, to something like its postface, one of its postfaces, since the drama I just alluded to also arose out of a certain postface, and even out of a sort of postscript added by Foucault to a postface in 1972.

While accepting wholeheartedly this generous invitation, I nonetheless declined the suggestion that came along with it to return to the discussion that began some twenty-eight years ago. I declined for numerous reasons, the first being the one I just mentioned: one does not carry on a stormy discussion after the other has departed. Second, because this whole thing is more than just overdetermined (so many difficult and intersecting texts, Descartes's, Foucault's, so many objections and responses, from me but also from all those, in France and elsewhere, who later came to act as arbiters); it has become too distant from me, and perhaps because of the drama just alluded to I no longer wished to return to it. In the end, the debate is archived and those who might be interested in it can analyze as much as they want and decide for themselves. By rereading all the texts of this discussion, right up to the last word, and especially the last word, one will be better able to understand, I imagine, why I prefer not to give it a new impetus today. There is no privileged witness for such a situation—which, moreover, only ever has the chance of forming, and this from the very origin, with the possible disappearance of the witness. This is perhaps one of the meanings of any history of madness, one of the problems for any project or discourse concerning a history of madness, or even a history of sexuality: is there any witnessing to madness? Who can witness? Does witnessing mean seeing? Is it to provide a reason *[rendre raison]*? Does it have an object? Is there any object? Is there a possible third that might provide a reason without objectifying, or even identifying, that is to say, without examining *[arraisoner]*?

Though I have decided not to return to what was debated close to thirty years ago, it would nevertheless be absurd, obsessional to the point of pathological, to say nothing of impossible, to give in to a sort of fetishistic denial and to think that I can protect myself from any contact with the place or meaning of this discussion. Although I intend to speak today of something else altogether, starting from a very recent rereading of *The History of Madness in the Classical Age*, I am not surprised, and you will probably not be either, to see the silhouette of certain questions reemerge: not their content, of course, to which I will in no way return, but their abstract type, the schema or specter of an analogous problematic. For example, if I speak not of Descartes but of Freud, if I thus avoid a figure who seems central to this book and who, because he is decisive as far as its center or centering of perspective is concerned, emerges right from the early pages on, right from the first border or approach,[1] if I

1. See Michel Foucault, *Folie et déraison: Historie de la folie à l'âge classique* (Paris, 1961), pp. 53–57; hereafter abbreviated *F.* Derrida refers here and throughout to the original edi-

thus avoid this Cartesian reference in order to move toward another (psychoanalysis, Freudian or some other) that is evoked only on the edges of the book and is named only right near the end, or ends, on the other border, this will perhaps be once again in order to pose a question that will resemble the one that imposed itself upon me thirty years ago, namely, that of the very possibility of a history of madness. The question will be, in the end, just about the same, though it will be posed from another border, and it still imposes itself upon me as the first tribute owed such a book. If this book was possible, if it had from the beginning and retains today a certain monumental value, the presence and undeniable necessity of a *monument,* that is, of what imposes itself by recalling and cautioning, it must tell us, teach us, or ask us something about its own possibility.

About its own possibility *today:* yes, we are saying *today,* a certain today. Whatever else one may think of this book, whatever questions or reservations it might inspire in those who come at it from some other point of view, its pathbreaking force seems incontestable. Just as incontestable, in fact, as the law according to which all pathbreaking opens the way only at a certain price, that is, by bolting shut other passages, by ligaturing, stitching up, or compressing, indeed repressing, at least provisionally, other veins. And so today, like yesterday, I mean in March of 1963, it is this question of the *today* that is important to me, the question such as I had tried to formulate it yesterday. I ask you to pardon me this once, then, since I will not make a habit of it, for citing a few lines that then defined, in its general form, a task that seems to me still necessary, on the side of *[du côté de]* Freud this time rather than on the side of Descartes. By saying "on the side of Freud" rather than "on the side of Descartes," let us not give in too quickly to the naivete that would precipitate

---

tion of this work. The book was reprinted with different pagination in 1972 and included as an appendix "Mon corps, ce papier, ce feu," Foucault's response to Derrida's "Cogito et histoire de la folie," a lecture first given in 1963 and reprinted in 1967 in Derrida, *L'Écriture et la différence* (Paris, 1967). A much abridged version of *Histoire de la folie* was published in 1964 and was translated into English by Richard Howard, under the title *Madness and Civilization: A History of Insanity in the Age of Reason* (New York, 1965); hereafter abbreviated *M.*

Since Derrida refers to the unabridged text of 1961 and works with the original title throughout, we have referred to this work as *The History of Madness* (or in some cases, *The History of Madness in the Classical Age*). This is in keeping with "Cogito and the History of Madness," *Writing and Difference,* trans. Alan Bass (Chicago, 1978), pp. 31–63. For the reader who wishes to follow Derrida's itinerary through *Folie et déraison: Histoire de la folie à l'âge classique,* we have given all references to the 1961 French version along with references to the English translation when they exist in the abridged version. Since all the other texts of Foucault cited by Derrida have been translated in their entirety, we have in each case given the French followed by the English page references. Translations have been slightly modified in several instances to fit the context of Derrida's argument.—TRANS.

us into believing that we are closer to a today with Freud than with Descartes, though this is the opinion of most historians.

Here, then, is the question of yesterday, of the today of yesterday, such as I would like to translate it today, on the side of Freud, transporting it in this way into the today of today:

> Therefore, if Foucault's book, despite all the acknowledged impossibilities and difficulties [acknowledged by him, of course], was capable of being written, we have the right to ask what, in the last resort, supports this language without recourse or support ["without recourse" and "without support" are expressions of Foucault that I had just cited]: who enunciates the possibility of nonrecourse? Who wrote and who is to understand, in what language and from what historical situation of logos, who wrote and who is to understand this history of madness? For it is not by chance that such a project could take shape today. Without forgetting, *quite to the contrary,* the audacity of Foucault's act in the *History of Madness,* we must assume that a certain liberation of madness has gotten underway, that psychiatry has opened itself up, however minimally [and, in the end, I would be tempted simply to replace *psychiatry* by *psychoanalysis* in order to translate the today of yesterday into the today of my question of today], and that the concept of madness as unreason, if it ever had a unity, has been dislocated. And that a project such as Foucault's can find its historical origin and passageway in the opening produced by this dislocation.
>
> If Foucault, more than anyone else, is attentive and sensitive to these kinds of questions, it nevertheless appears that he does not acknowledge their quality of being prerequisite methodological or philosophical considerations.[2]

If this type of question made any sense or had any legitimacy, if the point was then to question that which, today, in this time that is ours, this time in which Foucault's *History of Madness* was written, made possible the event of such a discourse, it would have been more appropriate for me to elaborate this problematic on the side of modernity, *a parte subjecti,* in some sense, on the side where the book was written, thus on the side, for example, of what must have happened to the modern psychiatry mentioned in the passage I just read. To modern psychiatry or, indeed, to psychoanalysis or rather to psychoanalyses or psychoanalysts, since the passage to the plural will be precisely what is at stake in this discussion. It would have thus been more imperative to insist on modern psychiatry or psychoanalysis than to direct the same question toward Descartes. To study the place and role of psychoanalysis in the Foucauldian project of

2. Derrida, "Cogito et histoire de la folie," p. 61; "Cogito and the History of Madness," p. 38.

a history of madness, as I am now going to try to do, might thus consist in correcting an oversight or in confronting more directly a problematic that I had left in a preliminary stage, as a general, programmatic frame, in the introduction to my lecture of 1963. That lecture made only one allusion to psychoanalysis. It is true, however, that it inscribed it from the very opening. In a protocol that laid out certain reading positions, I spoke of the way in which philosophical language is rooted in nonphilosophical language, and I recalled a rule of hermeneutical method that still seems to me valid for the historian of philosophy as well as for the psychoanalyst, namely, the necessity of first ascertaining a surface or manifest meaning and, thus, of speaking the language of the patient to whom one is listening: the necessity of gaining a good understanding, in a quasi-scholastic way, philologically and grammatically, by taking into account the dominant and stable conventions, of what Descartes *meant* on the already so difficult surface of his text, such as it is interpretable according to classical norms of reading; the necessity of gaining this understanding *before* submitting the first reading to a symptomatic and historical interpretation regulated by other axioms or protocols, *before and in order to* destabilize, wherever this is possible and if it is necessary, the authority of canonical interpretations. Whatever one ends up doing with it, one must begin by listening to the canon. It is in this context that I recalled Ferenczi's remark cited by Freud in *The Interpretation of Dreams* ("Every language has its own dream language") and Lagache's observations concerning polyglotism in analysis.[3]

In its general and historical form, my question concerned the *site* that *today* gives rise to a history of madness and thereby makes it possible. Such a question should have led me, it is true, toward the situation of psychiatry and psychoanalysis rather than toward a questioning of a reading of Descartes. This logic would have seemed more natural and the consequence more immediate. But if, in so strictly delimiting the field, I substituted Descartes for Freud, it was perhaps not only because of the significant and strategic place that Foucault confers upon the Cartesian moment in the interpretation of the *Great Confinement* and of the *Classical Age,* that is to say, in the layout of the very object of the book; it was already, at least implicitly, because of the role that the reference to a certain Descartes played in the thought of that time, in the early sixties, as close as possible to psychoanalysis, in the very element, in truth, of a certain psychoanalysis and Lacanian theory. This theory developed around the question of the subject and the subject of science. Whether it was a question of anticipated certainty and logical time (1945, in *Écrits*) or, some years later (1965–1966), of the role of the cogito and—precisely—of the deceitful God in "La Science et la vérité," Lacan returned time and again

3. See ibid., p. 53; p. 37.—Trans.

to a certain unsurpassability of Descartes.[4] In 1945, Lacan associated Descartes with Freud in his "Propos sur la causalité psychique" and concluded by saying that "neither Socrates, nor Descartes, nor Marx, nor Freud, can be 'surpassed' insofar as they led their research with this passion for unveiling whose object is the truth."[5]

The title I have proposed for the few reflections I will risk today, "The History of Madness in the Age of Psychoanalysis," clearly indicates a change—a change in tense, in mode or in voice. It is no longer a question of the age *described* by a *History of Madness*. It is no longer a question of an epoch or period, such as the classical age, that would, inasmuch as it is its very object, stand before the history of madness such as Foucault writes it. It is a question today of the age to which the book itself belongs, the age from out of which it takes place, the age that provides it its situation; it is a question of the age that is *describing* rather than the age that is *described*. In my title, it would be necessary to put "the history of madness" in quotation marks since the title designates the age of the book, *The History (historia rerum gestarum) of Madness*—as a book—in the age of psychoanalysis and not the history *(res gestae)* of madness, of madness itself, in the age of psychoanalysis, even though, as we will see, Foucault regularly attempts to objectify psychoanalysis and to reduce it to that of which he speaks rather than to that from out of which he speaks. What will interest me will thus be rather the time and historical conditions in which the book is rooted, those that it takes as its point of departure, and not so much the time or historical conditions that it recounts and tries in a certain sense to objectify. Were one to trust too readily in the opposition between subject and object, as well as in the category of objectification (something that I here believe to be neither possible nor just, and hardly faithful to Foucault's own intention), one would say for the sake of convenience that it is a question of considering the history of madness *a parte subjecti*, that is, from the side where it is written or inscribed and not from the side of what it describes.

Now, from the side where this history is written, there is, of course, a certain state of psychiatry—as well as psychoanalysis. Would Foucault's project have been possible without psychoanalysis, with which it is contemporary and of which it speaks little and in such an equivocal or ambivalent manner in the book? Does the project owe psychoanalysis anything? What? Would the debt, if it had been contracted, be essential? Or would it, on the contrary, define the very thing from which the project had to detach itself, and in a critical fashion, in order to take shape? In a word, what is the situation of psychoanalysis at the moment of, and with respect

---

4. See Jacques Lacan, "Propos sur la causalité psychique" and "La Science et la vérité," *Écrits* (Paris, 1966), p. 209, pp. 219–44. The latter was translated by Bruce Fink, under the title "Science and Truth," *Newsletter of the Freudian Field* 3, nos. 1–2 (1989):4–29.—TRANS.

5. Lacan, "Propos sur la causalité psychique," p. 193.

to, Foucault's book? And how does this book situate its project with re-spect to psychoanalysis?

Let us put our trust for a moment in this common name, psychoanal-ysis. And let us delay a bit the arrival of proper names, for example Freud or Lacan, and provisionally assume that there is indeed a psychoanalysis that is a single whole: as if it were not, already in Freud, sufficiently di-vided to make its localization and identification more than problematic. Yet the very thing whose coming due we are here trying to delay will no doubt form the very horizon, in any case the provisional conclusion, of this talk.

As you well know, Foucault speaks rather little of Freud in this book. This may seem justified, on the whole, by the very delimitation that a historian of madness in the classical age must impose upon himself. If one accepts the great caesura of this layout (even though this raises a question, or swarm of questions, that I prudently, and by economy, decide not to approach in order to get a better grasp on what Foucault *means* by Freud, situating myself, therefore, within the thesis or hypothesis of the partition between a classical and a postclassical age), then Freud does not have to be treated. He can and must be located at the very most on the borderline. The borderline is never a secure place, it never forms an indi-visible line, and it is always on the border that the most disconcerting problems of topology get posed. Where, in fact, would a problem of topol-ogy get posed if not *on the border?* Would one ever have to worry about the border if it formed an indivisible line? A borderline is, moreover, not a place per se. It is always risky, particularly for the historian, to assign to whatever happens on the borderline, to whatever happens between sites, the taking-place of a determinable event.

Now, Foucault *does and does not want* to situate Freud in a historical place that is stabilizable, identifiable, and open to a univocal understand-ing. The interpretation or topography that he presents us of the Freudian moment is always uncertain, divided, mobile, some would say ambiguous, others ambivalent, confused, or contradictory. Sometimes he wants to credit Freud, sometimes discredit him, unless he is actually doing both indiscernibly and at the same time. One will always have the choice of attributing this ambivalence to either Foucault or Freud; it can character-ize a motivation, the gesture of the interpreter and a certain state of his work, but it can also, or in the first place, refer simply to the interpreter or historian's taking account of a structural duplicity that his work reflects from the thing itself, namely, from the event of psychoanalysis. The moti-vation would thus be *justly* motivated, it would be *just that*—motivated; it would be called for and justified by the very thing that is in question. For the ambiguity of which we are going to speak could indeed be on the side of psychoanalysis, on the side of the event of this invention named psychoanalysis.

To begin, let us indicate a few telling signs. If most of the explicit references to Freud are grouped in the conclusions of the book (at the end of "The Birth of the Asylum" and in the beginning of "The Anthropological Circle"),[6] what I would here call a *charnière,* a *hinge,* comes earlier on, right in the middle of the volume, to divide at once the book and the book's relation to Freud.

Why a *charnière?* This word can be taken in the technical or anatomical sense of a central or cardinal articulation, a hinge pin *(cardo)* or pivot. A *charnière* or hinge is an axial device that enables the circuit, the trope, or the movement of rotation. But one might also dream a bit in the vicinity of its homonym, that is, in line with this other *artifact* that the code of falconry also calls a *charnière,* the place where the hunter attracts the bird by laying out the flesh of a lure.

This double articulation, this double movement or alternation between opening and closing that is assured by the workings of a hinge, this coming and going, indeed this *fort/da* of a pendulum *[pendule]* or balance *[balancier]*—that is what Freud means to Foucault. And this technico-historical hinge also remains the place of a possible simulacrum or lure—for both the body and the flesh. Taken at this level of generality, things will never change for Foucault. There will always be this interminable alternating movement that successively opens and closes, draws near and distances, rejects and accepts, excludes and includes, disqualifies and legitimates, masters and liberates. The Freudian place is not only the technico-historical apparatus, the *artifact* called *charnière* or hinge. Freud himself will in fact take on the ambiguous figure of a doorman or doorkeeper *[huissier].* Ushering in a new epoch of madness, our epoch, the one out of which is written *The History of Madness* (the book bearing this title), Freud also represents the best guardian of an epoch that comes to a close with him, the history of madness such as it is recounted by the book bearing this title.

Freud as the doorman of the today, the holder of the keys, of those that open as well as those that close the door, that is, the *huis:* onto the today *[l'aujourd'hui]* or onto madness. He *[Lui],* Freud, is the double figure of the door and the doorkeeper. He stands guard and ushers in. Alternatively or simultaneously, he closes one epoch and opens another. And as we will see, this double possibility is not alien to an institution, to what is called the analytic situation as a scene behind closed doors *[huis clos].* That is why—and this would be the paradox of a serial law—Freud does and does not belong to the different series in which Foucault inscribes him. What is outstanding, outside the series *[hors-série],* turns out to be regularly reinscribed within different series. I am not now going to get involved in formal questions concerning a quasi-transcendental law of seriality that could be illustrated in an analogous way by so many other

6. This final chapter of *Histoire de la folie* is not included in *Madness and Civilization.*—TRANS.

examples, each time, in fact, that the transcendental condition of a series is also, paradoxically, a part of that series, creating aporias for the constitution of any set or whole *[ensemble]*, particularly, of any historical configuration (age, *episteme*, paradigm, *themata*, epoch, and so on). These aporias are anything but accidental impasses that one should try to force at all cost into received theoretical models. The putting to the test of these aporias is also the chance of thinking.

To keep to the contract of this conference, I will restrict myself to a single example.

The first sign comes right in the middle of the book (*F*, pp. 410–11; *M*, pp. 197–98). It comes at the end of the second part, in the chapter entitled "Doctors and Patients." We have there a sort of epilogue, less than a page and a half long. Separated from the conclusion by asterisks,[7] the epilogue also signals the truth of a transition and the meaning of a passage. It seems to be firmly structured by two unequivocal statements:

1. Psychology does not exist in the classical age. It does *not yet* exist. Foucault says this without hesitation right at the beginning of the epilogue: "In the classical age, it is futile to try to distinguish physical therapeutics from psychological medications, for the simple reason that psychology did not exist."

2. But as for the psychology that was to be born after the classical age, psychoanalysis would not be a part, it would *no longer* be a part. Foucault writes: "It is not psychology that is involved in psychoanalysis."

In other words, if in the classical age there is *not yet* psychology, there is, in psychoanalysis, *already no more* psychology. But in order to affirm this, it is necessary, *on the one hand*, to resist a prejudice or a temptation, to resist that which continues to urge so many interpreters of good sense (and sometimes, in part, Foucault among them) to take psychoanalysis for a psychology (however original or new it may be). Foucault is going to show signs of this resistance, as we will see. But it is also necessary, *on the other hand*, to accept, within this historical schema, the hypothesis of a return: not the *return to Freud* but the *return of Freud* to—.

What return? Return to what? *Return* is Foucault's word, an underscored word. If psychoanalysis is already *no longer* a psychology, does it not, at least in this respect, seem to suggest a certain return to the time when psychology was *not yet*? Beyond eighteenth-century psychology and, very broadly, beyond the psychologistic modernity of the nineteenth century, beyond the positivist institution of psychology, does it not seem as if Freud were joining back up with a certain classical age or, at least, with whatever in this age does not determine madness as a physical illness but as unreason, that is, as something that has to do with reason? In the classical age, if such a thing exists (an hypothesis of Foucault that I take here, in this context, as such, as if it were not debatable), unreason is no

7. This is the case for the French versions but not for the English.—TRANS.

doubt reduced to silence; one does not speak with it. One interrupts or forbids dialogue; and this suspension or interdiction would have received from the Cartesian cogito the violent form of a sentence. For Freud *too* madness would be unreason (and in this sense, at least, there would be a neo-Cartesian logic at work in psychoanalysis). But this time one should resume speaking with it: one would reestablish a dialogue with unreason and lift the Cartesian interdiction. Like the word *return*, the expression "dialogue with unreason" is a quotation. The two expressions scan a final paragraph of this epilogue, in the middle of the book, that begins with the phrase with which I entitled this talk: "We must do justice to Freud" (*F*, p. 411; *M*, p. 198).

When one says, "one must do justice," "one has to be fair" *["il faut être juste"]*, it is often with the intention of correcting an impulse or reversing the direction of a tendency; one is also recommending resisting a temptation. Foucault had to have felt this temptation, the temptation to do an injustice to Freud, to be unfair to him, that is, in this case, to write him into the age of the psychopathological institution (which we will define in a moment). He must have felt it outside or within himself. Indeed, such a temptation must still be threatening and liable to reemerge since it is still necessary to call for vigilance and greater justice.

Here, then, is the paragraph, which I read in extenso, since its internal tension determines, it seems to me, the matrix of all future statements about psychoanalysis; it determines them in the very oscillation of their movement back and forth. It is like scales of justice *[la balance d'une justice]* that not even the death sentence *[arrêt de mort]* would ever be able to stop *[arrêterait]* in their even or just *[juste]* stability. It is as if justice were to remain its own movement:

> This is why we must do justice to Freud. Between Freud's *Five Case Histories* and Janet's scrupulous investigations of *Psychological Healing*, there is more than the density of a *discovery;* there is the sovereign violence of a *return.* Janet enumerated the elements of a division, drew up his inventory, annexed here and there, perhaps conquered. Freud went back to madness at the level of its *language*, reconstituted one of the essential elements of an experience reduced to silence by positivism; he did not make a major addition to the list of psychological treatments for madness; he restored, in medical thought, the possibility of a dialogue with unreason. Let us not be surprised that the most "psychological" of medications has so quickly encountered its converse and its organic confirmations. It is not psychology that is involved in psychoanalysis: but precisely an experience of unreason that it has been psychology's meaning, in the modern world, to mask. [*F*, p. 411; *M*, p. 198][8]

8. One will note in passing that we have here, along with very brief allusions to the *Three Essays on the Theory of Sexuality, Introductory Lectures on Psycho-Analysis,* and a couple of individual cases in *Mental Illness and Psychology,* and a reference just as brief to *Totem and*

"To mask": positivist psychology would thus have masked the experience of unreason: an imposition of the mask, a violent dissimulation of the face, of truth or of visibility. Such violence would have consisted in disrupting a certain unity, that which corresponded precisely *[justement]* to the presumed unity of the classical age: from then on, there would be, on the one hand, illness of an organic nature and, on the other, unreason, an unreason often tempered by this modernity under its "epithetic" form: the *unreasonable,* whose discursive manifestations will become the object of a psychology.[9] This psychology then loses all relation to a certain truth of madness, that is, to a certain truth of unreason. Psychoanalysis, on the contrary, breaks with psychology *by speaking with the Unreason* that speaks within madness and, thus, by returning through this exchange of words not to the classical age itself—which also determined madness as unreason, but, unlike psychology, did so only in order to exclude or confine it—but toward this eve of the classical age that still haunted it.

While this schema is firmly established by the page just cited, I was struck in rereading *The History of Madness* by a paradox in the form of a chiasm. I had not, in my first reading, given it the attention it deserves. What is the schema of this paradox? By reason of what we have just heard, in order to do "justice" to Freud we ought to give him credit—and this is what happens—for finding a place in the gallery of all those who, from one end of the book to the other, announce, like heralds of good tidings, the very possibility of the book: Nietzsche above all and, most frequently, Nietzsche and Artaud, who are often associated in the same sentence, Nietzsche, Artaud, Van Gogh, sometimes Nerval, and Hölderlin from time to time. Their excess, "the madness in which the work of art is engulfed," is the gulf or abyss out of which opens "the space of our enterprise" (*F,* p. 643; *M,* p. 288).

It is *before* this madness, in the fleeting moment when it is joined to the work, that we are *responsible.* We are far from being able to arraign it or make it appear, for it is we who must appear *before* it. Let us recognize,

---

Taboo in *The Order of Things,* one of the few times that Foucault mentions a work of Freud; beyond this, he does not, to my knowledge, cite or analyze any text of Freud, or of any other psychoanalyst, not even those of contemporary French psychoanalysts. Each time, only the proper name is pronounced—Freud, or the common name—psychoanalysis. See Foucault, *Maladie mentale et psychologie* (Paris, 1962), hereafter abbreviated *MM,* trans. Alan Sheridan, under the title *Mental Illness and Psychology* (Berkeley, 1987), p. 31, hereafter abbreviated *MI;* and *Les Mots et les choses: Une Archéologie des sciences humaines* (Paris, 1966), hereafter abbreviated *MC,* trans. pub., under the title *The Order of Things: An Archaeology of the Human Sciences* (New York, 1973), p. 379, hereafter abbreviated *OT.*

    Discovery is underscored by Foucault, along with *return* and *language.* Freud is the event of a *discovery*—the unconscious and psychoanalysis as a movement of *return*—and what relates the discovery to the return is language, the possibility of speaking with madness, "the possibility of a dialogue with unreason."

    9. Foucault had earlier noted this in *F,* p. 195.

then, that we are responsible before it rather than being authorized to examine it *[arraisonner]*, to objectify and demand an explanation from it. At the end of the last page, after having spent a good deal of time speaking of Nietzsche and after having mentioned Van Gogh, Foucault writes: "The moment when, together, the work of art and madness are born and fulfilled is the beginning of the time when the world finds itself arraigned by that work of art and responsible before it for what it is" (*F*, p. 643; *M*, p. 289). This is what *The History of Madness,* in responding to the summons, takes note of and assumes responsibility for. It assumes responsibility before that which is named by the names of Nietzsche and all these others who, as everyone knows, were deemed crazy by society (Artaud, and before him Van Gogh, and before him Nerval, and before him Hölderlin).

But what about Freud? Why is he, in the same book, sometimes associated with and sometimes opposed to these great witnesses of madness and excess, these great witnesses who are also great judges, our judges, those who judge us? Must we be arraigned before Freud? And why do things then get complicated?

I would see the chiasm of which I just spoke appearing in a place where Freud is in fact found near Nietzsche, on the same side as he, that is, on our side, on the side of what Foucault calls "contemporary man": this enigmatic "we" for whom a history of madness opens today, for whom the door of today *[l'huis d'aujourd'hui]* is cracked open so that its possibility may be glimpsed. Foucault has just described the loss of unreason, the background against which the classical age determined madness. It is the moment when unreason degenerates or disappears into the unreasonable; it is the tendency to pathologize, so to speak, madness. And there again, it is through a return to unreason, this time without exclusion, that Nietzsche and Freud reopen the dialogue with madness *itself* (assuming, along with Foucault, that one can here say "itself"). This dialogue had, in a sense, been *broken off* twice, and in two different ways: the second time, by a psychological positivism that no longer conceived of madness as unreason, and the first time, already by the classical age, which, while excluding madness and breaking off the dialogue with it, still determined it as unreason, and excluded it precisely because of this—but excluded it as close as possible to itself, as its other and its adversary: this is the Cartesian moment, such as it is determined, at least, in the three pages that were the object of our debate nearly thirty years ago.

I will underscore everything that marks the today, the present, the now, the contemporary, this time that is proper and common to us, the time of this fragile and divided "we" from which is decided the possibility of a book like *The History of Madness,* decided while scarcely being sketched out, while promising itself, in short, rather than giving itself over. Nietzsche *and* Freud are here conjoined, conjugated, like a couple, Nietzsche *and* Freud, and the conjunction of their coupling is also the copula-hinge or, if you prefer, the middle term of the modern proposition:

> If *contemporary* man, since Nietzsche and Freud, finds deep within himself the site for contesting all truth, being able to read, in what he *now* knows of himself, the signs of fragility through which unreason threatens, seventeenth-century man, on the contrary, discovers, in the immediate presence of his thought to itself, the certainty in which reason in its pure form is announced. [*F*, pp. 195–96]

Why did I speak of a chiasm? And why would we be fascinated by the multiple chiasm that organizes this entire interpretative scene?

It is because, in the three pages devoted to Descartes at the beginning of the second chapter "The Great Confinement," Foucault spoke of an *exclusion*. He described it, posed it, declared it unequivocally and firmly ("madness is excluded by the subject who doubts"). This exclusion was the result of a "decision," the result (and these are all his words) of a "strange act of force" that was going to "reduce to silence" the excluded madness and trace a very strict "line of division." In the part of the *Meditations* that he cited and focused on, Foucault left out all mention of the Evil Genius. It was thus in recalling the hyperbolic raising of the stakes in the fiction of the Evil Genius that I had then confessed my perplexity and proposed other questions. When Foucault responds to me nine years later in the afterword to the 1972 Gallimard edition of *The History of Madness,* he still firmly contests the way I used this Cartesian fiction of the Evil Genius and this hyperbolic moment of doubt. He accuses me of erasing "everything that shows that the episode of the evil genius is an exercise that is voluntary, controlled, mastered and carried out from start to finish by a meditating subject who never lets himself be surprised"[10] (*F*, p. 601; such a reproach was indeed unfair, unjust, since I had stressed that this methodical mastery of the voluntary subject is "almost always" at work and that Foucault, therefore, like Descartes, is "almost always right *[a . . . raison]*," and almost always wins out over *[a raison de]* the Evil Genius.[11] But that is not what is at issue here, and I said that I would not reopen the debate.) And by accusing me of erasing this methodical neutralization of the Evil Genius, Foucault—once again in his response of 1972—confirms the claims of the three pages in question and maintains that "if the evil genius again takes on the powers of *madness,* this is only after the exercise of meditation has excluded the risk of *being mad.*"[12] One might

10. Foucault, "My Body, This Paper, This Fire," trans. Geoff Bennington, *Oxford Literary Review* 4 (Autumn 1979): 26; trans. mod.; "Mon corps, ce papier, ce feu" was first published in *Paideia* (Sept. 1971) and was reissued as the appendix to the 1972 edition of *Histoire de la folie.*

11. Derrida, "Cogito et histoire de la folie," p. 91; "Cogito and the History of Madness," p. 58.

12. Foucault, "My Body, This Paper, This Fire," p. 26.

be tempted to respond that if the Evil Genius can *again take on* these pow-ers of madness, if he once "again takes them on" afterwards, after the fact, it is because the exclusion of the risk of being mad makes way for an *after.* The narrative is thus not interrupted during the exclusion alleged by Foucault, an exclusion that is, up to a certain point at least, attested to and incontestable (and I never in fact contested this exclusion in this re-gard, quite the contrary); neither the narrative nor the exercise of the meditation that it retraces are any more interrupted than the order of reasons is definitively stopped by this same exclusion. But let us move on. As I said earlier, I am not invoking this difficulty in order to return to an old discussion. I am doing it because Freud is going to be, as I will try to show, doubly situated, *twice* implicated in the chiasm that interests me: *on the one hand,* in the sentence that I cited a moment ago (where Freud was immediately associated with Nietzsche, the only one to be associated with him, on the "good" side, so to speak, on the side where "we" contempo-raries reopen the dialogue with unreason that was twice interrupted); this sentence is followed by a few references to the Evil Genius that com-plicate, as I myself had tried to do, the reading of the scene of Cartesian doubt as the moment of the great confinement; but also, and *on the other hand,* since I will later try, in a more indirect way—and this would be in the end the essence of my talk today—to recall the necessity of taking into account a certain Evil Genius *of* Freud, namely, the presence of the demonic, the devil, the devil's advocate, the limping devil, and so on in *Beyond the Pleasure Principle,* where psychoanalysis finds, it seems to me, its greatest speculative power but also the place of greatest resistance to psychoanalysis (death drive, repetition compulsion, and so on, and *fort/da!*).

Thus, just after having spoken of "contemporary man, since Nietzsche and Freud," Foucault offers a development *on the subject of the Evil Genius.* The logic of this sequence seems to me guided by a "One must not forget" that I would be tempted to relate to the "One must do justice" of a moment ago. What must one not forget? The Evil Genius, of course *[justement].* And especially, I emphasize, the fact that the Evil Ge-nius is *anterior* to the cogito, such that its threat remains *perpetual.*

This might contradict (as I had attempted to do) the thesis argued 150 pages earlier on the subject of the Cartesian cogito as the simple exclusion of madness. This could have, as a result, indeed this should have, spared us a long and dramatic debate. But it is too late now. Fou-cault reaffirms all the same, despite the recognized anteriority of the Evil Genius, that the cogito is the absolute beginning, even if, in this absolute beginning, "one must not forget" what has, in short, been forgotten or omitted in the discourse on the exclusion of madness by the cogito. The question thus still remains what a methodically absolute beginning would be that does not let us forget this anterior—and moreover perpetual—threat, nor the haunting backdrop that first lets it appear. As always, I prefer to cite, even though it is a long passage. Here is what Foucault says immediately after having evoked the "contemporary man" who, "since Nietzsche and Freud," meets in "what he now knows of himself" that "through which unreason threatens." He says, in effect, that what is called contemporary had already begun in the classical age and with the Evil Genius, which clearly, to my eyes at least, cannot leave intact the historical categories of reference and the presumed identity of something like the classical age (for example).

> But this does not mean that classical man was, in his experience of the truth, more distanced from unreason than we ourselves might be. It is true that the cogito is the absolute beginning [this statement thus confirms the thesis of *F,* pp. 54–57] *but one must not forget* [my emphasis] that the evil genius is anterior to it. And the evil genius is not the symbol in which are summed up and systematized all the dangers of such psychological events as dream images and sensory errors. Between God and man, the evil genius has an absolute meaning: he is in all his rigor the possibility of unreason and the totality of its powers. He is more than the refraction of human finitude; well beyond man, he signals the danger that could prevent man once and for all from gaining access to the truth: he is the main obstacle, not of such a spirit but of such reason. And it is not because the truth that gets illuminated in the cogito ends up entirely masking the shadow of the evil genius that one *ought to forget* its perpetually threatening power [my emphasis: Foucault had earlier said that *one must not forget* that the evil genius is anterior to the cogito, and he now says that *one must not forget* its perpetually threatening power, even after the passage, the moment, the experience, the certainty of the cogito, and the exclusion of madness that this brings about]: this danger will hover over Descartes' reflections right up until the establishment of the existence and truth of the external world. [*F,* p. 196]

One would have to ask, though we will not have the time and this is not the place, about the effects that the category of the "perpetual threat" (and this is Foucault's term) can have on indications of presence, positive markings, the determinations made by means of signs or statements, in short, the whole criteriology and symptomatology that can give assurance to a historical knowledge concerning a figure, an *episteme,* an age, an epoch, a paradigm, once all these determinations are found to be in effect *[justement]* threatened by a perpetual haunting. For, in principle, all these determinations are, for the historian, either presences or absences; as such, they thus exclude haunting; they allow themselves to be located by means of signs, one would almost say on a table of absences and presences; they come out of the logic of opposition, in this case, the logic of inclusion *or* exclusion, of the alternative between the inside and the outside, and so on. The perpetual threat, that is, the shadow of haunting (and haunting is, like the phantom or fiction of an Evil Genius, neither present nor absent, neither positive nor negative, neither inside nor outside) does not challenge only one thing or another; it threatens the logic that distinguishes between one thing and another, the very logic of exclusion or foreclosure, as well as the history that is founded upon this logic and its alternatives. What is excluded is, of course, never simply excluded, not by the cogito nor by anything else, without this eventually returning—and that is what a certain psychoanalysis will have also helped us to understand. Let me leave undeveloped this general problem, however, in order to return to a certain regulated functioning in the references to psychoanalysis and to the name of Freud in *The History of Madness in the Classical Age*.

Let us consider the couple Nietzsche/Freud, this *odd couple* about which there is so much else to say (I have attempted this elsewhere, especially in *The Post Card*, and precisely *[justement]* in relationship to *Beyond the Pleasure Principle*). The affiliation or filiation of this couple reappears elsewhere. It is again at a filial limit, in the introduction to the third and final part, when the "delirium" of *Rameau's Nephew* sets the tone or gives the key, just as the Cartesian cogito had, for a new arrangement or division *[partition]*. For the "delirium" of *Rameau's Nephew* "announces Freud and Nietzsche." Let us set aside all the questions that the concept of "announcing" might pose for the historian. It is not by accident that they resemble those raised a moment ago by the concept of *haunting*. As soon as that which *announces* already no longer completely belongs to a present configuration and already belongs to the future of another, its place, the taking-place of its event, calls for another logic; it disrupts, in any case, the axiomatics of a history that places too much trust in the opposition between absence and presence, outside and inside, inclusion and exclusion. Let us read, then, this sentence and note the recurring and thus all the more striking association of this *announcement* with the figure of the Evil Genius, but, this time, with the figure of "another evil genius":

> The delirium of Rameau's Nephew is a tragic confrontation of need and illusion in an oneiric mode, one that announces Freud and Nietzsche [the order of names is this time reversed]; it is also the ironic repetition of the world, its destructive reconstitution in the theater of illusion. [*F*, p. 422]

An Evil Genius then immediately reappears. And who will see this inevitable repetition as a coincidence? But it is not the same Evil Genius. It is another figure of the evil genius. There would thus be a recurring function of the Evil Genius, a function that, in making reference to a Platonic *hyperbole*, I had called hyperbolic in "Cogito and the History of Madness." This function had been fulfilled by the Evil Genius, under the guise as well as under the name that it takes on in Descartes. But another Evil Genius, which is also the same one, can reappear without this name and under a different guise, for example, in the vicinity or lineage of

Rameau's Nephew: a different Evil Genius, certainly, but bearing enough of a resemblance because of its recurring function that the historian, here Foucault, allows himself a metonymy that is legitimate enough in his eyes to continue calling it Evil Genius. This reappearance occurs after the second passage of Freud-and-Nietzsche, as they are furtively announced by *Rameau's Nephew,* whose laugh "prefigures in advance and reduces the whole movement of nineteenth-century anthropology" (*F*, p. 424). This time of prefiguration and announcement, this delay between the anticipatory lightning flash and the event of what is foreseen, is explained by the very structure of an experience of unreason, if there is any, namely, an experience in which one cannot maintain oneself and out of which one cannot but fall after having approached it. All this thus forbids us from making this history into a properly successive and sequential history of events. This is formulated in Foucault's question: "Why is it not possible to maintain oneself in the difference of unreason?" (*F*, p. 425).

> But in this vertigo where the truth of the world is maintained only on the inside of an absolute void, man also encounters the ironic perversion of his own truth, at the moment when it moves from the dreams of interiority to the forms of exchange. Unreason then takes on the figure of *another evil genius* [my emphasis]—no longer the one who exiles man from the truth of the world, but the one who at once mystifies and demystifies, enchants to the point of extreme disenchantment, this truth of man that man had entrusted to his hands, to his face, to his speech; an evil genius who no longer operates when man wants to accede to the truth but when he wants to restitute to the world a truth that is his own, when, thrown into the intoxication of the sensible realm where he is lost, he finally remains "immobile, stupid, astonished." It is no longer in *perception* that the possibility of the evil genius resides [that is, as in Descartes] but in *expression.* [*F*, p. 423]

But immediately after this appearance or arraignment of Freud next to Nietzsche and all the Evil Geniuses, the pendulum of the *fort/da* is put back in motion; from this point on, it will not cease to convoke and dismiss Freud from the two sides of the dividing line, both inside and outside of the series from out of which the history of madness is signed. For it is here, in the following pages, that we find Freud separated from the lineage in which are gathered all those worthy heirs of Rameau's Nephew. The name of the one who was not crazy, not crazy enough in any case, the name of Freud, is dissociated from that of Nietzsche. It is regularly passed over in silence when, according to another filiation, Hölderlin, Nerval, Nietzsche, Van Gogh, Roussel, and Artaud are at several reprieves named and renamed—renowned—within the same "family."

From this point on, things are going to deteriorate. "To do justice to Freud" will more and more come to mean putting on trial a psychoanalysis that will have participated, in its own way, however original that may be, in the order of the immemorial figures of the Father and the Judge, of Family and Law, in the order of Order, of Authority and Punishment, whose immemorial figures must, as Philippe Pinel had noted, be brought into play by the doctor, in order to cure (see *F,* p. 607; *M,* p. 272). There was already a disturbing sign of this long before the chapter on "The Birth of the Asylum" that will so strictly inscribe psychoanalysis into the tradition of Tuke and Pinel and will go so far as to say that "all nineteenth-century psychiatry really converges on Freud" (*F,* p. 611; *M,* p. 277). For the latter had already appeared in another chain, the chain of those who, since the nineteenth century, know that madness, like its counterpart reason, has a history. These will have been led astray by a sort of historicism of reason and madness, a risk that is avoided by those who, "from Sade to Hölderlin, to Nerval and to Nietzsche," are given over to a "repeated poetic and philosophical experience" and plunge into a language "that abolishes history." As a cultural historian of madness, like others are of reason, Freud thus appears between Janet and Brunschvicg (*F,* p. 456).

While accumulating the two errors, the rationalist historian of this cultural phenomenon called madness nonetheless continues to pay tribute to myth, magic, and thaumaturgy. Indeed *thaumaturgy* will be the word chosen by Foucault himself for the verdict. There is nothing surprising in this collusion of reason and a certain occultism. Montaigne and Pascal would have perhaps called it mystical authority; the history of reason and reason within history would exercise essentially the same violence, the same obscure, irrational, dictatorial violence, serving the same interests in the name of the same fictional allegation, as psychoanalysis does when it confers all powers to the doctor's speech. Freud would free the patient interned in the asylum only in order to reconstitute him "in his essential character" at the heart of the analytic situation. There is a continuity from Pinel and Tuke to psychoanalysis. There is an inevitable movement, right up to Freud, a persistence of what Foucault calls "the myth of Pinel, like that of Tuke" (*F,* p. 577). This same insistence is always concentrated in the figure of the doctor; it is, in the eyes of the patient who is always an accomplice, the becoming-thaumaturge of the doctor, of a doctor who is not even supposed to know. *Homo medicus* does not exercise his authority in the name of science but, as Pinel himself seems to recognize and to claim, in the name of order, law, and morality, specifically, by "relying upon that prestige that envelops the *secrets* of the Family, of Authority, of Punishment, and of Love; . . . by wearing the mask of Father and of Judge" (*F,* pp. 607–8; *M,* p. 273; my emphasis).

And when the walls of the asylum give way to psychoanalysis, it is in effect a certain concept of the *secret* that assures the tradition from Pinel to Freud. It would be necessary to follow throughout these pages all the ins and outs of the value—itself barely visible—of a secret, of a certain secrecy value. This value would come down, in the end, to a *technique* of the secret, and of the secret without knowledge. Wherever knowledge can only be supposed, wherever, as a result, one knows that supposition cannot give rise to knowledge, wherever no knowledge could ever be disputed, there is the production of a *secrecy effect*, of what we might be able to call a *speculation on the capital secret or on the capital of the secret*. The calculated and yet finally incalculable production of this secrecy effect relies on a simulacrum. This simulacrum recalls, from another point of view, the situation described at the opening of *Raymond Roussel*: the risk of "being deceived less by a secret than by the awareness that there is a secret."[13]

What persists from Pinel to Freud, in spite of all the differences, is the figure of the doctor as a man not of knowledge but of order. In this figure all *secret, magic, esoteric, thaumaturgical* powers are brought together—and these are all Foucault's words. The scientific objectivity that is claimed by this tradition is only a magical reification:

> If we wanted to analyze the profound structures of objectivity in the knowledge and practice of nineteenth-century psychiatry from Pinel to Freud [this is the definitive divorce between Nietzsche and Freud, the second coupling for the latter], we should have to show in fact that such objectivity was from the start a reification of a magical nature, which could only be accomplished with the complicity of the patient himself, and beginning from a transparent and clear moral practice, gradually forgotten as positivism imposed its myths of scientific objectivity. [*F,* p. 610; *M,* p. 276]

In the name of Freud, one can read the call for a note. At the bottom of the page, Foucault persists, dates and signs, but the note introduces a slight precaution; it is indeed a note of prudence, but Foucault insists nonetheless and speaks of persistence: "These structures still persist in non-psychoanalytic psychiatry, and in many aspects or on many sides *[par bien des côtés]* of psychoanalysis itself" (*F,* p. 610; *M,* p. 299).

Though too discreetly marked, there is indeed a limit to what persists "on many sides." The always divisible line of this limit situates, in its form, the totality of the stakes. More precisely, the stakes are nothing other than those of totality, and of the procedures of totalization: what does it mean to say psychoanalysis "itself"? What does one thereby identify in such a global way? Is it psychoanalysis *"itself,"* as Foucault says, that inherits from Pinel? What is psychoanalysis *itself*? And are the aspects or sides through which it inherits the essential and irreducible aspects or sides of psychoanalysis itself or the residual "asides" that it can win out over *[avoir raison de]*? or even, that it must, that it should, win out over?

If the answer to this last question still seems up in the air in this note, it is soon going to come in a more determined and less equivocal form:

13. Foucault, *Raymond Roussel* (Paris, 1963), p. 10; trans. Charles Ruas, under the title *Death and the Labyrinth: The World of Raymond Roussel* (New York, 1986), p. 3.

no, psychoanalysis will never free itself of the psychiatric heritage. Its essential historical situation is linked to what is called the *"analytic situation,"* that is, to the thaumaturgical mystification of the couple doctor-patient, regulated this time by institutional protocols. Before citing word for word a conclusion that will remain, I believe, without appeal not only in *The History of Madness* but in Foucault's entire oeuvre—and right up to its awful interruption—I will once again risk wearing out your patience in order to look for a moment at the way in which Foucault describes the thaumaturgical play whose *techne* Pinel would have passed down to Freud, a *techne* that would be at once art and technique, the secret, the secret of the secret, the secret that consists in knowing how to make one suppose knowledge and believe in the secret. It is worth pausing here in order to point out another paradoxical effect of the chiasm—one of the most significant for what concerns us here, namely, a certain diabolical repetition and the recurrence of the various figures of the Evil Genius. What does Foucault say? That in the couple doctor-patient "the doctor becomes a thaumaturge" (*F,* p. 609; *M,* p. 275). Now, to describe this thaumaturgy, Foucault does not hesitate to speak of the demonic and satanic, as if the Evil Genius resided this time not on the side of unreason, of absolute disorder and madness (to say it quickly and with a bit of a smile, using all the necessary quotation marks, "on the good side"), but on the side of order, on the side of a subtly authoritative violence, the side of the Father, the Judge, the Law, and so on:

> It was thought, and by the patient first of all, that it was in the esotericism of his knowledge, in some *almost* daemonic secret of knowledge [I emphasize "almost": Foucault will later say—his relation to Freud surely being anything but simple—that the philistine representation of mental illness in the nineteenth century would last "right up to Freud—or almost"] that the doctor had found the power to unravel insanity; and increasingly the patient would accept this self-surrender to a doctor both divine and satanic, beyond human measure in any case. [*F,* p. 609; *M,* p. 275]

Two pages later, it is said that Freud "amplified the thaumaturgical virtues" of the "medical personage," "preparing for his omnipotence a quasi-divine status." And Foucault continues:

> He focussed upon this single presence—concealed behind the patient and above him, in an absence that is also a total presence—all the powers that had been distributed in the collective existence of the asylum; he transformed this into an absolute Observation, a pure and circumspect Silence, a Judge who punishes and rewards in a judgment that does not even condescend to language; he made it the mirror in which madness, in an almost motionless movement, clings to and casts off itself.

> To the doctor, Freud transferred all the structures Pinel and
> Tuke had set up within confinement. [*F,* p. 611; *M,* pp. 277–78]

Fictive omnipotence and a divine, or rather "quasi-divine," power, divine
by simulacrum, at once divine and satanic—these are the very traits of
an Evil Genius that are now being attributed to the figure of the doctor.
The doctor suddenly begins to resemble in a troubling way the figure of
unreason that continued to haunt what is called the classical age after the
act of force [coup de force] of the *cogito.* And like the authority of the laws
whose "mystical foundation" is recalled by Montaigne and Pascal,[14] the
authority of the psychoanalyst-doctor is the result of a fiction; it is the
result, by transfer, of the credit given to a fiction; and this fiction appears
analogous to that which provisionally confers all powers—and even more
than knowledge—to the Evil Genius.

At the conclusion of "The Birth of the Asylum," Foucault is going to
dismiss without appeal this bad genius of the thaumaturgical doctor in
the figure of the psychoanalyst; he is going to do this—I believe one can
say without stretching the paradox—*against Descartes,* against a certain
Cartesian subject still represented in the filiation that runs from Descartes
to Pinel to Freud. But he is also going to do this, more or less willingly, *as
Descartes,* or, at least, as the Descartes whom he had accused of excluding
madness by excluding, mastering, or dismissing—since these all come
down to the same thing—the powers of the Evil Genius. Against Freud,
this descendant of Descartes, against Descartes, it is still the Cartesian
exclusion that is repeated in a deadly and devilish way, like a heritage
inscribed within a diabolical and almost all-powerful program that one
should admit one never gets rid of or frees oneself from without re-
mainder.

To substantiate what I have just said, I will cite the conclusion of this

14. "And so laws keep up their good standing, not because they are just, but because
they are laws: that is the mystical foundation of their authority, they have no other. . . .
Anyone who obeys them because they are just is not obeying them the way he ought to"
(quoted in Derrida, "Force of Law: The 'Mystical Foundation of Authority,'" trans. Mary
Quaintance, *Cardozo Law Review* 11 [July/Aug. 1990]: 939; Derrida's French text appears on
facing pages). Elsewhere, Montaigne had mentioned the "legitimate fictions" on which "our
law" "founds the truth of its justice" (ibid.). And Pascal cites Montaigne without naming
him when he recalls both the principle of justice and the fact that it should not be traced
back to its source unless one wants to ruin it. What is he himself doing, then, when he
speaks of "the mystical foundation of its authority," adding in the same breath, "Whoever
traces it to its source annihilates it" (ibid.)? Is he re-founding or ruining that of which he
speaks? Will one ever know? Must one know?

Power, authority, knowledge and non-knowledge, law, judgment, fiction, good standing or credit, transfer: from Montaigne to Pascal onto others, we recognize the same network of a critical problematic, an active, vigilant, hypercritical problematization. It is
difficult to be sure that the "classical age" did not thematize, reflect, and also deploy the
concepts of its symptoms: the concepts that one will later direct toward the symptoms that
it will one day be believed can be assigned to it.

chapter. It describes the transfer from Pinel to Freud (stroke of genius, "masterful short-circuit"—it is a question of Freud's genius, the good like the bad, the good as bad)—and it implacably judges psychoanalysis *in the past, in the present, and even in the future.* For psychoanalysis is condemned in advance. No future is promised that might allow it to escape its destiny once it has been determined both within the institutional (and supposedly inflexible) structure of what is called the *analytic situation* and in the figure of the doctor as *subject:*

> To the doctor, Freud transferred all the structures Pinel and Tuke had set up within confinement. He did deliver the patient from the existence of the asylum within which his "liberators" had alienated him; but he did not deliver him from what was essential in this existence; he regrouped its powers, extended them to the maximum by uniting them in the doctor's hands; he created the psychoanalytical situation where, by a masterful short-circuit [*court-circuit génial;* I underscore this allusion to the stroke of genius *(coup de génie)*, which, as soon as it confirms the evil of confinement and of the interior asylum, is diabolical and properly evil *(malin);* and as we will see, for more than twenty years Foucault never stopped seeing in Freud—and quite literally so—sometimes a good and sometimes a bad or evil *(mauvais)* genius], alienation becomes disalienating because, in the doctor, it becomes a subject.
>
> The doctor, as an alienating figure, remains the key to psychoanalysis. It is perhaps because it did not suppress this ultimate structure, and because it referred all the others to it, that psychoanalysis has not been able, *will not be able* [I thus emphasize this future; it announces the invariability of this verdict in Foucault's subsequent work], to hear the voices of unreason, nor to decipher in themselves the signs of the madman. Psychoanalysis can unravel some of the forms of madness; it remains a stranger to the sovereign enterprise of unreason. It can neither liberate nor transcribe, nor most certainly explain, what is essential in this enterprise. [*F,* pp. 611–12; *M,* p. 278]

And here, just after, are the very last lines of the chapter; we are far from the couple Nietzsche/Freud. They are now separated on both sides of what Foucault calls "moral imprisonment," and it will be difficult to say, in certain situations, who is to be found on the *inside* and who on the *outside*—and sometimes outside but inside. As opposed to Nietzsche and a few other great madmen, Freud no longer belongs to the space *from out of* which *The History of Madness* could be written. He belongs, rather, to this history of madness that the book in turn makes its *object:*

> Since the end of the eighteenth century, the life of unreason no longer manifests itself except in the lightning-flash of works such as those of Hölderlin, of Nerval, of Nietzsche, or of Artaud—forever irreducible to those alienations that can be cured, resisting by their

own strength that gigantic moral imprisonment which we are in the habit of calling, doubtless by antiphrasis, the liberation of the insane *[aliénés]* by Pinel and Tuke. [*F,* p. 612; *M,* p. 278]

This diagnosis, which is also a verdict, is confirmed in the last chapter of the book, "The Anthropological Circle." This chapter fixes the new distribution of names and places into the great series that form the grid of the book. When it is a question of showing that since the end of the eighteenth century the liberation of the mad has been replaced by an objectification of the concept of their freedom (within such categories as desire and will, determinism and responsibility, the automatic and the spontaneous) and that "one will now untiringly recount the trials and tribulations of freedom," which is also to say, of a certain humanization as anthropologization, Freud is then regularly included among the exemplary figures of this anthropologism of freedom. Foucault says, page after page: "From Esquirol to Janet, as from Reil to Freud or from Tuke to Jackson" (*F,* p. 616), or again, "From Esquirol to Freud" (*F,* p. 617), or again "since Esquirol and Broussais right up to Janet, Bleuler, and Freud" (*F,* p. 624). A slight yet troubling reservation comes just after to mitigate all these regroupings. Concerning general paralysis and neurosyphilis, philistinism is everywhere, "right up to Freud—or almost" (*F,* p. 626).

The chiasmatic effects multiply. Some two hundred pages earlier, what had inscribed both Freud *and* Nietzsche, like two accomplices of the same age, was the reopening of the dialogue with unreason, the lifting of the interdiction against *language,* the *return* to a proximity with madness. Yet it is precisely this or, rather, the silent double and hypocritical simulacrum of this, the mask of this language, the same freedom now objectified, that separates Freud from Nietzsche. It is this that now makes them unable to associate or to be associated with one another from the two sides of a wall that is all the more unsurmountable insofar as it consists of an asylum's partition, an invisible, interior, but eloquent partition, that of truth itself as the truth of man and his alienation. Foucault was able, much earlier, to say that Freudian psychoanalysis, to which one must be fair or *"do justice,"* is not a psychology as soon as it takes language into account. Now it is language itself that brings psychoanalysis back down to the status of a psycho-anthropology of alienation, "this language wherein man appears in madness as being other than himself," this "alterity," "a dialectic that is always begun anew between the *Same* and the *Other,*" revealing to man his truth "in the babbling movement of *alienation* or *madness*" (*F,* p. 631).

Concerning dialectic and alienation or madness—concerning everything, in fact, that happens in the circulation of this "anthropological circle" wherein psychoanalysis is caught up or held—one should, and I myself would have liked to have done this given more time, pause a bit longer than Foucault did on a passage from Hegel's *Encyclopedia.* I am referring to the Remark of §408 in which Hegel situates and deduces madness as a contradiction of the subject between the particular determination of self-feeling and the network of mediations that is called consciousness. Hegel makes in passing a spirited praise of Pinel (I do not understand why Foucault, in quickly citing this passage, replaces this praise for Pinel by an ellipsis). More important, perhaps, is the fact that Hegel also interprets madness as the taking control of a certain Evil Genius *(der böse Genius)* in man. Foucault elliptically cites a short phrase in translation ("méchant génie") without remarking on it and without linking these few extraordinary pages of Hegel to the great dramaturgy of the Evil Genius that concerns us here.

Let me be absolutely clear about this: my intention here is not at all to accuse or criticize Foucault, to say, for example, that he was wrong to confine *Freud himself (in general)* or *psychoanalysis itself (in general)* to this role and place; on the subject of Freud or psychoanalysis *themselves and in general,* I have in this form and place almost nothing to say or think, except perhaps that Foucault has some good arguments and that others would have some pretty good ones as well to oppose to his. It is also not my intention, in spite of what it may look like, to suggest that Foucault contradicts himself when he so firmly places the same Freud (in general) or the same psychoanalysis (in general) sometimes on one side and sometimes on the other of the dividing line, *and always on the side of the Evil Genius*—who is found sometimes on the side of madness, sometimes on the side of its exclusion-reappropriation, on the side of its confinement to the outside or the inside, with or without asylum walls. The contradiction is no doubt in the things themselves, so to speak. And we are in a region where the wrong (the *being-wrong* or the *doing-someone-wrong)* would want to be more than ever on the side of a certain reason, on the side of what is called *raison garder*—that is, on the side of keeping one's cool, keeping one's head—on the side, precisely, where one is right *[a raison],* and where *being right [avoir raison]* is to *win out over* or *prove someone wrong [avoir raison de],* with a violence whose subtlety, whose hyperdialectic and hyperchiasmatic resources, cannot be completely formalized, that is, can no longer be dominated by a metalanguage. Which means that we are always caught in the knots that are woven, before us and beyond us, by this powerful—all too powerful—logic. The history of reason embedded in all these turbulent idioms *(to prove someone wrong [donner tort]* or *to prove them right [donner raison], to be right [avoir raison], to be wrong [avoir tort], to win out over [avoir raison de], to do someone wrong [faire tort],* and so on) is also the history of madness that Foucault wished to recount to us. The fact that he was caught up, caught up even before setting out, in the snares of this logic—which he sometimes thematizes as having to do with a "system of contradictions" and "antinomies" whose "coherence" remains "hidden"—cannot be reduced to a fault or wrong on his part (*F,* p. 624). This does not mean, however, that we, without ever finding him to be radically wrong or at fault, have to subscribe a priori to all his statements. One would be able to master this entire problematic, assuming this were possible, only after having satisfactorily answered a few questions, questions as innocent—or as hardly innocent—as, What is reason? for example, or more narrowly, What is the principle of reason? What does it mean to be right *[avoir raison]*? What does it mean to be right or to prove someone right *[avoir ou donner raison]*? To be wrong, to prove someone wrong, or to do them wrong *[avoir, donner ou faire tort]*? You will forgive me here, I hope, for leaving these enigmas as they are.

I will restrict myself to a modest and more accessible question. The distribution of statements, such as it appears to be set out before us, should lead us to think two apparently incompatible things: the book entitled *The History of Madness,* as the history of madness itself, is and is not the same age as Freudian psychoanalysis. The project of this book thus does and does not belong to the age of psychoanalysis; it already belongs to it and already no longer belongs to it. This division without division would put us back on the track of another logic of division, one that would urge us to think the internal partitions of wholes, partitions that would make such things as madness, reason, history, and age—especially the whole we call age—but also psychoanalysis, Freud, and so on, into rather dubious identities, sufficiently divided from within to threaten in advance all our statements and all our references with parasitism: it would be a bit as if a virus were introduced into the matrix of language, the way such things are today introduced into computer software, the difference being that we are—and for a very good reason—very far from having at our disposal any of these diagnostic and remedial antiviral programs that are available on the market today, even though these same programs—and for a very good reason—have a hard time keeping pace with the industrial production of these viruses, which are themselves sometimes produced by those who produce the intercepting programs. A maddening situation for any discourse, certainly, but a certain mad panic is not necessarily the worst thing that can happen to a discourse on madness as soon as it does not go all out to confine or exclude its object, that is, in the sense Foucault gives to this word, to *objectify* it.

Does one have the right to stop here and be content with this as an internal reading of Foucault's great book? Is an *internal* reading possible? Is it legitimate to privilege to this extent its relation to something like an "age" of psychoanalysis "itself"? The reservations that such presumptions of identity might arouse (the unity of an "age," the indivisibility of psychoanalysis "itself," and so on)—and I've made more than one allusion to them—would be enough to make us question this.

One would be able to justify a response to this question, in any case, only by continuing to read and to analyze, by continuing to take into account particularly Foucault's corpus, his archive, what this archive says on the subject of the archive. Without limiting ourselves to this, think in particular of the problems posed some five to eight years later: (1) by *The Order of Things* concerning something that has always seemed enigmatic to me and that Foucault calls for a time *episteme* (there where it is said, "We think in that place" [*MC*, p. 396; *OT*, p. 384]); a place that, and I will return to this in a moment, encompasses or comprehends the psychoanalysis that does not comprehend it, or more precisely, that comprehends it without comprehending it and without acceding to it; (2) by *The Archaeology of Knowledge* concerning "The Historical *a priori* and the Archive" (this is the title of the central chapter) and archaeology in its relation to the history of ideas.

It is out of the question to get involved here, in so short a time, in such difficult readings. I will thus be content to conclude, if you will still allow me, with a few indications (two at the most) along one of the paths I would have wanted to follow on the basis of these readings.

1. On the one hand, I would have tried to identify the signs of an imperturbable constancy in this movement of the pendulum or balance. The oscillation *regularly* leads from one topological assignation to the other: as if psychoanalysis had *two places* or took place *two times.* Yet it seems to me that the law of this displacement operates without the structural possibility of an event or a place being analyzed for itself, and without the consequences being drawn with regard to the identity of all the concepts at work in this history that does not want to be a history of ideas and representations.

This constancy in the oscillation of the pendulum is first marked, of course, in books that are more or less contemporary with *The History of Madness. Maladie mentale et psychologie [Mental Illness and Psychology]* (1962) intersects and coincides at many points with *The History of Madness.* In the history of mental illness, Freud appears as "the first to open up once again the possibility for reason and unreason to communicate in the danger of a common language, ever ready to break down and disintegrate into the inaccessible" (*MM*, p. 82; *MI*, p. 69). In truth, though profoundly in accord with the movement and logic of *The History of Madness,* this book of 1962 is, in the end, a bit more precise and differentiated in its references to Freud, although *Beyond the Pleasure Principle* is never mentioned. Foucault speaks both of Freud's "stroke of genius" (and this is indeed his word) and of the dividing line that runs down his work. Freud's "stroke of genius" was to have escaped the evolutionist horizon of John Hughlings Jackson (*MM*, p. 37; *MI*, p. 31), whose model can nevertheless be found in the description of the evolutive forms of neurosis and the history libidinal stages,[15] the libido being mythological (a myth to destroy, often a biopsychological myth that is abandoned, Foucault

---

15. Insofar as, and to the extent that, it follows Jackson's model (for the "stroke of genius" also consists in escaping from this), psychoanalysis is *credulous,* it *will have been* credu-

then thinks, by psychoanalysts), just as mythological as Janet's "'psychic force,'" with which Foucault associates it more than once (*MM*, p. 29; *MI*, p. 24).[16]

If the assignation of Freud is thus double, it is because his work is divided: "In psychoanalysis, it is always possible," says Foucault, "to separate that which pertains to a psychology of evolution (as in *Three Essays on the Theory of Sexuality*) and that which belongs to a psychology of individual history (as in *Five Psychoanalyses* and the accompanying texts)" (*MM*, p. 37; *MI*, p. 31).

Despite this consideration for the "stroke of genius," Foucault is indeed speaking here of an analytic psychology. This is what he calls it. Insofar as it remains a psychology, it remains speechless before the language of madness. Indeed, "there is a very good reason why psychology can never master madness; it is because psychology became possible in our world only when madness had already been mastered and excluded from the drama" (*MM*, p. 104; *MI*, p. 87—a few lines before the end of the book).

In other words, the logic at work in this conclusion, the consequences—the ruinous consequences—of which one would ceaselessly have to take into account, is that what has already been mastered can no longer be mastered, and that too much mastery (in the form of exclusion but also of objectification) deprives one of mastery (in the form of access, knowledge, competence). The concept of mastery is an impossible concept to manipulate, as we know: the more there is, the less there is, and vice versa. The conclusion drawn in the few lines I just cited thus excludes

---

lous, for it is in this that it is outdated, a credulous presumption: "it believed that it could," "Freud believed." After having cited Jackson's *The Factors of Insanities*, Foucault in fact adds (I emphasize the verb and tense of *to believe*):

> Jackson's entire work tended to give right of place to evolutionism in neuro- and psycho-pathology. Since the *Croonian Lectures* (1874), it has no longer been possible to omit the regressive aspects of illness; evolution is now one of the dimensions by which one gains access to the pathological fact.
> A whole side of Freud's work consists of a commentary on the evolutive forms of neurosis. The history of the libido, of its development, of its successive fixations, resembles a collection of the pathological possibilities of the individual: each type of neurosis is a return to a libidinal stage of evolution. And psychoanalysis *believed that it could* write a psychology of the child by carrying out a pathology of the adult. . . . This is the celebrated Oedipus complex, in which Freud *believed* that he could read the enigma of man and the key to his destiny, in which one must find the most comprehensive analysis of the conflicts experienced by the child in his relations with his parents and the point at which many neuroses became fixated.
> In short, every libidinal stage is a potential pathological structure. Neurosis is a spontaneous archaeology of the libido. [*MM*, pp. 23–26; *MI*, pp. 19–21]

16. For example: "It is not a question of invalidating the analyses of pathological regression; all that is required is to free them of the myths that neither Janet nor Freud succeeded in separating from them" (*MM*, p. 31; *MI*, p. 26).

both Freud's "stroke of genius" *and* psychology, be it analytic or some other. Freudian man remains a *homo psychologicus*. Freud is once again passed over in silence, cut out of both the lineage and the work of mad geniuses. He is given over to a forgetfulness where one can then accuse him of silence and forgetting.

> And when, in lightning flashes and cries, madness reappears, as in Nerval or Artaud, Nietzsche or Roussel, it is psychology that remains silent, *speechless*, before this language that borrows a meaning of its own from that *tragic split* [I emphasize this phrase; this is a tragic and romantic discourse on the essence of madness and the birth of tragedy, a discourse just as close, literally, to that of a certain Novalis as to that of Hölderlin], from that freedom, that, for contemporary man, only the existence of "psychologists" allows him to forget. [*MM*, p. 104; *MI*, pp. 87–88][17]

And yet. Still according to the interminable and inexhaustible *fort/da* that we have been following for some time now, the same *Freudian man* is reinscribed into the noble lineage at the end of *Naissance de la clinique [The Birth of the Clinic]* (a book published in 1963 but clearly written during the same creative period). Why single out this occurrence of the reinscription rather than another? Because it might give us (and this is, in fact, the hypothesis that interests me) a rule for reading this *fort/da;* it might provide us with a criterion for interpreting this untiring exclusion/inclusion. It is a question of another divide, within psychoanalysis, or, in any case, a divide that seems somewhat different than the one I spoke of a moment ago between Freud, the psychologist of evolution, and Freud, the psychologist of individual history. I say "seems somewhat different" because the one perhaps leads back to the other.

The line of this second divide is, quite simply—if one can say this—death. The Freud who breaks with psychology, with evolutionism and biologism, the tragic Freud, really, who shows himself *hospitable* to madness (and I take the risk of this word) because he is foreign to the space of the hospital, the tragic Freud who deserves hospitality in the great lineage of mad geniuses, is the Freud who talks it out with death. This would especially be the Freud, then, of *Beyond the Pleasure Principle*, although Foucault never, to my knowledge, mentions this work and makes only a very ambiguous allusion in *Mental Illness and Psychology* to what he calls a death instinct, the one by which Freud wished to explain the war,

---

17. A literally identical schema was at work a few pages earlier: "Psychology can never tell the truth about madness because it is madness that holds the truth of psychology." It is again a tragic vision, a tragic discourse on the tragic. Hölderlin, Nerval, Roussel, and Artaud are again named through their works as witnesses of a "tragic confrontation with madness" free of all psychology (*MM*, p. 89; *MI*, pp. 74, 75). No reconciliation is possible between psychology, even if analytic, and tragedy.

although "it was war that was dreamed in this shift in Freud's thinking" (*MM*, p. 99; *MI*, p. 83).

Death alone, along with war, introduces the power of the negative into psychology and into its evolutionist optimism. On the basis of this experience of death, on the basis of what is called in the final pages of *The Birth of the Clinic* "originary finitude" [18] (a vocabulary and theme that then take over Foucault's text and that always seemed to me difficult to dissociate from Heidegger, who as you know is practically never evoked, nor even named, by Foucault), [19] Freud is reintegrated into this modernity from out of which *The History of Madness* is written and from which he had been banished at regular intervals. It is by taking account of death as "the concrete a priori of medical experience" that "the beginning of that fundamental relation that binds modern man to his originary finitude" comes about (*N*, pp. 198, 199; *B*, pp. 196, 197). This modern man is also a "Freudian man":

> the experience of individuality in modern culture is bound up with that of death: from Hölderlin's Empedocles to Nietzsche's Zarathustra, and on to Freudian man, an obstinate relation to death prescribes to the universal its singular face, and lends to each individual the power of being heard forever. [*N*, p. 199; *B*, p. 197]

Originary finitude is a finitude that no longer arises out of the infinity of a divine presence. It now unfolds "in the void left by the absence of the gods" (*N*, p. 200; *B*, p. 198). What we have here, then, is, in the name of death, so to speak, a reinscription of Freudian man into a "modern" grouping or whole from which he was sometimes excluded.

One can then follow *two* new but equally ambiguous consequences. *On the one hand*, the grouping in question is going to be restructured. One should not be surprised to see reappear, as on the very last page of *The Birth of the Clinic*, the name of Jackson—and, before him, Bichat, whose

---

18. Foucault, *Naissance de la clinique: Une Archéologie du regard médical* (Paris, 1963), p. 199; hereafter abbreviated *N;* trans. A. M. Sheridan Smith, under the title *The Birth of the Clinic: An Archeology of Medical Perception* (New York, 1975), p. 197; hereafter abbreviated *B*.

19. Except perhaps in passing in *Les Mots et les choses:* "the experience of Hölderlin, Nietzsche, and Heidegger, in which the return is posited only in the extreme recession of the origin" (*MC*, p. 345; *OT*, p. 334).

This ponderous silence would last, I believe, right up until an interview that he gave not long before his death. Faithful to the Foucauldian style of interpretation, one might say that the spacing of this omission, of this blank silence—like the silence that reigns over the name of Lacan, whom one can associate with Heidegger up to a certain point, and thus with a few others who never stopped, in France and elsewhere, to dialogue with these two— is anything but the empty and inoperative sign of an absence. It *gives rise* or *gives the place [donne lieu]*, on the contrary, it marks out the place and the age. The dotted lines of a suspended writing *situate* with a formidable precision. No attention to the age or to the problem of the age should lose sight of this.

Traité des membranes (1827) and *Recherches physiologiques* would have allowed death to be seen and thought. This vitalism would have arisen against the backdrop of "'mortalism'" (*N*, p. 147; *B*, p. 145). It would be a characteristic of the entire European nineteenth century, and it could be attested to just as well by Goya, Géricault, Delacroix, or Baudelaire, to name just a few: "The importance of Bichat, Jackson, and Freud in European culture does not prove that they were philosophers as well as doctors, but that, in this culture, medical thought is fully engaged in the philosophical status of man" (*N*, p. 200; *B*, p. 198).

But there is a second ambiguous consequence of this relation to death as originary finitude. And so, *on the other hand*, the figure or face that is then fixed, and in which one believes one recognizes the traits of "Freudian man," comes to occupy a rather singular place with respect to what Foucault calls the analytic of finitude and the modern *episteme* at the end of *Les Mots et les choses* [*The Order of Things*] (1966). From the standpoint of a certain epistemological trihedron (life, work, and language, or biology, economy, and philology), the human sciences are seen to be at once *inclusive* and *exclusive;* these are Foucault's words (see *MC*, p. 358; *OT*, p. 347).

As for this inclusive exclusion, Freud's work, to which Foucault unwaveringly assigns a model that is more philological than biological, still occupies the place of the *hinge;* Foucault in fact speaks about the place and workings of a *"pivot":* "all this knowledge, within which Western culture had given itself in one century a certain image of man, pivots on the work of Freud, though without, for all that, leaving its fundamental arrangement" (*MC*, p. 372; *OT*, p. 361).

"Though without, for all that, leaving its fundamental arrangement": that is how everything turns round the event or the invention of psychoanalysis. It turns in circles and in place, endlessly returning to the same. It is a revolution that changes nothing. Hence this is not, as Foucault adds at this point, "the most decisive importance of psychoanalysis."

In what, then does this "most decisive importance of psychoanalysis" consist? In exceeding both consciousness and representation—and, as a result, the human sciences, which do not go beyond the realm of the representable. It is in this respect that psychoanalysis, like ethnology in fact, does not belong to the field of the human sciences. It "relates the knowledge of man to the finitude that gives man its foundation" (*MC*, p. 392; *OT*, p. 381). We are far from its earlier determination as an analytic psychology. And this same excessive character leads psychoanalysis toward the very forms of finitude that Foucault writes in capital letters, that is, toward Death, Desire, Law or Law-Language (see *MC*, p. 386; *OT*, p. 375). It would be necessary to devote a more detailed and more probing reading to these few pages, something I cannot do here. To keep to the surest schema, let us simply say that, from this point of view and to this degree at least, psychoanalysis, as an analytic of finitude, is now granted an intimacy with the madness that it had sometimes been conceded but had most often been emphatically denied in *The History of Madness*. And this intimacy is a sort of complicity with the madness of the day, the madness of today, "madness in its present form, madness as it is posited in the modern experience, as its truth and its alterity" (*MC*, p. 387; *OT*, p. 375).

But let us not oversimplify things. What Foucault generously grants psychoanalytic experience is now nothing other than what is denied it; more precisely, it is the being able to see what is denied it. Indeed, the only privilege that is here granted to psychoanalysis is that of the experience *that accedes to that to which it can never accede*. If Foucault here mentions, under the name of madness, only schizophrenia and psychosis, it is because psychoanalysis most often approaches these only in order to acknowledge its own limit: a forbidden or impossible access. *This limit defines psychoanalysis*. Its intimacy with madness par excellence is an intimacy with the least intimate, a nonintimacy that relates it to what is most heterogeneous, to that which in no way lets itself be interiorized, nor even subjectified: neither alienated, I would say, nor inalienable.

> This is why psychoanalysis finds in that madness *par excellence* ["madness *par excellence*" is also the title given by Blanchot many years earlier to a text on Hölderlin, and Foucault is no doubt echoing this without saying so]—which psychiatrists term schizophrenia—its intimate, its most invincible torture: for, given in this form of madness, in an absolutely manifest and absolutely withdrawn form [this absolute identity of the manifest and the withdrawn, of the open and the secret, is no doubt the key to this double gesture of interpretation and evaluation], are the forms of finitude towards which it usually advances unceasingly (and interminably) from the starting-point of that which is voluntarily-involuntarily offered to it in the patient's language. So psychoanalysis 'recognizes itself' when it is confronted with those very psychoses to which, nevertheless (or rather, for that very reason), it has scarcely any means of access: as if the psychosis were displaying in a savage illumination, and offering in a mode not too distant but precisely too close, that towards which analysis must make its laborious way. [*MC*, p. 387; *OT*, pp. 375–76]

This displacement, as ambiguous as it is, leads Foucault to adopt the exact opposite position of certain theses of *The History of Madness* and *Mental Illness and Psychology* concerning the couple patient-doctor, concerning transference or alienation. This time, psychoanalysis not only has nothing to do with a psychology but it constitutes neither a general theory of man—since it is above all else a knowledge linked to a practice—nor an anthropology (see *MC*, pp. 388, 390; *OT*, pp. 376, 378–79). Even better: in the movement where he clearly affirms this, Foucault challenges the very thing of which he had unequivocally accused psychoanalysis, namely, of being a mythology and a thaumaturgy. He now wants to explain why psychologists and philosophers were so quick, and so naive, to

denounce a Freudian mythology there where that which exceeds representation and consciousness must have in fact *resembled*, but only resembled, something mythological (see *MC*, p. 386; *OT*, p. 374). As for the
thaumaturgy of transference, the logic of alienation, and the subtly or
sublimely asylumlike violence of the analytic situation, they are no longer,
Foucault now says, essential to psychoanalysis, no longer "constitutive" of
it. It is not that all violence is absent from this rehabilitated psychoanalysis, but it is, I hardly dare say it, a good violence, or in any case what
Foucault calls a "calm" violence, one that, in the singular experience of
singularity, allows access to "the concrete figures of finitude":

> neither hypnosis, nor the patient's alienation within the fantasmatic
> character of the doctor, is constitutive of psychoanalysis; . . . the lat-
> ter can be deployed only in the calm violence of a particular relation-
> ship and the transference it produces. . . . Psychoanalysis makes use
> of the particular relation of the transference in order to reveal, on
> the outer confines of representation. Desire, Law, and Death, which
> outline, at the extremity of analytic language and practice, the con-
> crete figures of finitude. [*MC*, pp. 388–89; *OT*, pp. 377–78]

Things have indeed changed—or so it appears—between *The History
of Madness* and *The Order of Things*.

From where does the theme of finitude that seems to govern this new
displacement of the pendulum come? To what philosophical event is this
analytic of finitude to be attributed—this analytic in which is inscribed
the trihedron of knowledges or models of the modern *episteme*, with its
nonsciences, the "'human sciences,'" according to Foucault (*MC*, p. 378;
OT, p. 366), and its "'counter-sciences,'" which Foucault says psychoanalysis and ethnology also are (*MC*, p. 391; *OT*, p. 379)?

As a project, the analytic of finitude would belong to the tradition of
the Kantian critique. Foucault insists on this Kantian filiation by speci-
fying, to cite it once again: "We think in that place." Here is again and
for a time, according to Foucault, *our* age, *our* contemporaneity. It is true
that if originary finitude obviously makes us think of Kant, it would be
unable to do so alone, that is—to summarize an enormous venture in a
word, in a name—without the active interpretation of the Heideggerian
repetition and all its repercussions, particularly, since this is our topic
today, in the discourse of French philosophy and psychoanalysis, and especially Lacanian psychoanalysis; and when I say Lacanian, I am also
referring to all the debates *with* Lacan during the past few decades. This
would have perhaps deserved some mention here on the part of Foucault,
especially when he speaks of originary finitude. For Kantian finitude is
precisely not "originary," as is, on the contrary, the one to which the Heideggerian interpretation leads. Finitude in Kant's sense is instead derived, as is the intuition bearing the same name. But let us leave all this
aside, since it would, as we say, take us a bit too far afield.

The "we" who is saying "we think in that place" is evidently, tautolog-ically, the "we" from out of which the signatory of these lines, the author of the *The History of Madness* and *The Order of Things*, speaks, writes, and thinks. But this "we" never stops dividing, and the places of its signature are displaced in being divided up. A certain untimeliness always disturbs the contemporary who reassures him or herself in a "we." This "we," our "we," is not its own contemporary. The self-identity of its age, or of any age, appears as divided, and thus problematic, *problematizable* (I under-score this word for a reason that will perhaps become apparent in a mo-ment), as the age of madness or an age of psychoanalysis—as well as, in fact, all the historical or archeological categories that promise us the determinable stability of a configurable whole. In fact, from the moment a couple separates, from the moment, for example, just to locate here a symptom or a simple indication, the couple Freud/Nietzsche forms and then unforms, this decoupling fissures the identity of the epoch, of the age, of the *episteme* or the paradigm of which one or the other, or both together, might have been the significant representatives. This is even more true when this decoupling comes to fissure the self-identity of some individual, or some presumed individuality, for example, of Freud. What allows one to presume the non–self-difference of Freud, for example? And of psychoanalysis? These decouplings and self-differences no doubt introduce a good deal of disorder into the unity of any configuration, whole, epoch, or historical age. Such disturbances make the historians' work rather difficult, even and especially the work of the most original and refined among them. This self-difference, this difference *to self [à soi]*, and not simply *with self*, makes life hard if not impossible for historical science. But inversely, would there be any history, would anything ever *happen*, without this principle of disturbance? Would there ever be any event without this disturbance of the principality?

At the point where we are, the age of finitude is being de-identified for at least one reason, from which I can here abstract only the general schema: the thought of finitude, as the thought of finite man, speaks *both* of the tradition, the memory of the Kantian critique or of the knowledges rooted in it, *and* of the end *[fin]* of this finite man, this man who is "near-ing its end," as Foucault's most famous sentence would have it in this final wager, placed on the edge of a promise that has yet to take shape, in the final lines of *The Order of Things:* "then one can certainly wager that man would be effaced, like a face drawn in sand at the edge or limit of the sea" (*MC*, p., 398; *OT*, p. 387). The *trait* (the trait of the face, the line or the limit) that then runs the risk of being effaced in the sand would per-haps also be the one that separates an end from itself, thereby multiplying it endlessly and making it, once again, into a limit: the self-relation of a limit at once erases and multiples the limit; it cannot but divide it in inventing it. The limit only comes to be effaced—it only comes to efface itself—as soon as it is inscribed.

2. I'm finished with this point, and so I should really finish it up right here. Assuming that I haven't already worn out your patience, I will conclude with a second indication as a sort of *postscript*—and even more schematically—in order to point once again in the direction of psycho-analysis and to put these hypotheses to the test of *The History of Sexuality* (1976–1984).[20]

If one is still willing to follow this figure of the pendulum *[balancier]* making a scene before psychoanalysis, then one will observe that the *fort/ da* here gives a new impetus to the movement, a movement with the same rhythm but with a greater amplitude and range than ever before. Psycho-analysis is here reduced, more than it ever was, to a very circumscribed and dependent moment in a history of the "strategies of knowledge and power" (juridical, familial, psychiatric) (*VS*, p. 210; *HS*, p. 159). Psycho-analysis is taken by and interested in these strategies, but it does not think them through. The praises of Freud fall decisively and irreversibly: one hears, for example, of "how wonderfully effective he was—worthy of the greatest spiritual fathers and directors of the classical period—in giving a new impetus to the secular injunction to study sex and transform it into discourse" (*VS*, p. 210; *HS*, p. 159). This time, in other words, in reinscribing the invention of psychoanalysis into the history of a disciplin-ary dynamic, one no longer indicts only the ruses of objectivization and psychiatric alienation, as in *The History of Madness,* and no longer only the stratagems that would have allowed the *confinement without confinement* of the patient in the invisible asylum of the analytic situation. This time, it is a question of going much further back, and more radically than the "repressive hypothesis" ever did, towards the harsh ruses of the monar-chy of sex and the agencies of power that support it. These latter invest in and take charge of sexuality, so that there is no need to oppose, as one so often and naively believes, power and pleasure.

And since we have been following for so long now the obsessive avatars of the Evil Genius, the irresistible, demonic, and metamorphic returns of this quasi-God, of God's second in command, this metem-psychotic Satan, we here find Freud himself once again, Freud, to whom Foucault leaves a choice between only two roles: the bad genius and the good one. And what we have here is another chiasm: in the rhetoric of the few lines that I will read in a moment, one will not be surprised to see that the accused, the one who is the most directly targeted by the indictment—for no amount of denying will make us forget that we are dealing here with a trial and a verdict—is the "good genius of Freud"

20. *Histoire de la sexualité* is the name given by Foucault to his entire project on sexual-ity, of which three volumes have now been published: *La Volonté de savoir* (Paris, 1976), here-after abbreviated *VS*, trans. Robert Hurley, under the title *The History of Sexuality: An Introduction* (New York, 1978), hereafter abbreviated *HS; L'Usage des plaisirs* (Paris, 1984), trans. Hurley, under the title *The Use of Pleasure* (New York, 1985); and *Le Souci de soi* (Paris, 1984), trans. Hurley, under the title *The Care of the Self* (New York, 1986).

and not his "bad genius." Why so? In the final pages of the first volume of *The History of Sexuality*, the accusation of pansexualism that was often leveled against psychoanalysis naturally comes up. Those most blind in this regard, says Foucault, were not those who denounced pansexualism out of prudishness. Their only error was to have attributed "solely to the *bad genius [mauvais génie]* of Freud what had already gone through a long stage of preparation" (*VS*, p. 210; *HS*, p. 159; my emphasis). The opposite error, the symmetrical lure, corresponds to a more serious mystification. It is the illusion that could be called emancipatory, the aberration of the Enlightenment, the misguided notion on the part of those who believed that Freud, the "*good genius*" of Freud, had finally freed sex from its repression by power. These

were mistaken concerning the nature of the process; they believed that Freud had at last, through a sudden reversal, restored to sex the rightful share which it had been denied for so long; they had not seen how the *good genius* of Freud had placed it at one of the critical points marked out for it since the eighteenth century by the strategies of knowledge and power, how wonderfully effective he was . . . in giving a new impetus to the secular injunction to study sex and transform it into discourse. [*VS*, p. 210; *HS*, p. 159; my emphasis][21]

21. It is perhaps appropriate to recall here the lines immediately following this, the last in the first volume of *The History of Sexuality*. They unequivocally describe this sort of Christian teleology or, more precisely, modern Christianity (as opposed to "an old Christianity") whose completion would, in some sense, be marked by psychoanalysis:

the secular injunction to study sex and transform it into discourse. We are often reminded of the countless procedures which an old Christianity once employed to make us detest the body; but let us ponder all the ruses that were employed for centuries to make us love sex, to make the knowledge of it desirable and everything said about it precious. Let us consider the stratagems by which we were induced to apply all our skills to discovering its secrets, by which we were attached to the obligation to draw out its truth, and made guilty for having failed to recognize it for so long. These devices are what ought to make us wonder today. Moreover, we need to consider the possibility that one day, perhaps, in a different economy of bodies and pleasures, people will no longer quite understand how the ruses of sexuality, and the power that sustains its organization, were able to subject us to that austere monarchy of sex, so that we became dedicated to the endless task for forcing its secret, of exacting the truest of confessions from a shadow.

The irony of this deployment is in having us believe that our "liberation" is in the balance. [*VS*, pp. 210–11; *HS*, p. 159]

Some might be tempted to relate this conclusion to that of *The Order of Things*, to everything that is said there about the *end* and about its *tomorrow*, about man "nearing his end" right up to this "day" when, as *The History of Sexuality* says, "in a different economy of bodies and pleasures, people will no longer quite understand how," and so on. It is difficult not to hear in the rhetoric and tonality of such a call, in the apocalyptic and eschatological tone of this promise (even if "we can at the moment do no more than sense the possibility [of this event]—without knowing either what its form will be or what it promises" [*MC*, p. 398; *OT*, p. 387]), a certain resonance with the Christianity and Christian humanism whose end is being announced.

The "good genius" of Freud would thus be worse than the bad one. It would have consisted in getting itself well placed, in spotting the best place in an old strategy of knowledge and power.

Whatever questions it might leave unanswered—and I will speak in just a moment of one of those it suscitates in me—this project appears nonetheless exciting, necessary, and courageous. And I would not want any particular reservation on my part to be too quickly classified among the reactions of those who hastened to defend the threatened privilege of the pure invention of psychoanalysis, that is, of an invention that would be *pure,* of a psychoanalysis that one might still dream would have innocently sprung forth already outfitted, helmeted, armed, in short, outside all history, after the epistemological cutting of the cord, as one used to say, indeed, after the unraveling of the navel of the dream. Foucault himself during an interview seemed to be ready for some sort of compromise on this issue, readily and good-spiritedly acknowledging the "impasses" (this was his word) of his concept of *episteme* and the difficulties into which this new project had led him.[22] But only those who work, only those who take risks in working, encounter difficulties. One only ever thinks and takes responsibility—if indeed one ever does—in the testing of the aporia; without this, one is content to follow an inclination or apply a program. And it would not be very generous, indeed it would be especially naive and imprudent, to take advantage of these avowals, to take them literally, and to forget what Foucault himself tells us about the confessional scene.

The question that I would have liked to formulate would thus not aim to protect psychoanalysis against some new attack, nor even to cast the slightest doubt upon the importance, necessity, and legitimacy of Foucault's extremely interesting project concerning this great history of sexuality. My question would only seek—and this would be, in sum, a sort of modest contribution—to complicate somewhat an axiomatic and, on the basis of this perhaps, certain discursive or conceptual procedures, particularly regarding the way in which this axiomatic is inscribed in its age, in the historical field that serves as a point of departure, and in its reference to psychoanalysis. In a word, without compromising in the least the necessity of reinscribing almost "all" psychoanalysis (assuming one could seriously say such a thing, which I do not believe one can: psychoanalysis *itself, all* psychoanalysis, *the whole truth about all* psychoanalysis) into a history that precedes and exceeds it, it would be a question of becoming interested in certain gestures, in certain works, in certain moments of certain works of psychoanalysis, Freudian and post-Freudian (for one cannot, especially in France, seriously treat this subject by limiting oneself

22. See "Le Jeu de Michel Foucault," *Ornicar?* 10 (July 1977): 62–93; ed. Alain Grosrichard, under the title "The Confessions of the Flesh," *Power/Knowledge: Selected Interviews and Other Writings, 1972–77,* trans. Colin Gordon et al., ed. Gordon (New York, 1980), esp. pp. 196–97.

to a strictly Freudian discourse and apparatus), in certain traits of a conse-quently nonglobalizable psychoanalysis, one that is divided and multiple (like the powers that Foucault ceaselessly reminds us are essentially dis-persed). It would then be a question of admitting that these necessarily fragmentary or disjointed movements say and do, provide resources for saying and doing, what *The History of Sexuality (The Will to Knowledge)* wishes to say, what it *means [veut dire]*, and what it wishes to do (to know and to make known) with regard to psychoanalysis. In other words, if one still wanted to speak in terms of age—something that I would only ever do in the form of citation—at this point, here on this line, concerning some trait that is on the side from out of which the history of sexuality is written rather than on the side of what it describes or objectifies, one would have to say that Foucault's project belongs too much to "the age of psychoanalysis" in its possibility for it, when claiming to thematize psy-choanalysis, to do anything other than let psychoanalysis continue to speak obliquely of itself and to mark one of its folds in a scene that I will not call self-referential or specular but whose structural complication I will not here try to describe (I have tried to do this elsewhere). This is not only because of what withdraws this history from the regime of represen-tation (because of what already inscribes the possibility of this history in and since the age of Freud and Heidegger—to use these names as mere indications for the sake of convenience). It is also for a reason that inter-ests us here more directly: what Foucault announces and denounces about the relation between pleasure and power, in what he calls the "dou-ble impetus: pleasure and power" (*VS,* p. 62; *HS,* p. 45), would find, al-ready in Freud, to say nothing of those who followed, discussed, transformed, and displaced him, the very resources for the objection lev-eled against the "good genius," the so very bad "good genius," of the father of psychoanalysis. I will situate this with just a word in order to con-clude.

Foucault had clearly cautioned us: this history of sexuality was not be a historian's history. A "genealogy of desiring man" was to be neither a history of representations nor a history of behaviors or sexual practices. This would lead one to think that sexuality cannot become an object of history without seriously affecting the historian's practice and the concept of history. Moreover, Foucault puts quotation marks around the word *sexuality:* "the quotation marks have a certain importance," he adds.[23] We are thus also dealing here with the history of a word, with its usages start-ing in the nineteenth century and the reformulation of the vocabulary in relation to a large number of other phenomena, from biological mecha-nisms to traditional and new norms, to the institutions that support these, be they religious, juridical, pedagogical, or medical (for example, psycho-analytic). This history of the uses of a word is neither nominalist nor

23. Foucault, *L'Usage des plaisirs,* p. 9; *The Use of Pleasure,* p. 3.

essentialist. It concerns procedures and, more precisely, zones of "problematization." It is a "history of truth" as a history of *problematizations*, and even as an "archaeology of problematizations," "through which being offers itself as something that can and must be thought."[24] The point is to analyze not simply behaviors, ideas, or ideologies but, first of all, these *problematizations* in which a thought of being intersects "practices" and "practices of the self," a "genealogy of practices of the self" through which these problematizations are formed. With its reflexive vigilance and care in thinking itself in its rigorous specificity, such an analysis thus calls for the *problematization of its own problematization*. This latter must *itself* also question itself, and with the same archaeological and genealogical care, the same care that it itself methodically prescribes.

When confronted with a historical problematization of such scope and thematic richness, one should not be satisfied with a mere survey, nor with asking in just a few minutes an overarching question so as to insure some sort of synoptic mastery. What we can and must try to do in such a situation is to pay tribute to a work that is this great and this uncertain by means of a question that it itself raises, by means of a question that it carries within itself, that it keeps in reserve in its unlimited potential, one of the questions that can thus be deciphered within it, a question that keeps it in suspense, holding its breath *[tient . . . en haleine]*— and, thus, keeps it alive.

One of these questions, for me, for example, would be the one I had tried to formulate a few years ago during a conference honoring Foucault at New York University.[25] It was developed by means of a problematization of the concept of power and of the theme of what Foucault calls the *spiral* in the duality power/pleasure. Leaving aside the huge question of the concept of power and of what gives it its alleged unity under the essential dispersion rightly recalled by Foucault himself, I will pull out only a thread: it would lead to that which, in a certain Freud and at the center of a certain—let's say for the sake of convenience—French heritage of Freud, would not only not let itself be objectified by the Foucauldian problematization but would actually contribute to it in the most determinate and efficient way, thereby deserving to be inscribed on the thematizing rather than on the thematized border of this history of sexuality. I thus have to wonder what Foucault would have said, in this perspective and were he to have taken this into account, not of "Freud" or of psychoanalysis "itself" *in general*—which does not exist any more than power does as one big central and homogeneous corpus—but, for example, since this is only one example, about an undertaking like *Beyond the Pleasure Principle*, about something in its lineage or between its filial

24. Ibid., pp. 17–19; pp. 11–13.
25. The following analysis thus intersects a much longer treatment of the subject in an unpublished paper entitled "Beyond the Power Principle" that I presented during this conference at New York University, organized by Thomas Bishop, in April 1986.

connections—along with everything that has been inherited, repeated, or discussed from it since then. In following one of these threads or filial connections, one of the most discreet, in following the abyssal, unassignable, and unmasterable strategy of this text, a strategy that is finally without strategy, one begins to see that this text not only opens up the horizon of a beyond of the pleasure principle (the hypothesis of such a beyond never really seeming to be of interest to Foucault) against which the whole economy of pleasure needs to be rethought, complicated, pursued in its most unrecognizable ruses and detours. By means of one of these filiations—another one unwinding the spool of the *fort/da* that continues to interest us—this text also problematizes, in its greatest radicality, the agency of power and mastery. In a discreet and difficult passage, an original drive for power or drive for mastery *(Bemächtigungstrieb)* is mentioned. It is very difficult to know if this drive for power is still dependent upon the pleasure principle, indeed, upon sexuality as such, upon the austere monarchy of sex that Foucault speaks of on the last page of his book.

How would Foucault have situated this drive for mastery in his discourse on power or on irreducibly plural powers? How would he have read this drive, had he read it, in this extremely enigmatic text of Freud? How would he have interpreted the recurring references to the demonic from someone who then makes himself, according to his own terms, the "devil's advocate" and who becomes interested in the hypothesis of a late or derived appearance of sex and sexual pleasure? In the whole problematization whose history he describes, how would Foucault have inscribed this passage from *Beyond the Pleasure Principle,* and this concept and these questions (with all the debates to which this book of Freud either directly or indirectly gave rise, in a sort of critical capitalization, particularly in the France of our age, beginning with everything in Lacan that takes its point of departure in the repetition compulsion *[Wiederholungszwang]*)? Would he have inscribed this problematic matrix *within* the whole whose history he describes? Or would he have put it on the other side, on the side of what allows one on the contrary to delimit the whole, indeed to problematize it? And thus on a side that no longer belongs to the whole, nor, as I would be tempted to think, to any whole, such that the very idea of a gathering of problematization or procedure, to say nothing any longer of age, *episteme,* paradigm, or epoch, would make for so many problematic names, just as problematic as the very idea of problematization?

This is one of the questions that I would have liked to ask him. I am trying, since this is, unfortunately, the only recourse left us in the solitude of questioning, to imagine the principle of the reply. It would perhaps be something like this: what one must stop believing in is principality or principleness, in the problematic of the principle, in the principled unity of pleasure and power, or of some drive that is thought to be more originary than the other. The theme of the *spiral* would be that of a drive duality (power/pleasure) that is *without principle*.

It is *the spirit of this spiral* that keeps one in suspense, holding one's breath—and, thus, keeps one alive.

The question would thus once again be given a new impetus: is not the duality in question, this spiralled duality, what Freud tried to oppose to all monisms by speaking of a dual drive and of a death drive, of a death drive that was no doubt not alien to the drive for mastery? And, thus, to what is most alive in life, to its very living on *[survivance]*?

I am still trying to imagine Foucault's response. I can't quite do it. I would need him to take it on himself.

But in this place where no one can answer for him, in the absolute silence where we remain nonetheless turned toward him, I would venture to bet that, in a sentence that I will not construct for him, he would have associated and yet also dissociated, he would have placed back to back, mastery and death, that is, the same—death *and* the master, death *as* the master.

Madness, the Absence of Work

Michel Foucault

Translated by Peter Stastny and Deniz Şengel

Perhaps some day we will no longer really know what madness was. Its face will have closed upon itself, no longer allowing us to decipher the traces it may have left behind. Will these traces themselves have become anything to the unknowing gaze but simple black marks? Or will they at the most have become part of the configurations that we others now cannot sketch but that in the future would constitute the indispensable grids through which we and our culture become legible? Artaud will belong to the foundation of our language, not to its rupture; the neuroses will belong among the constitutive forms (and not the deviations) of our society. Everything we experience today in the mode of a limit, or as foreign, or as intolerable will have returned to the serenity of the positive. And whatever currently designates this exteriority to us may well one day designate us.

Only the enigma of this exteriority will remain. What was, then, this strange demarcation, one will ask, that was at work from the heart of the Middle Ages until the twentieth century and possibly beyond? Why did Western culture cast from its field that in which it might just as well have recognized itself, where in fact it had recognized itself obliquely? Why has it formulated so clearly since the nineteenth century, but in a way already since the classical age, that madness was the truth of the human laid bare while nevertheless placing it in a space, neutralized and pale, where it was as it were canceled? What was the point of collecting the texts of Nerval or Artaud? Why discover oneself in their utterances and not in themselves?

So the sharp image of reason will wither in flames. The familiar game of mirroring the other side of ourselves in madness and of eavesdropping from our listening posts on voices that, coming from very far, tell us more nearly what we are—this game with its rules, its strategies, its contrivances, its tricks, its tolerated illegalities will once and for all have become nothing but a complex ritual whose significations will have been reduced to ashes. Something like the great ceremonies of barter and combat in archaic societies. Something like the ambiguous attention Greek reason paid to its oracles. Or like the latter's twin institution, starting with the fourteenth century A.D., of the practices and trials of witchcraft. Nothing will remain in the hands of cultural historians except the codified methods of confinement, the techniques of medicine, and, on the other hand, the sudden, irruptive inclusion in our language of the speech of the excluded.

What will the technical support for this radical change be? The possibility that medicine may master mental illness just like other organic ailments? Precise pharmacological control of all mental symptoms? Or a more or less rigorous definition of behavioral deviations for each of which society might be at leisure to anticipate the most convenient method of neutralization? Or still other modes of intervention, perhaps none of which will in fact suppress mental illness but which will all have the purpose of eliminating the very face of madness from our culture?

I know well that by proposing this latter hypothesis I am contesting something that is ordinarily accepted: that the advances of medicine could indeed succeed in eradicating mental illness just as they have done away with leprosy and tuberculosis but that the one thing to remain is the relationship of humankind to its ghosts, to its impossible, to its bodiless pain, to its carcass of the night; that once pathology is removed from circulation, the dark link of the human to madness will become the ageless memory of an evil that has been effaced as a form of illness but persists as misfortune. To tell the truth, this idea assumes as inalterable what is undoubtedly most precarious, even more precarious than the constants of pathology: the relationship of a culture to the very thing it excludes or, more precisely, the relationship of our culture to this truth about itself, far away and inverted, which it discovers over and over in madness.

That which will not take long to die, that which is already dying in us (and whose very death bears our current language) is *homo dialecticus*—the being of departure, of return, and of time; the animal that loses its truth only in order to find it again, illuminated; the self-estranged who once again recovers the unity of the self-same. This figure has been the master subject and the object slave of all the discourses concerning the human, in particular human alienation, which have persisted for quite some time. And fortunately it is dying beneath the babble of these discourses.

So that it will no longer be known how humanity had been able to place this figure of itself at a distance; how it could have let pass from the other side of the limit even that which belonged to it and which it resembled? No thought will be able to contemplate this movement from which until all too recently the West took its liberties. It is this relationship to madness (and not some knowledge about mental illness or some position taken on human alienation) that will be lost forever. The only thing that will be known is that we others, five-century-old Westerners, had been those people upon the face of the earth who, among many other fundamental traits, had borne the strangest trait of them all: we maintained a profound, passionate relationship to mental illness, perhaps difficult to formulate for ourselves but impenetrable to anyone else, in which we confronted dangers most vivid to us as well as what was perhaps the truth closest to us. It will not be said that we were *at a distance* from madness but *within distance* of it. The Greeks, similarly, were not distanced from ΰβρισ [hubris] because they condemned it; they were rather within reach of this excess located at the heart of the distance where they kept it.

Those who will no longer be what we are will face the task of contemplating this enigma (somewhat as we do today when we try to grasp how Athena could have fallen in love with and detached herself from the irrationality of Alcibiades). How could humans search for their truth, their essential speech, and their signs in the face of a peril that made them tremble and from which they were compelled to avert their eyes once they had caught sight of it? And this will appear even more strange to them than asking death the truth of humanity, for death says what will happen to everyone. Madness, in turn, is the rarer danger, a chance that weighs little compared to the obsessions it has engendered and the questions it has been asked. How could it be, in a culture, that such a slight contingency held such great power of revelation and terror?

Those who will be looking at us over their shoulder will certainly not have many clues at their disposal to answer this question. Only a few charred signs: the endlessly examined, centuries-old fear of seeing the level of madness rise and submerge the world; the rituals of excluding and including the mad; and, since the nineteenth century, the alert ear bent on overhearing something in madness that could tell the truth about the human; the same impatience with which the utterances of madness are rejected and collected, the hesitation in recognizing their emptiness or their meaningfulness.

And all the rest—this unique movement by which we come to meet madness while distancing ourselves from it; this terrifying recognition; this desire to establish the limit yet at once to compensate for it through the framework of a unitary meaning—all this will be reduced to silence, just as the Greek trilogy μανία, ΰβρισ, ἀλογία [mania, hubris, alogia] or the posture of shamanic deviation in some primitive societies are mute to us today.

We are now at that point in time, in that fold of time, where a certain technical control of illness conceals rather than points to the movement that closes the experience of madness upon itself. But it is precisely this fold, too, that allows us to disentangle two different configurations that remained bound up with one another for centuries. Mental illness and madness, merged with and mistaken for each other from the seventeenth century on, are now becoming separated under our very eyes or, rather, in our language.

To say that madness is disappearing today means that its implication both in psychiatric knowledge and thought of an anthropological kind is coming undone. But this is not to say that the general form of transgression, whose visible face madness has been for centuries, is also disappearing. Nor does it mean that this transgression is not giving rise to a new experience even as we are asking ourselves what madness is.

There is not a single culture in the world where everything is permitted. And we have known for a long time that humanity does not start out from freedom but from limitation and the line not to be crossed. We know the systems of rules with which forbidden acts are to comply; we have been able to discern the rules of the incest taboo in every culture. But we still do not know much about the organization of the prohibitions in language. It seems that these two systems of restriction do not overlap as if one were nothing but the verbal version of the other; what is not allowed to appear at the level of the word is not necessarily what is forbidden in the realm of deed. The Zuni narrate incest between brother and sister, which they outlaw, and the Greeks tell the legend of Oedipus. On the other hand, the Code of 1808 abolished extant criminal laws against sodomy, but the language of the nineteenth century was much more intolerant of homosexuality, at least of its male manifestation, than had been that of preceding eras. And it is likely that the psychological concepts of compensation and symbolic expression cannot in the least explain such phenomena.

The domain of the prohibitions in language should in itself be studied some day. It is today undoubtedly too early to know just how to carry out such an analysis. Should we employ the categories that are presently admitted into language? Should we first identify, regarding the limits of the forbidden and the impossible, the laws that are relevant to the linguistic code (what we so clearly refer to as *linguistic errors*); and then, within this code and among extant words or expressions, locate those that are affected by the rule forbidding the utterance of certain words or expressions (the entire religious, sexual, magical series of *blasphemous words*); and then, among those words and expressions that may be uttered, identify which ones are permitted by the code, permitted in the act of speech, but whose meaning is not tolerated by the culture in question at a given time. At this point, the metaphoric detour would no longer be possible, since it is the meaning itself that is the object of *censorship*. Finally, there is a fourth form of language that is excluded; it consists of subjecting an utterance, which appears to conform to the accepted code, to another code whose key is contained within that same utterance so that this utterance becomes divided within itself. It says what it says, but it adds a silent surplus that quietly enunciates what it says and according to which code it says what it says. This is not the case of an encoded language but of one that is structurally esoteric. That is to say, it does not communicate a forbidden meaning by concealing its meaning; it positions itself from the start in an essential fold of the utterance. A fold that hollows it out from within and perhaps to infinity. Therefore it matters little what is said in such a language and what meaning is being delivered there. It is this obscure and central liberation at the very heart of the utterance, its uncontrollable flight toward a source that is always without light, that no culture can readily accept. Such utterance is transgressive not in its meaning, not in its verbal property, but in its *play*.

It is quite likely that any culture, whatever it may be, knows, practices, and tolerates (to a certain extent) but equally represses and excludes these four types of forbidden language.

In Western history, the experience of madness has been displaced along this vector. In fact, it has long occupied an indeterminate area, difficult for us to specify, between the prohibition directed at action and that directed at language. Hence the exemplary importance of the pair *furor-inanitas,* which had practically organized the world of madness along the registers of deed and word up to the end of the Renaissance. The period of confinement (the general hospitals, Charenton, Saint-Lazare, established in the seventeenth century) marks a displacement of madness toward the realm of the insane; with forbidden acts, madness now maintains hardly more than a moral kinship (primarily, it stays attached to sexual prohibitions), but it is included in the universe of the prohibitions of language. Classical confinement envelopes, along with madness, the libertinism of thought and of speech, the obstinacy within impiety or heterodoxy, blasphemy, sorcery, alchemy—in short, everything that characterizes the *spoken* and forbidden world of unreason; madness is language that is excluded—those who, against the code of language, pronounce words without meaning (the "insane," the "imbeciles," the "demented"), or those who utter sanctified words (the "violent ones," the "furious"), or yet still, those who bring forth forbidden meanings (the "libertines," the "headstrong"). Pinel's reform is a conspicuous completion rather than a modification of this repression of madness as forbidden language.

The latter does not actually occur until Freud, when the experience of madness becomes displaced toward the last type of language prohibition of which we spoke earlier. Madness, then, ceases to be a linguistic error, a spoken blasphemy, or an intolerable meaning (and in that sense psychoanalysis actually constitutes the great catalogue of prohibitions as defined by Freud himself). Madness appears as an utterance wrapped up in itself, articulating something else beneath what it says, of which it is at the same time the only possible code—an esoteric language, if you will, since it confines its linguistic code within an utterance that ultimately does not articulate anything other than this implication.

Therefore Freud's work ought to be taken for what it is; it does not discover that madness is apprehended in a web of significations it shares with everyday language, thereby granting the license to speak of it in the common platitudes of a psychological vocabulary. It dislodges the European experience of madness in order to situate it in this perilous region, still transgressive (therefore still forbidden but in a rather peculiar fashion), which is the region of languages that implicate themselves; that is to say, they enunciate in their utterances the linguistic code in which they enunciate those utterances. Freud did not discover the lost identity of a meaning; he carved out the disruptive image of a signifier that is *absolutely not* like the others. This should have sufficed to shield his work from all psychologizing interpretations wherein our half of the century has buried it in the (derisive) name of the "human sciences" and their asexual union.

And, for the same reason, madness has appeared not like the ruse of a hidden signification but like a prodigious *reserve* of meaning. We still have to grasp how fitting this word *reserve* is. Much more than a mere supply, it is a figure that retains and suspends meaning, laying out an emptiness where nothing is proposed but the yet-incomplete possibility that some meaning or another may come to lodge there, or still a third, and this may perhaps continue to infinity. Madness opens up a lacunar reserve that designates and exposes that chasm where linguistic code and utterance become entangled, shaping each other and speaking of nothing but their still silent rapport. Since Freud, Western madness has become a nonlanguage as it turned into a double language (a linguistic code that does not exist except in this utterance, an utterance that does not say anything other than its linguistic code)—that is to say, a matrix of a language that, in a strict sense, does not say anything. A fold of the spoken that is an absence of work.

One day we ought to do the justice to Freud of acknowledging that he did not make a madness *speak* that had been for centuries precisely a language (excluded language, babbling inanity, speech circulating indeterminately outside of the pondered silence of reason); to the contrary, he exhausted its meaningless logos; he dried it out; he returned its words to their source—to that blank region of self-implication where nothing is said.

What is occurring today still appears to us in an uncertain light, yet we are able to take note of a strange movement in our language. Literature itself (undoubtedly since Mallarmé) is in the midst of becoming in its turn, step by step, a language of which the utterance enunciates—at the same time and in the same movement that it says whatever it says—the linguistic code that renders it intelligible as utterance. Before Mallarmé, writing consisted of establishing one's utterance within a given linguistic code, as if the work of that language were of the same nature as that of the rest of language, close to the familiar signs (and they were certainly majestic) of rhetoric, of the subject, or of images. By the end of the nineteenth century (around the time of the discovery of psychoanalysis, when there was certainly no dearth of discoveries), literature had become utterance that inscribed in itself its own principle of decipherment. Or, in any case, it implied, in every sentence and in every word, the power to modify in sovereign fashion the values and significations of the linguistic code to which in spite of everything (and in fact) it belonged; it suspended the reign of that code in one actual gesture of writing.

Hence the necessity of secondary languages (what is called, in brief, criticism). Today, they no longer function as external supplements to literature (judgments, mediations, stepping-stones that were deemed useful links between a work indexed to the psychological enigma of its creation and the act of its consumption in reading). At the heart of literature, they now partake of the void that literature installs within its own language; they constitute the necessary movement—albeit one that by necessity will remain incomplete—by which the utterance is returned to its linguistic code, and by which the code is founded upon the utterance. Hence, too, that strange proximity between madness and literature, which ought not be taken in the sense of a relation of common psychological parentage now finally exposed. Once uncovered as a language silenced by its superposition upon itself, madness neither manifests nor narrates the birth of a work (or of something which, by genius or by chance, could have become a work); it outlines an empty form from where this work comes, in other words, the place from where it never ceases to be absent, where it will never be found because it had never been located there to begin with. There, in that pale region, in that essential hiding place, the twinlike incompatibility of the work and of madness becomes unveiled; this is the blind spot of the possibility of each to become the other and of their mutual exclusion.

But since Raymond Roussel, since Artaud, it is also the place from where the language of literature comes. But it does not come from there as if from something that might have borne the task of enunciating. It is time to recognize that the language of literature is not defined by what it says, nor by the structures that render it significant. Rather, it has a being, and it is about this being that it ought to be questioned. What, in fact, is this being? Undoubtedly something connected to self-implication, to the double and the void that expands within it. In this sense, the being of literature, as it has been produced from Mallarmé to today, obtains the region where, since Freud, the experience of madness figures.

In the eyes of some unknown future culture—one possibly already quite near—we shall be those that have come closest to those two sentences never really pronounced, those two sentences equally contradictory and impossible as the famous "I am lying" and both pointing to the same empty self-reference: "I am writing" and "I am delirious." We shall thus figure next to countless other cultures that placed the "I am mad" near an "I am an animal," or "I am a god," or "I am a sign," or yet near an "I am a truth" as was the case in the entire nineteenth century up to Freud. And if that culture should have a feeling for history, it will in effect remember that Nietzsche, becoming mad, had proclaimed (in 1887) that he was the truth (why I am so wise, why I have known of it so long, why I write such great books, why I am fate); and that less than fifty years later, on the eve of his suicide, Roussel would write in *Comment j'ai écrit certains de mes livres*, the systematically divided account of his madness and his procedures of writing. And they will be astonished, no doubt, that we were capable of identifying such a strange kinship between what, for a long time, was dreaded like a scream and what, for a long time, was considered a song.

But it is quite possible that precisely this transformation will not seem to merit any astonishment. It is we today who are astonished to see two languages communicate with each other (that of madness and that of literature) whose incompatibility has been established by our history. Since the seventeenth century, madness and mental illness have occupied the same space in the realm of forbidden languages (in general, the realm of the insane). Entering another domain of excluded language (a language that is circumscribed, consecrated, dreaded, erected, and elevated far above itself, whose reference is but a self-reference within that useless and transgressive fold we call literature), madness dissolves its kinship, ancient or recent according to the chosen scale, to mental illness.

The latter will no doubt enter into a technical space of ever increasing control. In the hospitals, pharmacology has already transformed the wards of the agitated into vast, tepid aquariums. But underneath these transformations and for reasons that will seem strange to them (at least according to our current views), a *dénouement* is already in process: madness and mental illness are undoing their affiliation to the same anthropological unit. This unity itself is disappearing along with the human as a transitory postulate. Madness, the lyrical halo of illness, continues to extinguish itself. And at a distance from pathology, from the vicinity where language folds in upon itself still saying nothing, an experience is about to be born where our thought is headed. This imminence, already visible but absolutely empty, remains to be named.

HISTORY, DIAGNOSTICS, POWER

Human Nature: Justice versus Power

Noam Chomsky and Michel Foucault

ELDERS: Ladies and gentlemen, welcome to the third debate of the International Philosophers' Project. Tonight's debaters are Mr. Michel Foucault, of the Collège de France, and Mr. Noam Chomsky, of the Massachusetts Institute of Technology. Both philosophers have points in common and points of difference. Perhaps the best way to compare both philosophers would be to see them as tunnellers through a mountain working at opposite sides of the same mountain with different tools, without even knowing if they are working in each other's direction.

But both are doing their jobs with quite new ideas, digging as profoundly as possible with an equal commitment in philosophy as in politics: enough reasons, it seems to me, for us to expect a fascinating debate about philosophy and about politics.

I intend, therefore, not to lose any time and to start off with a central, perennial question: the question of human nature.

All studies of man, from history to linguistics and psychology, are faced with the question of whether, in the last instance, we are the product of all kinds of external factors, or if, in spite of our differences, we have something we could call a common human nature, by which we can recognize each other as human beings.

So my first question is to you Mr. Chomsky, because you often employ the concept of human nature, in which connection you even use terms like "innate ideas" and "innate structures." Which arguments can you derive from linguistics to give such a central position to this concept of human nature ?

CHOMSKY: Well, let me begin in a slightly technical way.

A person who is interested in studying languages is faced with a very definite empirical problem. He's faced with an organism, a mature, let's say adult, speaker, who has somehow acquired an amazing range of abilities, which enable him in particular to say what he means, to understand what people say to him, to do this in a fashion that I think is proper to call highly creative . . . that is, much of what a person says in his normal intercourse with others is novel, much of what you hear is new, it doesn't bear any close resemblance to anything in your experience; it's not random novel behavior, clearly, it's behavior which is in some sense, which is very hard to characterize, appropriate to situations. And in fact it has many of the characteristics of what I think might very well be called creativity.

Now, the person who has acquired this intricate and highly articulated and organized collection of abilities—the collection of abilities that we call knowing a language—has been exposed to a certain experience; he has been presented in the course of his lifetime with a certain amount of data, of direct experience with a language.

We can investigate the data that's available to this person; having done so, in principle, we're faced with a reasonably clear and well-delineated scientific problem, namely that of accounting for the gap between the really quite small quantity of data, small and rather degenerate in quality, that's presented to the child, and the very highly articulated, highly systematic, profoundly organized resulting knowledge that he somehow derives from these data.

Furthermore we notice that varying individuals with very varied experience in a particular language nevertheless arrive at systems which are very much congruent to one another. The systems that two speakers of English arrive at on the basis of their very different experiences are congruent in the sense that, over an overwhelming range, what one of them says, the other can understand.

Furthermore, even more remarkable, we notice that in a wide range of languages, in fact all that have been studied seriously, there are remarkable limitations on the kind of systems that emerge from the very different kinds of experiences to which people are exposed.

There is only one possible explanation, which I have to give in a rather schematic fashion, for this remarkable phenomenon, namely the assumption that the individual himself contributes a good deal, an overwhelming part in fact, of the general schematic structure and perhaps even of the specific content of the knowledge that he ultimately derives from this very scattered and limited experience.

A person who knows a language has acquired that knowledge because he approached the learning experience with a very explicit and detailed schematism that tells him what kind of language it is that he is being exposed to. That is, to put it rather loosely: the child must begin with the knowledge, certainly not with the knowledge that he's hearing English or Dutch or French or something else, but he *does* start with the knowledge that he's hearing a human language of a very narrow and explicit type, that permits a very small range of variation. And it is because he begins with that highly organized and very restrictive schematism, that he is able to make the huge leap from scattered and degenerate data to highly organized knowledge. And furthermore I should add that we can go a certain distance, I think a rather long distance, towards presenting the properties of this system of knowledge, that I would call innate language or instinctive knowledge, that the child brings to language learning; and also we can go a long way towards describing the system that is mentally represented when he has acquired this knowledge.

I would claim then that this instinctive knowledge, if you like, this schematism that makes it possible to derive complex and intricate knowledge on the basis of very partial data, is one fundamental constituent of human nature. In this case I think a fundamental constituent because of the role that language plays, not merely in communication, but also in expression of thought and interaction between persons; and I assume that in other domains of human intelligence, in other domains of human cognition and behavior, something of the same sort must be true.

Well, this collection, this mass of schematisms, innate organizing principles, which guides our social and intellectual and individual behavior, that's what I mean to refer to by the concept of human nature.

ELDERS: Well, Mr. Foucault, when I think of your books like *The History of Madness* and *Words and Objects,* I get the impression that you are working on a completely different level and with a totally opposite aim and goal; when I think of the word schematism in relation to human nature, I suppose you are trying to elaborate several periods with several schematisms. What do you say to this ?

FOUCAULT: Well, if you don't mind I will answer in French, because my English is so poor that I would be ashamed of answering in English.

It is true that I mistrust the notion of human nature a little, and for the following reason: I believe that of the concepts or notions which a science can use, not all have the same degree of elaboration, and that in general they have neither the same function nor the same type of possible use in scientific discourse. Let's take the example of biology. You will find concepts with a classifying function, concepts with a differentiating function, and concepts with an analytical function: some of them enable us to characterize objects, for example that of "tissue"; others to isolate elements, like that of "hereditary feature"; others to fix relations, such as that of "reflex." There are at the same time elements which play a role in the discourse and in the internal rules of the reasoning practice. But there also exist "peripheral" notions, those by which scientific practice designates itself, differentiates itself in relation to other practices, delimits its domain of objects, and designates what it considers to be the totality of its future tasks. The notion of life played this role to some extent in biology during a certain period.

In the seventeenth and eighteenth centuries, the notion of life was hardly used in studying nature: one classified natural beings, whether living or nonliving, in a vast hierarchical tableau which went from minerals to man; the break between the minerals and the plants or animals was relatively undecided; epistemologically it was only important to fix their positions once and for all in an indisputable way.

At the end of the eighteenth century, the description and analysis of these natural beings showed, through the use of more highly perfected instruments and the latest techniques, an entire domain of objects, an entire field of relations and processes which have enabled us to define the specificity of biology in the knowledge of nature. Can one say that research into life has finally constituted itself in biological science? Has the concept of life been responsible for the organization of biological knowledge? I don't think so. It seems to me more likely that the transformations of biological knowledge at the end of the eighteenth century were demonstrated on one hand by a whole series of new concepts for use in scientific discourse and on the other hand gave rise to a notion like that of life which has enabled us to designate, to delimit and to situate a certain type of scientific discourse, among other things. I would say that the notion of life is not a *scientific concept;* it has been an *epistemological indicator* of which the classifying, delimiting and other functions had an effect on scientific discussions, and not on what they were talking about.

Well, it seems to me that the notion of human nature is of the same type. It was not by studying human nature that linguists discovered the laws of consonant mutation, or Freud the principles of the analysis of dreams, or cultural anthropologists the structure of myths. In the history of knowledge, the notion of human nature seems to me mainly to have played the role of an epistemological indicator to designate certain types of discourse in relation to or in opposition to theology or biology or history. I would find it difficult to see in this a scientific concept.

CHOMSKY: Well, in the first place, if we were able to specify in terms of, let's say, neural networks the properties of human cognitive structure that make it possible for the child to acquire these complicated systems, then I at least would have no hesitation in describing those properties as being a constituent element of human nature. That is, there is something biologically given, unchangeable, a foundation for whatever it is that we do with our mental capacities in this case.

But I would like to pursue a little further the line of development that you outlined, with which in fact I entirely agree, about the concept of life as an organizing concept in the biological sciences.

It seems to me that one might speculate a bit further—speculate in this case, since we're talking about the future, not the past—and ask whether the concept of human nature or of innate organizing mechanisms or of intrinsic mental schematism or whatever we want to call it, I don't see much difference between them, but let's call it human nature for shorthand, might not provide for biology the next peak to try to scale, after having—at least in the minds of the biologists, though one might perhaps question this—already answered to the satisfaction of some the question of what is life.

In other words, to be precise, is it possible to give a biological explanation or a physical explanation . . . is it possible to characterize, in terms of the physical concepts presently available to us, the ability of the child to acquire complex systems of knowledge; and furthermore, critically, having acquired such systems of knowledge, to make use of this knowledge in the free and creative and remarkably varied ways in which he does?

Can we explain in biological terms, ultimately in physical terms, these properties of both acquiring knowledge in the first place and making use of it in the second? I really see no reason to believe that we can; that is, it's an article of faith on the part of scientists that since science has explained many other things it will also explain this.

In a sense one might say that this is a variant of the body–mind problem. But if we look back at the way in which science has scaled various peaks, and at the way in which the concept of life was finally acquired by science after having been beyond its vision for a long period, then I think we notice at many points in history—and in fact the seventeenth and eighteenth centuries are particularly clear examples—that scientific advances were possible precisely because the domain of physical science was itself enlarged. Classic cases are Newton's gravitational forces. To the Cartesians, action at a distance was a mystical concept, and in fact to Newton himself it was an occult quality, a mystical entity, which didn't belong within science. To the common sense of a later generation, action at a distance has been incorporated within science.

What happened was that the notion of body, the notion of the physical had changed. To a Cartesian, a strict Cartesian, if such a person appeared today, it would appear that there is no explanation for the behavior of the heavenly bodies. Certainly there is no explanation for the phenomena that are explained in terms of electromagnetic force, let's say. But by the extension of physical science to incorporate hitherto unavailable concepts, entirely new ideas, it became possible to successively build more and more complicated structures that incorporated a larger range of phenomena.

For example, it's certainly not true that the physics of the Cartesians is able to explain, let's say, the behavior of elementary particles in physics, just as it's unable to explain the concepts of life.

Similarly, I think, one might ask the question whether physical science as known today, including biology, incorporates within itself the principles and the concepts that will enable it to give an account of innate human intellectual capacities and, even more profoundly, of the ability to make use of those capacities under conditions of freedom in the way which humans do. I see no particular reason to believe that biology or physics now contain those concepts, and it may be that to scale the next peak, to make the next step, they will have to focus on this organizing concept, and may very well have to broaden their scope in order to come to grips with it.

FOUCAULT: Yes.

ELDERS: Perhaps I may try to ask one more specific question leading out of both your answers, because I'm afraid otherwise the debate will become too technical. I have the impression that one of the main differences between you both has its origin in a difference in approach. You, Mr. Foucault, are especially interested in the way science or scientists function in a certain period, whereas Mr. Chomsky is more interested in the so-called what-questions: why we possess language—not just how language functions, but what's the *reason* for our having language. We can try to elucidate this in a more general way: you, Mr. Foucault, are delimiting eighteenth-century rationalism, whereas you, Mr. Chomsky, are combining eighteenth-century rationalism with notions like freedom and creativity.

Perhaps we could illustrate this in a more general way with examples from the seventeenth and eighteenth centuries.

CHOMSKY: Well, first I should say that I approach classical rationalism not really as a historian of science or a historian of philosophy, but from the rather different point of view of someone who has a certain range of scientific notions and is interested in seeing how at an earlier stage people may have been groping towards these notions, possibly without even realizing what they were groping towards.

So one might say that I'm looking at history not as an antiquarian, who is interested in finding out and giving a precisely accurate account of what the thinking of the seventeenth century was—I don't mean to demean that activity, it's just not mine—but rather from the point of view of, let's say, an art lover, who wants to look at the seventeenth century to find in it things that are of particular value, and that obtain part of their value in part because of the perspective with which he approaches them.

And I think that, without objecting to the other approach, my approach is legitimate; that is, I think it is perfectly possible to go back to earlier stages of scientific thinking on the basis of our present understanding, and to perceive how great thinkers were, within the limitations of their time, groping towards concepts and ideas and insights that they themselves could not be clearly aware of.

For example, I think that anyone can do this about his own thought. Without trying to compare oneself to the great thinkers of the past, anyone can . . .

ELDERS: Why not?

CHOMSKY: . . . look at . . .

ELDERS: Why not?

CHOMSKY: All right *[laughs]*, anyone can consider what he now knows and can ask what he knew twenty years ago, and can see that in some unclear fashion he was striving towards something which he can only now understand . . . if he is fortunate.

Similarly I think it's possible to look at the past, without distorting your view, and it is in these terms that I want to look at the seventeenth century. Now, when I look back at the seventeenth and eighteenth centuries, what strikes me particularly is the way in which, for example, Descartes and his followers were led to postulate mind as a thinking substance independent of the body. If you look at their reasons for postulating this second substance, mind, thinking entity, they were that Descartes was able to convince himself, rightly or wrongly, it doesn't matter at the moment, that events in the physical world and even much of the behavioral and psychological world, for example a good deal of sensation, were explicable in terms of what he considered to be physics—wrongly, as we now believe—that is, in terms of things bumping into each other and turning and moving and so on.

He thought that in those terms, in terms of the mechanical principle, he could explain a certain domain of phenomena; and then he observed that there was a range of phenomena that he argued could not be explained in those terms. And he therefore postulated a creative principle to account for that domain of phenomena, the principle of mind with its own properties. And then later followers, many who didn't regard themselves as Cartesians, for example many who regarded themselves as strongly antirationalistic, developed the concept of creation within a system of rule.

I won't bother with the details, but my own research into the subject led me ultimately to Wilhelm von Humboldt, who certainly didn't consider himself a Cartesian, but nevertheless in a rather different framework and within a different historical period and with different insight, in a remarkable and ingenious way, which, I think, is of lasting importance, also developed the concept of internalized form—fundamentally the concept of free creation within a system of rule—in an effort to come to grips with some of the same difficulties and problems that the Cartesians faced in their terms.

Now I believe, and here I would differ from a lot of my colleagues, that the move of Descartes to the postulation of a second substance was a very scientific move; it was not a metaphysical or an antiscientific move. In fact, in many ways it was very much like Newton's intellectual move when he postulated action at a distance; he was moving into the domain of the occult, if you like. He was moving into the domain of something that went beyond well-established science, and was trying to integrate it with well-established science by developing a theory in which these notions could be properly clarified and explained.

Now Descartes, I think, made a similar intellectual move in postulating a second substance. Of course he failed where Newton succeeded; that is, he was unable to lay the groundworks for a mathematical theory of mind, as achieved by Newton and his followers, which laid the groundwork for a mathematical theory of physical entities that incorporated such occult notions as action at a distance and later electromagnetic forces and so on.

But then that poses for us, I think, the task of carrying on and developing this, if you like, mathematical theory of mind; by that I simply mean a precisely articulated, clearly formulated, abstract theory which will have empirical consequences, which will let us know whether the theory is right or wrong, or on the wrong track or the right track, and at the same time will have the properties of mathematical science, that is, the properties of rigor and precision and a structure that makes it possible for us to deduce conclusions from assumptions and so on.

Now it's from that point of view that I try to look back at the seventeenth and eighteenth centuries and to pick out points, which I think are really there, even though I certainly recognize, and in fact would want to insist, that the individuals in question may not have seen it this way.

ELDERS: Mr. Foucault, I suppose you will have a severe criticism of this?

FOUCAULT: No . . . there are just one or two little historical points. I cannot object to the account which you have given in your historical analysis of their reasons and of their modality. But there is one thing one could nevertheless add: when you speak of creativity as conceived by Descartes, I wonder if you don't transpose to Descartes an idea which is to be found among his successors or even certain of his contemporaries. According to Descartes, the mind was not so very creative. It saw, it perceived, it was illuminated by the evidence.

Moreover, the problem which Descartes never resolved nor entirely mastered, was that of understanding how one could pass from one of these clear and distinct ideas, one of these intuitions, to another, and what status should be given to the evidence of the passage between them. I can't see exactly either the creation in the moment where the mind grasped the truth for Descartes, or even the real creation in the passage from one truth to another.

On the contrary, you can find, I think, at the same time in Pascal and Leibniz, something which is much closer to what you are looking for: in other words in Pascal and in the whole Augustinian stream of Christian thought, you find this idea of a mind in profundity; of a mind folded back in the intimacy of itself which is touched by a sort of unconsciousness, and which can develop its potentialities by the deepening of the self. And that is why the grammar of Port Royal, to which you refer, is, I think, much more Augustinian than Cartesian.

And furthermore you will find in Leibniz something which you will certainly like: the idea that in the profundity of the mind is incorporated a whole web of logical relations which constitutes, in a certain sense, the rational unconscious of the consciousness, the not yet clarified and visible form of the reason itself, which the monad or the individual develops little by little, and with which he understands the whole world.

That's where I would make a very small criticism.

ELDERS: Mr. Chomsky, one moment please. I don't think it's a question of making a historical criticism, but of formulating your own opinions on these quite fundamental concepts. . . .

FOUCAULT: But one's fundamental opinions can be demonstrated in precise analyses such as these.

ELDERS: Yes, all right. But I remember some passages in your *History of Madness*, which give a description of the seventeenth and eighteenth centuries in terms of repression, suppression and exclusion, while for Mr. Chomsky this period is full of creativity and individuality.

Why do we have at that period, for the first time, closed psychiatric or insane asylums? I think this is a very fundamental question. . . .

FOUCAULT: . . . on creativity, yes!

But I don't know, perhaps Mr. Chomsky would like to speak about it . . .

ELDERS: No, no, no, please go on. Continue.

FOUCAULT: No, I would like to say this: in the historical studies that I have been able to make, or have tried to make, I have without any doubt given very little room to what you might call the creativity of individuals, to their capacity for creation, to their aptitude for inventing by themselves, for originating concepts, theories or scientific truths by themselves.

But I believe that my problem is different to that of Mr. Chomsky. Mr. Chomsky has been fighting against linguistic behaviorism, which attributed almost nothing to the creativity of the speaking subject; the speaking subject was a kind of surface on which information came together little by little, which he afterwards combined.

In the field of the history of science or, more generally, the history of thought, the problem was completely different.

The history of knowledge has tried for a long time to obey two claims. One is the claim of *attribution:* each discovery should not only be situated and dated, but should also be attributed to someone; it should have an inventor and someone responsible for it. General or collective phenomena on the other hand, those which by definition can't be "attributed," are normally devalued: they are still traditionally described through words like *tradition, mentality, modes;* and one lets them play the negative role of a brake in relation to the "originality" of the inventor. In brief, this has to do with the principle of the sovereignty of the subject applied to the history of knowledge. The other claim is that which no longer allows us to save the subject, but the truth: so that it won't be compromised by history, it is necessary not that the truth constitutes itself in history, but only that it reveals itself in it; hidden to men's eyes, provisionally inaccessible, sitting in the shadows, it will wait to be unveiled. The history of truth would be essentially its delay, its fall or the disappearance of the obstacles which have impeded it until now from coming to light. The historical dimension of knowledge is always negative in relation to the truth. It isn't difficult to see how these two claims were adjusted, one to the other: the phenomena of collective order, the "common thought," the "prejudices" of the "myths" of a period, constituted the obstacles which the subject of knowledge had to surmount or to outlive in order to have access finally to the truth; he had to be in an "eccentric" position in order to "discover." At one level this seems to be invoking a certain "romanticism" about the history of science: the solitude of the man of truth, the originality which reopened itself onto the original through history and despite it. I think that, more fundamentally, it's a matter of superimposing the theory of knowledge and the subject of knowledge on the history of knowledge.

And what if understanding the relation of the subject to the truth, were just an effect of knowledge? What if understanding were a complex, multiple, nonindividual formation, not "subjected to the subject," which produced effects of truth? One should then put forward positively this entire dimension which the history of science has negativized; analyze the productive capacity of knowledge as a collective practice; and consequently replace individuals and their "knowledge" in the development of a knowledge which at a given moment functions according to certain rules which one can register and describe.

You will say to me that all the Marxist historians of science have been doing this for a long time. But when one sees how they work with these facts and especially what use they make of the notions of consciousness, of ideology as opposed to science, one realizes that they are for the main part more or less detached from the theory of knowledge.

In any case, what I am anxious about is substituting transformations of the understanding for the history of the discoveries of knowledge. Therefore I have, in appearance at least, a completely different attitude to Mr. Chomsky apropos creativity, because for me it is a matter of effacing the dilemma of the knowing subject, while for him it is a matter of allowing the dilemma of the speaking subject to reappear.

But if he has made it reappear, if he has described it, it is because he can do so. The linguists have for a long time now analyzed language as a system with a collective value. The understanding as a collective totality of rules allowing such and such a knowledge to be produced in a certain period has hardly been studied until now. Nevertheless, it presents some fairly positive characteristics to the observer. Take for example medicine at the end of the eighteenth century: read twenty medical works, it doesn't matter which, of the years 1770 to 1780, then twenty others from the years 1820 to 1830, and I would say, quite at random, that in forty or fifty years everything had changed; what one talked about, the way one talked about it, not just the remedies, of course, not just the maladies and their classifications, but the outlook itself. Who was responsible for that? Who was the author of it? It is artificial, I think, to say Bichat, or even to expand a little and to say the first anatomical clinicians. It's a matter of a collective and complex transformation of medical understanding in its practice and its rules. And this transformation is far from a negative phenomenon: it is the suppression of a negativity, the effacement of an obstacle, the disappearance of prejudices, the abandonment of old myths, the retreat of irrational beliefs, and access finally freed to experience and to reason; it represents the application of an entirely new *grille*, with its choices and exclusions; a new play with its own rules, decisions and limitations, with its own inner logic, its parameters and its blind alleys, all of which lead to the modification of the point of origin. And it is in this functioning that the understanding itself exists. So, if one studies the history of knowledge, one sees that there are two broad directions of analysis: according to one, one has to show how, under what conditions and for what reasons, the understanding modifies itself in its formative rules, without passing through an original "inventor" discovering the "truth"; and according to the other, one has to show how the working of the rules of an understanding can produce in an individual new and unpublished knowledge. Here my aim rejoins, with imperfect methods and in a quite inferior mode, Mr. Chomsky's project: accounting for the fact that with a few rules or definite elements, unknown totalities, never even produced, can be brought to light by individuals. To resolve this problem, Mr. Chomsky has to reintroduce the dilemma of the subject in the field of grammatical analysis. To resolve an analogous problem in the field of history with which I am involved, one has to do the opposite, in a way: to introduce the point of view of understanding, of its rules, of its systems, of its transformations of totalities in the game of individual knowledge. Here and there the problem of creativity cannot be resolved in the same way, or rather, it can't be formulated in the same terms, given the state of disciplines inside which it is put.

CHOMSKY: I think in part we're slightly talking at cross purposes, because of a different use of the term *creativity*. In fact, I should say that my use of the term *creativity* is a little bit idiosyncratic and therefore the onus falls on me in this case, not on you. But when I speak of creativity, I'm not attributing to the concept the notion of value that is normal when we speak of creativity. That is, when you speak of scientific creativity, you're speaking, properly, of the achievements of a Newton. But in the context in which I have been speaking about creativity, it's a normal human act.

I'm speaking of the kind of creativity that any child demonstrates when he's able to come to grips with a new situation: to describe it properly, react to it properly, tell one something about it, think about it in a new fashion for him and so on. I think it's appropriate to call those acts creative, but of course without thinking of those acts as being the acts of a Newton.

In fact it may very well be *true* that creativity in the arts or the sciences, that which goes beyond the normal, may really involve properties of, well, I would also say of human nature, which may not exist fully developed in the mass of mankind, and may not constitute part of the normal creativity of everyday life.

Now my belief is that science can look forward to the problem of normal creativity as a topic that it can perhaps incorporate within itself. But I don't believe, and I suspect you will agree, that science can look forward, at least in the reasonable future, to coming to grips with true creativity, the achievements of the great artist and the great scientist. It has no hope of accommodating these unique phenomena within its grasp. It's the lower levels of creativity that I've been speaking of.

Now, as far as what you say about the history of science is concerned, I think that's correct and illuminating and particularly relevant in fact to the kinds of enterprise that I see lying before us in psychology and linguistics and the philosophy of the mind.

That is, I think there are certain topics that have been repressed or put aside during the scientific advances of the past few centuries.

For example, this concern with low-level creativity that I'm referring to was really present in Descartes also. For example, when he speaks of the difference between a parrot, who can mimic what is said, and a human, who can say new things that are appropriate to the situation, and when he specifies that as being the distinctive property that designates the limits of physics and carries us into the science of the mind, to use modern terms, I think he really is referring to the kind of creativity that I have in mind; and I quite agree with your comments about the other sources of such notions.

Well, these concepts, even in fact the whole notion of the organization of sentence structure, were put aside during the period of great advances that followed from Sir William Jones and others and the development of comparative philology as a whole.

But now, I think, we can go beyond that period when it was necessary to forget and to pretend that these phenomena did not exist and to turn to something else. In this period of comparative philology and also, in my view, structural linguistics, and much of behavioral psychology, and in fact much of what grows out of the empiricist tradition in the study of mind and behavior, it is possible to put aside those limitations and bring into our consideration just those topics that animated a good deal of the thinking and speculation of the seventeenth and eighteenth centuries, and to incorporate them within a much broader and I think deeper science of man that will give a fuller role—though it is certainly not expected to give a complete understanding—to such notions as innovation and creativity and freedom and the production of new entities, new elements of thought and behavior within some system of rule and schematism. Those are concepts that I think we can come to grips with.

ELDERS: Well, may I first of all ask you not to make your answers so lengthy. *[Foucault laughs.]*

When you discuss creativity and freedom, I think that one of the misunderstandings, if any misunderstandings have arisen, has to do with the fact that Mr. Chomsky is starting from a limited number of rules with infinite possibilities of application, whereas you, Mr. Foucault, are stressing the inevitability of the "grille" of our historical and psychological determinisms, which also applies to the way in which we discover new ideas.

Perhaps we can sort this out, not by analyzing the scientific process, but just by analyzing our own thought process.

When you discover a new fundamental idea, Mr. Foucault, do you believe, that as far as your own personal creativity is concerned something is happening that makes you feel that you are being liberated; that something new has been developed? Perhaps afterwards you discover that it was not so new. But do you yourself believe that, within your own personality, creativity and freedom are working together, or not?

FOUCAULT: Oh, you know, I don't believe that the problem of personal experience is so very important . . .

ELDERS: Why not?

FOUCAULT: . . . in a question like this. No, I believe that there is in reality quite a strong similarity between what Mr. Chomsky said and what I tried to show: in other words there exist in fact only possible creations, possible innovations. One can only, in terms of language or of knowledge, produce something new by putting into play a certain number of rules which will define the acceptability or the grammaticality of these statements, or which will define, in the case of knowledge, the scientific character of the statements.

Thus we can roughly say that linguists before Mr. Chomsky mainly insisted on the rules of construction of statements and less on the innovation represented by every new statement, or the hearing of a new statement. And in the history of science or in the history of thought, we placed more emphasis on individual creation, and we had kept aside and left in the shadows these communal, general rules, which obscurely manifest themselves through every scientific discovery, every scientific invention, and even every philosophical innovation.

And to that degree, when I no doubt wrongly believe that I am saying something new, I am nevertheless conscious of the fact that in my statement there are rules at work, not only linguistic rules, but also epistemological rules, and those rules characterize contemporary knowledge.

CHOMSKY: Well, perhaps I can try to react to those comments within my own framework in a way which will maybe shed some light on this.

Let's think again of a human child, who has in his mind some schematism that determines the kind of language he can learn. Okay. And then, given experience, he very quickly knows the language, of which this experience is a part, or in which it is included.

Now this is a normal act; that is, it's an act of normal intelligence, but it's a highly creative act.

If a Martian were to look at this process of acquiring this vast and complicated and intricate system of knowledge on the basis of this ridiculously small quantity of data, he would think of it as an immense act of invention and creation. In fact, a Martian would, I think, consider it as much of an achievement as the invention of, let's say, any aspect of a physical theory on the basis of the data that was presented to the physicist.

However, if this hypothetical Martian were then to observe that every normal human child immediately carries out this creative act and they all do it in the same way and without any difficulty, whereas it takes centuries of genius to slowly carry out the creative act of going from evidence to a scientific theory, then this Martian would, if he were rational, conclude that the structure of the knowledge that is acquired in the case of language is basically internal to the human mind; whereas the structure of physics is not, in so direct a way, internal to the human mind. Our minds are not constructed so that when we look at the phenomena of the world theoretical physics comes forth, and we write it down and produce it; that's not the way our minds are constructed.

Nevertheless, I think there is a possible point of connection and it might be useful to elaborate it: that is, how is it that we are able to construct any kind of scientific theory at all? How is it that, given a small amount of data, it's possible for various scientists, for various geniuses even, over a long period of time, to arrive at some kind of a theory, at least in some cases, that is more or less profound and more or less empirically adequate.

This is a remarkable fact.

And, in fact, if it were not the case that these scientists, including the geniuses, were beginning with a very narrow limitation on the class of possible scientific theories, if they didn't have built into their minds somehow an obviously unconscious specification of what is a possible scientific theory, then this inductive leap would certainly be quite impossible: just as if each child did not have built into his mind the concept of human language in a very restricted way, then the inductive leap from data to knowledge of a language would be impossible.

So even though the process of, let's say, deriving knowledge of physics from data is far more complex, far more difficult for an organism such as ours, far more drawn out in time, requiring intervention of genius and so on and so forth, nevertheless in a certain sense the achievement of discovering physical science or biology or whatever you like, is based on something rather similar to the achievement of the normal child in discovering the structure of his language: that is, it *must* be achieved on the basis of an initial limitation, an initial restriction on the class of possible theories. If you didn't begin by knowing that only certain things are possible theories, then no induction would be possible at all. You could go from data anywhere, in any direction. And the fact that science converges and progresses itself shows us that such initial limitations and structures exist.

If we really want to develop a theory of scientific creation, or for that matter artistic creation, I think we have to focus attention precisely on that set of conditions that, on the one hand, delimits and restricts the scope of our possible knowledge, while at the same time permitting the inductive leap to complicated systems of knowledge on the basis of a small amount of data. That, it seems to me, would be the way to progress towards a theory of scientific creativity, or in fact towards any question of epistemology.

ELDERS: Well, I think if we take this point of the initial limitation with all its creative possibilities, I have the impression that for Mr. Chomsky rules and freedom are not opposed to each other, but more or less imply each other. Whereas I get the impression that it is just the reverse for you, Mr. Foucault. What are your reasons for putting it the opposite way, for this really is a very fundamental point in the debate, and I hope we can elaborate it.

To formulate the same problem in other terms: can you think of universal knowledge without any form of repression?

FOUCAULT: Well, in what Mr. Chomsky has just said there is something which seems to me to create a little difficulty; perhaps I understood it badly.

I believe that you have been talking about a limited number of possibilities in the order of a scientific theory. That is true if you limit yourself to a fairly short period of time, whatever it may be. But if you consider a longer period, it seems to me that what is striking is the proliferation of possibilities by divergences.

For a long time the idea has existed that the sciences, knowledge, followed a certain line of "progress," obeying the principle of "growth," and the principle of the convergence of all these kinds of knowledge. And yet when one sees how the European understanding, which turned out to be a worldwide and universal understanding in a historical and geographical sense, developed, can one say that there has been growth? I, myself, would say that it has been much more a matter of transformation.

Take, as an example, animal and plant classifications. How often have they not been rewritten since the Middle Ages according to completely different rules: by symbolism, by natural history, by comparative anatomy, by the theory of evolution. Each time this rewriting makes the knowledge completely different in its functions, in its economy, in its internal relations. You have there a principle of divergence, much more than one of growth. I would much rather say that there are many different ways of making possible simultaneously a few types of knowledge. There is, therefore, from a certain point of view, always an excess of *data* in relation to possible systems in a given period, which causes them to be experienced within their boundaries, even in their deficiency, which means that one fails to realize their creativity; and from another point of view, that of the historian, there is an excess, a proliferation of systems for a small amount of *data,* from which originates the widespread idea that it is the discovery of new facts which determines movement in the history of science.

CHOMSKY: Here perhaps again, let me try to synthesize a bit. I agree with your conception of scientific progress; that is, I don't think that scientific progress is simply a matter of the accumulated addition of new knowledge and the absorption of new theories and so on. Rather I think that it has this sort of jagged pattern that you describe, forgetting certain problems and leaping to new theories . . .

FOUCAULT: And transforming the same knowledge.

CHOMSKY: Right. But I think that one can perhaps hazard an explanation for that. Oversimplifying grossly, I really don't mean what I'm going to say now literally, one might suppose that the following general lines of an explanation are accurate: it is as if, as human beings of a particular biologically given organization, we have in our heads, to start with, a certain set of possible intellectual structures, possible sciences. Okay?

Now, in the lucky event that some aspect of reality happens to have the character of one of these structures in our mind, then we have a science: that is to say that, fortunately, the structure of our mind and the structure of some aspect of reality coincide sufficiently so that we develop an intelligible science.

It is precisely this initial limitation in our minds to a certain kind of possible science which provides the tremendous richness and creativity of scientific knowledge. It is important to stress—and this has to do with your point about limitation and freedom—that were it not for these limitations, we would not have the creative act of going from a little bit of knowledge, a little bit of experience, to a rich and highly articulated and complicated array of knowledge. Because if anything could be possible, then nothing would be possible.

But it is precisely because of this property of our minds, which in detail we don't understand, but which, I think, in a general way we can begin to perceive, which presents us with certain possible intelligible structures, and which in the course of history and insight and experience begin to come into focus or fall out of focus and so on; it is precisely because of this property of our minds that the progress of science, I think, has this erratic and jagged character that you describe.

That doesn't mean that everything is ultimately going to fall within the domain of science. Personally I believe that many of the things we would like to understand, and maybe the things we would *most* like to understand, such as the nature of man, or the nature of a decent society, or lots of other things, might really fall outside the scope of possible human science.

ELDERS: Well, I think that we are confronted again with the question of the inner relation between limitation and freedom. Do you agree, Mr. Foucault, with the statement about the combination of limitation, fundamental limitation . . .

FOUCAULT: It is not a matter of combination. Only creativity is possible in putting into play of a system of rules; it is not a mixture of order and freedom.

Where perhaps I don't completely agree with Mr. Chomsky, is when he places the principle of these regularities, in a way, in the interior of the mind or of human nature.

If it is a matter of whether these rules are effectively put to work by the human mind, all right; all right, too, if it is a question of whether the historian and the linguist can think it in their turn; it is all right also to say that these rules should allow us to realize what is said or thought by these individuals. But to say that these regularities are connected, as conditions of existence, to the human mind or its nature, is difficult for me to accept: it seems to me that one must, before reaching that point—and in any case I am talking only about the understanding—replace it in the field of other human practices, such as economics, technology, politics, sociology, which can serve them as conditions of formation, of models, of place, of apparition, etc. I would like to know whether one cannot discover the system of regularity, of constraint, which makes science possible, somewhere else, even outside the human mind, in social forms, in the relations of production, in the class struggles, etc.

For example, the fact that at a certain time madness became an object for scientific study, and an object of knowledge in the West, seems to me to be linked to a particular economic and social situation.

Perhaps the point of difference between Mr. Chomsky and myself is that when he speaks of science he probably thinks of the formal organization of knowledge, whereas I am speaking of knowledge itself, that is to say, I think of the content of various knowledges which is dispersed into a particular society, permeates through that society, and asserts itself as the foundation for education, for theories, for practices, etc.

ELDERS: But what does this theory of knowledge mean for your theme of the death of man or the end of the period of the nineteenth–twentieth centuries?

FOUCAULT: But this doesn't have any relation to what we are talking about.

ELDERS: I don't know, because I was trying to apply what you have said to your anthropological notion. You have already refused to speak about your own creativity and freedom, haven't you? Well, I'm wondering what are the psychological reasons for this . . .

FOUCAULT: *[Protesting.]* Well, you can wonder about it, but I can't help that.

ELDERS: Ah, well.

FOUCAULT: I am not wondering about it.

ELDERS: But what are the objective reasons, in relation to your conception of understanding, of knowledge, of science, for refusing to answer these personal questions?

When there is a problem for you to answer, what are your reasons for making a problem out of a personal question?

FOUCAULT: No, I'm not making a problem out of a personal question, I make of a personal question an absence of a problem.

Let me take a very simple example, which I will not analyze, but which is this: How was it possible that men began, at the end of the eighteenth century, for the first time in the history of Western thought and of Western knowledge, to open up the corpses of people in order to know what was the source, the origin, the anatomical needle, of the particular malady which was responsible for their deaths?

The idea seems simple enough. Well, four or five thousand years of medicine in the West were needed before we had the idea of looking for the cause of the malady in the lesion of a corpse.

If you tried to explain this by the personality of Bichat, I believe that would be without interest. If, on the contrary, you tried to establish the place of disease and of death in society at the end of the eighteenth century, and what interest industrial society effectively had in quadrupling the entire population in order to expand and develop itself, as a result of which medical surveys of society were made, big hospitals were opened, etc.; if you tried to find out how medical knowledge became institutionalized in that period, how its relations with other kinds of knowledge were ordered, well, then you could see how the relationship between disease, the hospitalized, ill person, the corpse, and pathological anatomy were made possible.

Here is, I believe, a form of analysis which I don't say is new, but which in any case has been much too neglected; and personal events have almost nothing to do with it.

ELDERS: Yes, but nevertheless it would have been very interesting for us to know a little bit more about your arguments to refute this.

Could you, Mr. Chomsky—and as far as I'm concerned, it's my last question about this philosophical part of the debate—give your ideas about, for example, the way the social sciences are working? I'm thinking here especially about your severe attacks on behaviorism. And perhaps you could even explain a little the way Mr. Foucault is now working in a more or less behavioristic way. *[Both philosophers laugh.]*

CHOMSKY: I would like to depart from your injunction very briefly, just to make one comment about what Mr. Foucault just said.

I think that illustrates very nicely the way in which we're digging into the mountain from opposite directions, to use your original image. That is, I think that an act of scientific creation depends on two facts: one, some intrinsic property of the mind, another, some set of social and intellectual conditions that exist. And it is not a question, as I see it, of which of these we should study; rather we will understand scientific discovery, and similarly any other kind of discovery, when we know what these factors are and can therefore explain how they interact in a particular fashion.

My particular interest, in this connection at least, is with the intrinsic capacities of the mind; yours, as you say, is in the particular arrangement of social and economic and other conditions.

FOUCAULT: But I don't believe that difference is connected to our characters—because at this moment it would make Mr. Elders right, and he must not be right.

CHOMSKY: No, I agree, and . . .

FOUCAULT: It's connected to the state of knowledge, of knowing, in which we are working. The linguistics with which you have been familiar, and which you have succeeded in transforming, excluded the importance of the creative subject, of the creative speaking subject; while the history of science such as it existed when people of my generation were starting to work, on the contrary, exalted individual creativity . . .

CHOMSKY: Yes.

FOUCAULT: . . . and put aside these collective rules.

CHOMSKY: Yes, yes.

QUESTION: Ah . . .

ELDERS: Yes, please go on.

QUESTION: It goes a bit back in your discussion, but what I should like to know, Mr. Chomsky, is this: you suppose a basic system of what must be in a way elementary limitations that are present in what you call human nature; to what extent do you think these are subject to historical change? Do you think, for instance, that they have changed substantially since, let's say, the seventeenth century? In that case, you could perhaps connect this with the ideas of Mr. Foucault?

CHOMSKY: Well, I think that as a matter of biological and anthropological fact, the nature of human intelligence certainly has not changed in any substantial way, at least since the seventeenth century, or probably since Cro-Magnon man. That is, I think that the fundamental properties of our intelligence, those that are within the domain of what we are discussing tonight, are certainly very ancient; and that if you took a man from five thousand or maybe twenty thousand years ago, and placed him as a child within today's society, he would learn what everyone else learns, and he would be a genius or a fool or something else, but he wouldn't be fundamentally different.

But, of course, the level of acquired knowledge changes, social conditions change—those conditions that permit a person to think freely and break through the bonds of, let's say, superstitious constraint. And as those conditions change, a given human intelligence will progress to new forms of creation. In fact this relates very closely to the last question that Mr. Elders put, if I can perhaps say a word about that.

Take behavioral science, and think of it in these contexts. It seems to me that the fundamental property of behaviorism, which is in a way suggested by the odd term behavioral science, is that it is a negation of the possibility of developing a scientific theory. That is, what defines behaviorism is the very curious and self-destructive assumption that you are *not* permitted to create an interesting theory.

If physics, for example, had made the assumption that you have to keep to phenomena and their arrangement and such things, we would be doing Babylonian astronomy today. Fortunately physicists never made this ridiculous, extraneous assumption, which has its own historical reasons and had to do with all sorts of curious facts about the historical context in which behaviorism evolved.

But looking at it purely intellectually, behaviorism is the arbitrary insistence that one must not create a scientific theory of human behavior; rather one must deal directly with phenomena and their interrelation, and no more—something which is totally impossible in any other domain, and I assume impossible in the domain of human intelligence or human behavior as well. So in this sense I don't think that behaviorism is a science. Here is a case in point of just the kind of thing that you mentioned and that Mr. Foucault is discussing: under certain historical circumstances, for example those in which experimental psychology developed, it was—for some reason which I won't go into—interesting and maybe important to impose some very strange limitations on the kind of scientific theory construction that was permitted, and those very strange limitations are known as behaviorism. Well, it has long since run its course, I think. Whatever value it may have had in 1880, it has no function today except constraining and limiting scientific inquiry and should therefore simply be dispensed with, in the same way one would dispense with a physicist who said: you're not allowed to develop a general physical theory, you're only allowed to plot the motions of the planets and make up more epicycles and so on and so forth. One forgets about that and puts it aside. Similarly one should put aside the very curious restrictions that define behaviorism; restrictions which are, as I said before, very much suggested by the term *behavioral science* itself.

We can agree, perhaps, that behavior in some broad sense constitutes the data for the science of man. But to define a science by its data, would be to define physics as the theory of meter readings. And if a physicist were to say: yes, I'm involved in meter-reading science, we could be pretty sure that he was not going to get very far. They might talk about meter readings and correlations between them and such things, but they wouldn't ever create physical theory.

And so the term itself is symptomatic of the disease in this case. We should understand the historical context in which these curious limitations developed, and having understood them, I believe, discard them and proceed in the science of man as we would in any other domain, that is by discarding entirely behaviorism and in fact, in my view, the entire empiricist tradition from which it evolved.

QUESTION: So you are not willing to link your theory about innate limitations with Mr. Foucault's theory of the "grille." There might be a certain connection. You see, Mr. Foucault says that an upsurge of creativity in a certain direction automatically removes knowledge in another direction, by a system of "grilles." Well, if you had a changing system of limitations, this might be connected.

CHOMSKY: Well, the reason for what he describes, I think, is different. Again, I'm oversimplifying. We have more possible sciences available intellectually. When we try out those intellectual constructions in a changing world of fact, we will not find cumulative growth. What we will find are strange leaps: here is a domain of phenomena, a certain science applies very nicely; now slightly broaden the range of phenomena, then another science, which is very different, happens to apply very beautifully, perhaps leaving out some of these other phenomena. Okay, that's scientific progress and that leads to the omission or forgetting of certain domains. But I think the reason for this is precisely this set of principles, which unfortunately, we don't know, which makes the whole discussion rather abstract, which defines for us what is a possible intellectual structure, a possible deep science, if you like.

ELDERS: Well, let's move over now to the second part of the discussion, to politics. First of all I would like to ask Mr. Foucault why he is so interested in politics, because he told me that in fact he likes politics much more than philosophy.

FOUCAULT: I've never concerned myself, in any case, with philosophy. But that is not a problem. *[He laughs.]*

Your question is: why am I so interested in politics? But if I were to answer you very simply, I would say this: *why* shouldn't I be interested? That is to say, what blindness, what deafness, what density of ideology would have to weigh me down to prevent me from being interested in what is probably the most crucial subject to our existence, that is to say the society in which we live, the economic relations within which it functions, and the system of power which defines the regular forms and the regular permissions and prohibitions of our conduct. The essence of our life consists, after all, of the political functioning of the society in which we find ourselves.

So I can't answer the question of why I should be interested; I could only answer it by asking why shouldn't I be interested?

ELDERS: You are obliged to be interested, isn't that so?

FOUCAULT: Yes, at least, there isn't anything odd here which is worth question or answer. Not to be interested in politics, that's what constitutes a problem. So instead of asking me, you should ask someone who is not interested in politics and then your question would be well-founded, and you would have the right to say "Why, damn it, are you not interested?" *[They laugh and the audience laughs.]*

ELDERS: Well, yes, perhaps. Mr. Chomsky, we are all very interested to know your political objectives, especially in relation to your well-known anarcho-syndicalism or, as you formulated it, libertarian socialism. What are the most important goals of your libertarian socialism?

CHOMSKY: I'll overcome the urge to answer the earlier very interesting question that you asked me and turn to this one.

Let me begin by referring to something that we have already discussed, that is, *if* it is correct, as I believe it is, that a fundamental element of human nature is the need for creative work, for creative inquiry, for free creation without the arbitrary limiting effect of coercive institutions, then, of course, it will follow that a decent society should maximize the possibilities for this fundamental human characteristic to be realized. That means trying to overcome the elements of repression and oppression and destruction and coercion that exist in any existing society, ours for example, as a historical residue.

Now any form of coercion or repression, any form of autocratic control of some domain of existence, let's say private ownership of capital or state control of some aspects of human life, any such autocratic restriction on some area of human endeavor, can be justified, *if at all, only* in terms of the need for subsistence, or the need for survival, or the need for defense against some horrible fate or something of that sort. It cannot be justified intrinsically. Rather it must be overcome and eliminated.

And I think that, at least in the technologically advanced societies of the West we are now certainly in a position where meaningless drudgery can very largely be eliminated and, to the marginal extent that it's necessary, can be shared among the population; where centralized autocratic control of, in the first place, economic institutions, by which I mean either private capitalism or state totalitarianism or the various mixed forms of state capitalism that exist here and there, has become a destructive vestige of history.

They are all vestiges that have to be overthrown, eliminated in favor of direct participation in the form of workers' councils or other free associations that individuals will constitute themselves for the purpose of their social existence and their productive labor.

Now a federated, decentralized system of free associations, incorporating economic as well as other social institutions, would be what I refer to as anarcho-syndicalism; and it seems to me that this is the appropriate form of social organization for an advanced technological society, in which human beings do *not* have to be forced into the position of tools, of cogs in the machine. There is no longer any social necessity for human beings to be treated as mechanical elements in the productive process; that can be overcome and we must overcome it by a society of freedom and free association, in which the creative urge that I consider intrinsic to human nature, will in fact be able to realize itself in whatever way it will.

And again, like Mr. Foucault, I don't see how any human being can fail to be interested in this question. *[Foucault laughs.]*

ELDERS: Do you believe, Mr. Foucault, that we can call our societies in any way democratic, after listening to this statement from Mr. Chomsky?

FOUCAULT: No, I don't have the least belief that one could consider our society democratic. *[Laughs.]*

If one understands by democracy the effective exercise of power by a population which is neither divided nor hierarchically ordered in classes, it is quite clear that we are very far from democracy. It is only too clear that we are living under a regime of a dictatorship of class, of a power of class which imposes itself by violence, even when the instruments of this violence are institutional and constitutional; and to that degree, there isn't any question of democracy for us.

Well. When you asked me why I was interested in politics, I refused to answer because it seemed evident to me, but perhaps your question was How am I interested in it?

And had you asked me that question, and in a certain sense I could say you have, I would say to you that I am much less advanced in my way, I go much less far than Mr. Chomsky. That is to say that I admit to not being able to define, nor for even stronger reasons to propose, an ideal social model for the functioning of our scientific or technological society.

On the other hand, one of the tasks that seems immediate and urgent to me, over and above anything else, is this: that we should indicate and show up, even where they are hidden, all the relationships of political power which actually control the social body and oppress or repress it.

What I want to say is this: it is the custom, at least in European society, to consider that power is localized in the hands of the government and that it is exercised through a certain number of particular institutions, such as the administration, the police, the army, and the apparatus of the state. One knows that all these institutions are made to elaborate and to transmit a certain number of decisions, in the name of the nation or of the state, to have them applied and to punish those who don't obey. But I believe that political power also exercises itself through the mediation of a certain number of institutions which look as if they have nothing in common with the political power, and as if they are independent of it, while they are not.

One knows this in relation to the family; and one knows that the university, and in a general way, all teaching systems, which appear simply to disseminate knowledge, are made to maintain a certain social class in power; and to exclude the instruments of power of another social class. Institutions of knowledge, of foresight and care, such as medicine, also help to support the political power. It's also obvious, even to the point of scandal, in certain cases related to psychiatry.

It seems to me that the real political task in a society such as ours is to criticize the workings of institutions, which appear to be both neutral and independent; to criticize and attack them in such a manner that the political violence which has always exercised itself obscurely through them will be unmasked, so that one can fight against them.

This critique and this fight seem essential to me for different reasons: firstly, because political power goes much deeper than one suspects; there are centers and invisible, little-known points of support; its true resistance, its true solidity is perhaps where one doesn't expect it. Probably it's insufficient to say that behind the governments, behind the apparatus of the State, there is the dominant class; one must locate the point of activity, the places and forms in which its domination is exercised. And because this domination is not simply the expression in political terms of economic exploitation, it is its instrument and, to a large extent, the condition which makes it possible; the suppression of the one is achieved through the exhaustive discernment of the other. Well, if one fails to recognize these points of support of class power, one risks allowing them to continue to exist; and to see this class power reconstitute itself even after an apparent revolutionary process.

CHOMSKY: Yes, I would certainly agree with that, not only in theory but also in action. That is, there are two intellectual tasks: one, and the one that I was discussing, is to try to create the vision of a future just society; that is to create, if you like, a humanistic social theory that is based, if possible, on some firm and humane concept of the human essence or human nature. That's one task.

Another task is to understand very clearly the nature of power and oppression and terror and destruction in our own society. And that certainly includes the institutions you mentioned, as well as the central institutions of any industrial society, namely the economic, commercial and financial institutions and in particular, in the coming period, the great multinational corporations, which are not very far from us physically tonight [that is, Philips at Eindhoven].

Those are the basic institutions of oppression and coercion and autocratic rule that appear to be neutral despite everything they say: well, we're subject to the democracy of the market place, and that must be understood precisely in terms of their autocratic power, including the particular form of autocratic control that comes from the domination of market forces in an inegalitarian society.

Surely we must understand these facts, and not only understand them but combat them. And in fact, as far as one's own political involvements are concerned, in which one spends the majority of one's energy and effort, it seems to me that they must certainly be in that area. I don't want to get personal about it, but my own certainly are in that area, and I assume everyone's are.

Still, I think it would be a great shame to put aside entirely the somewhat more abstract and philosophical task of trying to draw the connections between a concept of human nature that gives full scope to freedom and dignity and creativity and other fundamental human characteristics, and to relate that to some notion of social structure in which those properties could be realized and in which meaningful human life could take place.

And in fact, if we are thinking of social transformation or social revolution, though it would be absurd, of course, to try to sketch out in detail the goal that we are hoping to reach, still we should know something about where we think we are going, and such a theory may tell it to us.

FOUCAULT: Yes, but then isn't there a danger here? If you say that a certain human nature exists, that this human nature has not been given in actual society the rights and the possibilities which allow it to realize itself . . . that's really what you have said, I believe.

CHOMSKY: Yes.

FOUCAULT: And if one admits that, doesn't one risk defining this human nature—which is at the same time ideal and real, and has been hidden and repressed until now—in terms borrowed from our society, from our civilization, from our culture?

I will take an example by greatly simplifying it. The socialism of a certain period, at the end of the nineteenth century, and the beginning of the twentieth century, admitted in effect that in capitalist societies man hadn't realized the full potential for his development and self-realization; that human nature was effectively alienated in the capitalist system. And it dreamed of an ultimately liberated human nature.

What model did it use to conceive, project, and eventually realize that human nature? It was in fact the bourgeois model.

It considered that an alienated society was a society which, for example, gave pride of place to the benefit of all, to a sexuality of a bourgeois type, to a family of a bourgeois type, to an aesthetic of a bourgeois type. And it is moreover very true that this has happened in the Soviet Union and in the popular democracies: a kind of society has been reconstituted which has been transposed from the bourgeois society of the nineteenth century. The universalization of the model of the bourgeois has been the utopia which has animated the constitution of Soviet society.

The result is that you too realized, I think, that it is difficult to say exactly what human nature is.

Isn't there a risk that we will be led into error? Mao Tse-tung spoke of bourgeois human nature and proletarian human nature, and he considers that they are not the same thing.

CHOMSKY: Well, you see, I think that in the intellectual domain of political action, that is the domain of trying to construct a vision of a just and free society on the basis of some notion of human nature, we face the very same problem that we face in immediate political action, namely, that of being impelled to do something, because the problems are so great, and yet knowing that whatever we do is on the basis of a very partial understanding of the social realities, and the human realities in this case.

For example, to be quite concrete, a lot of my own activity really has to do with the Vietnam War, and some of my own energy goes into civil disobedience. Well, civil disobedience in the U.S. is an action undertaken in the face of considerable uncertainties about its effects. For example, it threatens the social order in ways which might, one might argue, bring about fascism; and that would be a very bad thing for America, for Vietnam, for Holland and for everyone else. You know, if a great Leviathan like the United States were really to become fascist, a lot of problems would result; so that is one danger in undertaking this concrete act.

On the other hand there is a great danger in not undertaking it, namely, if you don't undertake it, the society of Indochina will be torn to shreds by American power. In the face of these uncertainties one has to choose a course of action.

Well, similarly in the intellectual domain, one is faced with the uncertainties that you correctly pose. Our concept of human nature is certainly limited; it's partially socially conditioned, constrained by our own character defects and the limitations of the intellectual culture in which we exist. Yet at the same time it is of critical importance that we know what impossible goals we're trying to achieve, if we hope to achieve some of the possible goals. And that means that we have to be bold enough to speculate and create social theories on the basis of partial knowledge, while remaining very open to the strong possibility, and in fact overwhelming probability, that at least in some respects we're very far off the mark.

ELDERS: Well, perhaps it would be interesting to delve a little deeper into this problem of strategy. I suppose that what you call civil disobedience is probably the same as what we call extraparliamentary action?

CHOMSKY: No, I think it goes beyond that.

Extraparliamentary action would include, let's say, a mass legal demonstration, but civil disobedience is narrower than all extraparliamentary action, in that it means direct defiance of what is alleged, incorrectly in my view, by the state to be law.

ELDERS: So, for example, in the case of Holland, we had something like a population census. One was obliged to answer questions on official forms. You would call it civil disobedience if one refused to fill in the forms?

CHOMSKY: Right. I would be a little bit careful about that, because, going back to a very important point that Mr. Foucault made, one does not necessarily allow the state to define what is legal. Now the state has the power to enforce a certain concept of what is legal, but power doesn't imply justice or even correctness; so that the state may define something as civil disobedience and may be wrong in doing so.

For example, in the United States the state defines it as civil disobedience to, let's say, derail an ammunition train that's going to Vietnam; and the state is *wrong* in defining that as civil disobedience, because it's legal and proper and should be done. It's proper to carry out actions that will prevent the criminal acts of the state, just as it is proper to violate a traffic ordinance in order to prevent a murder.

If I had stopped my car in front of a traffic light which was red, and then I drove through the red traffic light to prevent somebody from, let's say, machine-gunning a group of people, of course that's not an illegal act, it's an appropriate and proper action; no sane judge would convict you for such an action.

Similarly, a good deal of what the state authorities define as civil disobedience is not really civil disobedience: in fact, it's legal, obligatory behavior in violation of the commands of the state, which may or may not be legal commands.

So one has to be rather careful about calling things illegal, I think.

FOUCAULT: Yes, but I would like to ask you a question. When, in the United States, you commit an illegal act, do you justify it in terms of justice or of a superior legality, or do you justify it by the necessity of the class struggle, which is at the present time essential for the proletariat in their struggle against the ruling class?

CHOMSKY: Well, here I would like to take the point of view which is taken by the American Supreme Court and probably other courts in such circumstances; that is, to try to settle the issue on the narrowest possible grounds. I would think that ultimately it would make very good sense, in many cases, to act against the legal institutions of a given society, if in so doing you're striking at the sources of power and oppression in that society.

However, to a very large extent existing law represents certain human values, which are decent human values; and existing law, correctly interpreted, permits much of what the state commands you not to do. And I think it's important to exploit the fact . . .

FOUCAULT: Yeah.

CHOMSKY: . . . it's important to exploit the areas of law which are properly formulated and then perhaps to act directly against those areas of law which simply ratify some system of power.

FOUCAULT: But, but, I, I . . .

CHOMSKY: Let me get . . .

FOUCAULT: My question, my question was this: when you commit a clearly illegal act . . .

CHOMSKY: . . . which I regard as illegal, not just the state.

FOUCAULT: No, no, well, the state's . . .

CHOMSKY: . . . that the state regards as illegal . . .

FOUCAULT: . . . that the state considers as illegal.

CHOMSKY: Yeah.

FOUCAULT: Are you committing this act in virtue of an ideal justice, or because the class struggle makes it useful and necessary? Do you refer to ideal justice, that's my problem.

CHOMSKY: Again, very often when I do something which the state regards as illegal, I regard it as legal: that is, I regard the state as criminal. But in some instances that's not true. Let me be quite concrete about it and move from the area of class war to imperialist war, where the situation is somewhat clearer and easier. Take international law, a very weak instrument as we know, but nevertheless one that incorporates some very interesting principles. Well, international law is, in many respects, the instrument of the powerful: it is a creation of states and their representatives. In developing the presently existing body of international law, there was no participation by mass movements of peasants.

The structure of international law reflects that fact; that is, international law permits much too wide a range of forceful intervention in support of existing power structures that define themselves as states against the interests of masses of people who happen to be organized in opposition to states.

Now that's a fundamental defect of international law and I think one is justified in opposing that aspect of international law as having no validity, as having no more validity than the divine right of kings. It's simply an instrument of the powerful to retain their power.

But, in fact, international law is not *solely* of that kind. And in fact there are interesting elements of international law, for example, embedded in the Nuremberg principles and the United Nations Charter, which permit, in fact, I believe, *require* the citizen to act against his own state in ways which the state will falsely regard as criminal. Nevertheless, he's acting legally, because international law also happens to prohibit the threat or use of force in international affairs, except under some very narrow circumstances, of which, for example, the war in Vietnam is not one. This means that in the particular case of the Vietnam War, which interests me most, the American state is acting in a criminal capacity. And the people have the right to stop criminals from committing murder. Just because the criminal happens to call your action illegal when you try to stop him, it doesn't mean it *is* illegal.

A perfectly clear case of that is the present case of the Pentagon Papers in the United States, which, I suppose, you know about.

Reduced to its essentials and forgetting legalisms, what is happening is that the state is trying to prosecute people for exposing its crimes. That's what it amounts to.

Now, obviously that's absurd, and one must pay no attention whatsoever to that distortion of any reasonable judicial process. Furthermore, I think that the existing system of law even explains *why* it is absurd. But if it didn't, we would then have to oppose that system of law.

FOUCAULT: So it is in the name of a purer justice that you criticize the functioning of justice?

There is an important question for us here. It is true that in all social struggles, there is a question of "justice." To put it more precisely, the fight against class justice, against its injustice, is always part of the social struggle: to dismiss the judges, to change the tribunals, to amnesty the condemned, to open the prisons, has always been part of social transformations as soon as they become slightly violent. At the present time in France the function of justice and the police is the target of many attacks from those whom we call the "gauchistes." But if justice is at stake in a struggle, then it is as an instrument of power; it is not in the hope that finally one day, in this or another society, people will be rewarded according to their merits, or punished according to their faults. Rather than thinking of the social struggle in terms of "justice," one has to emphasize justice in terms of the social struggle.

CHOMSKY: Yeah, but surely you believe that your role in the war is a just role, that you are fighting a just war, to bring in a concept from another domain. And that, I think, is important. If you thought that you were fighting an unjust war, you couldn't follow that line of reasoning.

I would like to slightly reformulate what you said. It seems to me that the difference isn't between legality and ideal justice; it's rather between legality and better justice.

I would agree that we are certainly in no position to create a system of ideal justice, just as we are in no position to create an ideal society in our minds. We don't know enough and we're too limited and too biased and all sorts of other things. But we are in a position—and we must act as sensitive and responsible human beings in that position—to imagine and move towards the creation of a better society and also a better system of justice. Now this better system will certainly have its defects. But if one compares the better system with the existing system, without being confused into thinking that our better system is the ideal system, we can then argue, I think, as follows:

The concept of legality and the concept of justice are not identical; they're not entirely distinct either. Insofar as legality incorporates justice in this sense of better justice, referring to a better society, then we should follow and obey the law, and force the state to obey the law and force the great corporations to obey the law, and force the police to obey the law, if we have the power to do so.

Of course, in those areas where the legal system happens to represent not better justice, but rather the techniques of oppression that have been codified in a particular autocratic system, well, then a reasonable human being should disregard and oppose them, at least in principle; he may not, for some reason, do it in fact.

FOUCAULT: But I would merely like to reply to your first sentence, in which you said that if you didn't consider the war you make against the police to be just, you wouldn't make it.

I would like to reply to you in terms of Spinoza and say that the proletariat doesn't wage war against the ruling class because it considers such a war to be just. The proletariat makes war with the ruling class because, for the first time in history, it wants to take power. And because it will overthrow the power of the ruling class it considers such a war to be just.

CHOMSKY: Yeah, I don't agree.

FOUCAULT: One makes war to win, not because it is just.

CHOMSKY: I don't, personally, agree with that.

For example, if I could convince myself that attainment of power by the proletariat would lead to a terrorist police state, in which freedom and dignity and decent human relations would be destroyed, then I wouldn't want the proletariat to take power. In fact the only reason for wanting any such thing, I believe, is because one thinks, rightly or wrongly, that some fundamental human values will be achieved by that transfer of power.

FOUCAULT: When the proletariat takes power, it may be quite possible that the proletariat will exert towards the classes over which it has just triumphed, a violent, dictatorial and even bloody power. I can't see what objection one could make to this.

But if you ask me what would be the case if the proletariat exerted bloody, tyrannical and unjust power towards itself, then I would say that this could only occur if the proletariat hadn't really taken power, but that a class outside the proletariat, a group of people inside the proletariat, a bureaucracy or petit bourgeois elements had taken power.

CHOMSKY: Well, I'm not at all satisfied with that theory of revolution for a lot of reasons, historical and others. But even if one were to accept it for the sake of argument, still that theory maintains that it is proper for the proletariat to take power and exercise it in a violent and bloody and unjust fashion, because it is claimed, and in my opinion falsely, that that will lead to a more just society, in which the state will wither away, in which the proletariat will be a universal class and so on and so forth. If it weren't for that future justification, the concept of a violent and bloody dictatorship of the proletariat would certainly be unjust. Now this is another issue, but I'm very skeptical about the idea of a violent and bloody dictatorship of the proletariat, especially when expressed by self-appointed representatives of a vanguard party, who, we have enough historical experience to know and might have predicted in advance, will simply be the new rulers over this society.

FOUCAULT: Yes, but I haven't been talking about the power of the proletariat, which in itself would be an unjust power; you are right in saying that this would obviously be too easy. I would like to say that the power of the proletariat could, in a certain period, imply violence and a prolonged war against a social class over which its triumph or victory was not yet totally assured.

CHOMSKY: Well, look, I'm not saying there is an absolute. . . . For example, I am not a committed pacifist. I would not hold that it is under all imaginable circumstances wrong to use violence, even though use of violence is in some sense unjust. I believe that one has to estimate relative justices.

But the use of violence and the creation of some degree of injustice can only be justified on the basis of the claim and the assessment— which always ought to be undertaken very, very seriously and with a good deal of skepticism—that this violence is being exercised because a more just result is going to be achieved. If it does not have such a grounding, it is really totally immoral, in my opinion.

FOUCAULT: I don't think that as far as the aim which the proletariat proposes for itself in leading a class struggle is concerned, it would be sufficient to say that it is in itself a greater justice. What the proletariat will achieve by expelling the class which is at present in power and by taking over power itself, is precisely the suppression of the power of class in general.

CHOMSKY: Okay, but that's the further justification.

FOUCAULT: That is the justification, but one doesn't speak in terms of justice but in terms of power.

CHOMSKY: But it *is* in terms of justice; it's because the end that will be achieved is claimed as a just one.

No Leninist or whatever you like would dare to say "We, the proletariat, have a right to take power, and then throw everyone else into crematoria." If that were the consequence of the proletariat taking power, of course it would not be appropriate.

The idea is—and for the reasons I mentioned I'm skeptical about it—that a period of violent dictatorship, or perhaps violent and bloody dictatorship, is justified because it will mean the submergence and termination of class oppression, a proper end to achieve in human life; it is because of that final qualification that the whole enterprise might be justified. Whether it is or not is another issue.

FOUCAULT: If you like, I will be a little bit Nietzschean about this; in other words, it seems to me that the idea of justice in itself is an idea which in effect has been invented and put to work in different types of societies as an instrument of a certain political and economic power or as a weapon against that power. But it seems to me that, in any case, the notion of justice itself functions within a society of classes as a claim made by the oppressed class and as justification for it.

CHOMSKY: I don't agree with that.

FOUCAULT: And in a classless society, I am not sure that we would still use this notion of justice.

CHOMSKY: Well, here I really disagree. I think there is some sort of an absolute basis—if you press me too hard I'll be in trouble, because I can't sketch it out—ultimately residing in fundamental human qualities, in terms of which a "real" notion of justice is grounded.

I think it's too hasty to characterize our existing systems of justice as merely systems of class oppression; I don't think that they are that. I think that they embody systems of class oppression and elements of other kinds of oppression, but they also embody a kind of groping towards the true humanly, valuable concepts of justice and decency and love and kindness and sympathy, which I think are real.

And I think that in any future society, which will, of course, never be the perfect society, we'll have such concepts again, which we hope will come closer to incorporating a defense of fundamental human needs, including such needs as those for solidarity and sympathy and whatever, but will probably still reflect in some manner the inequities and the elements of oppression of the existing society.

However, I think what you're describing only holds for a very different kind of situation.

For example, let's take a case of national conflict. Here are two societies, each trying to destroy the other. No question of justice arises. The only question that arises is Which side are you on? Are you going to defend your own society and destroy the other?

I mean, in a certain sense, abstracting away from a lot of historical problems, that's what faced the soldiers who were massacring each other in the trenches in the First World War. They were fighting for nothing. They were fighting for the right to destroy each other. And in that kind of circumstance no questions of justice arise.

And of course there were rational people, most of them in jail, like Karl Liebknecht, for example, who pointed that out and were in jail because they did so, or Bertrand Russell, to take another example on the other side. There were people who understood that there was no point to that mutual massacre in terms of any sort of justice and that they ought to just call it off.

Now those people were regarded as madmen or lunatics and criminals or whatever, but of course they were the only sane people around.

And in such a circumstance, the kind that you describe, where there is no question of justice, just the question of who's going to win a struggle to the death, then I think the proper human reaction is: call it off, don't win either way, try to stop it—and of course if you say that, you'll immediately be thrown in jail or killed or something of that sort, the fate of a lot of rational people.

But I don't think that's the typical situation in human affairs, and I don't think that's the situation in the case of class conflict or social revolution. There I think that one can and *must* give an argument, if you can't give an argument you should extract yourself from the struggle. Give an argument that the social revolution that you're trying to achieve *is* in the ends of justice, *is* in the ends of realizing fundamental human needs, not merely in the ends of putting some other group into power, because they want it.

FOUCAULT: Well, do I have time to answer?

ELDERS: Yes.

FOUCAULT: How much? Because . . .

ELDERS: Two minutes. *[Foucault laughs.]*

FOUCAULT: But I would say that that is unjust. *[Everybody laughs.]*

CHOMSKY: Absolutely, yes.

FOUCAULT: No, but I don't want to answer in so little time. I would simply say this, that finally this problem of human nature, when put simply in theoretical terms, hasn't led to an argument between us; ultimately we understand each other very well on these theoretical problems.

On the other hand, when we discussed the problem of human nature and political problems, then differences arose between us. And contrary to what you think, you can't prevent me from believing that these notions of human nature, of justice, of the realization of the essence of human beings, are all notions and concepts which have been formed within our civilization, within our type of knowledge and our form of philosophy, and that as a result form part of our class system; and one can't, however regrettable it may be, put forward these notions to describe or justify a fight which should—and shall in principle— overthrow the very fundaments of our society. This is an extrapolation for which I can't find the historical justification. That's the point . . .

CHOMSKY: It's clear.

ELDERS: Mr. Foucault, if you were obliged to describe our actual society in pathological terms, which of its kinds of madness would most impress you?

FOUCAULT: In our contemporary society?

ELDERS: Yes.

FOUCAULT: If I were to say with which malady contemporary society is most afflicted?

ELDERS: Yes.

FOUCAULT: The definition of disease and of the insane, and the classification of the insane has been made in such a way as to exclude from our society a certain number of people. If our society characterized itself as insane, it would exclude itself. It pretends to do so for reasons of internal reform. Nobody is more conservative than those people who tell you that the modern world is afflicted by nervous anxiety or schizophrenia. It is in fact a cunning way of excluding certain people or certain patterns of behavior.

So I don't think that one can, except as a metaphor or a game, validly say that our society is schizophrenic or paranoid, unless one gives these words a nonpsychiatric meaning. But if you were to push me to an extreme, I would say that our society has been afflicted by a disease, a very curious, a very paradoxical disease, for which we haven't yet found a name; and this mental disease has a very curious symptom, which is that the symptom itself brought the mental disease into being. There you have it.

ELDERS: Great. Well, I think we can immediately start the discussion.

QUESTION: Mr. Chomsky, I would like to ask you one question. In your discussion you used the term *proletariat;* what do you mean by *proletariat* in a highly developed technological society? I think this is a Marxist notion, which doesn't represent the exact sociological state of affairs.

CHOMSKY: Yes, I think you are right, and that is one of the reasons why I kept hedging on that issue and saying I'm very skeptical about the whole idea, because I think the notion of a proletariat, if we want to use it, has to be given a new interpretation fitting to our present social conditions. Really, I'd even like to drop the word, since it's so loaded with specific historical connotations, and think instead of the people who do the productive work of the society, manual and intellectual work. I think those people should be in a position to organize the conditions of their work, and to determine the ends of their work and the uses to which it's put; and, because of my concept of human nature, I really think of that as partially including everyone. Because I think that any human being who is not physically or mentally deformed—and here I again must disagree with Monsieur Foucault and express my belief that the concept of mental illness probably *does* have an absolute character, to some extent at least—is not only capable of, but is insistent upon doing productive, creative work, if given the opportunity to do so.

I've never seen a child who didn't want to build something out of blocks, or learn something new, or try the next task. And the only reason why adults aren't like that is, I suppose, that they have been sent to school and other oppressive institutions, which have driven that out of them.

Now if that's the case, then the proletariat, or whatever you want to call it, can really be universal, that is, it can be all those human beings who are impelled by what I believe to be the fundamental human need to be yourself, which means to be creative, to be exploratory, to be inquisitive . . .

QUESTION: May I interrupt?

CHOMSKY: . . . to do useful things, you know.

QUESTION: If you use such a category, which has another meaning in Marxist . . .

CHOMSKY: That's why I say maybe we ought to drop the concept.

QUESTION: Wouldn't you do better to use another term? In this situation I would like to ask another question: which groups, do you think, will make the revolution?

CHOMSKY: Yes, that's a different question.

QUESTION: It's an irony of history that at this moment young intellectuals, coming from the middle and upper classes, call themselves proletarians and say we must join the proletarians. But I don't see any class-conscious proletarians. And that's the great dilemma.

CHOMSKY: Okay. Now I think you're asking a concrete and specific question, and a very reasonable one.

It is not true in our given society that all people are doing useful, productive work, or self-satisfying work—obviously that's very far from true—or that, if they were to do the kind of work they're doing under conditions of freedom, it would thereby become productive and satisfying.

Rather there are a very large number of people who are involved in other kinds of work. For example, the people who are involved in the management of exploitation, or the people who are involved in the creation of artificial consumption, or the people who are involved in the creation of mechanisms of destruction and oppression, or the people who are simply not given any place in a stagnating industrial economy. Lots of people are excluded from the possibility of productive labor.

And I think that the revolution, if you like, should be in the *name* of all human beings; but it will have to be conducted by certain categories of human beings, and those will be, I think, the human beings who really *are* involved in the productive work of society. Now *what* this is will differ, depending upon the society. In our society it includes, I think, intellectual workers; it includes a spectrum of people that runs from manual laborers to skilled workers, to engineers, to scientists, to a very large class of professionals, to many people in the so-called service occupations, which really do constitute the overwhelming mass of the population, at least in the United States, and I suppose probably here too, and will become the mass of the population in the future.

And so I think that the student-revolutionaries, if you like, have a point, a partial point: that is to say, it's a very important thing in a modern advanced industrial society how the trained intelligentsia identifies itself. It's very important to ask whether they are going to identify themselves as social managers, whether they are going to be technocrats, or servants of either the state or private power, or, alternatively, whether they are going to identify themselves as part of the workforce, who happen to be doing intellectual labor.

If the latter, then they can and should play a decent role in a progressive social revolution. If the former, then they're part of the class of oppressors.

QUESTION: Thank you.

ELDERS: Yes, go on please.

QUESTION: I was struck, Mr. Chomsky, by what you said about the intellectual necessity of creating new models of society. One of the problems we have in doing this with student groups in Utrecht is that we are looking for consistency of values. One of the values you more or less mentioned is the necessity of decentralization of power. People on the spot should participate in decision making.

That's the value of decentralization and participation: but on the other hand we're living in a society that makes it more and more necessary—or seems to make it more and more necessary—that decisions are made on a worldwide scale. And in order to have, for example, a more equal distribution of welfare, etc., it might be necessary to have more centralization. These problems should be solved on a higher level. Well, that's one of the inconsistencies we found in creating your models of society, and we should like to hear some of your ideas on it.

I've one small additional question—or rather a remark—to make to you. That is: how can you, with your very courageous attitude towards the war in Vietnam, survive in an institution like MIT, which is known here as one of the great war contractors and intellectual makers of this war?

CHOMSKY: Well, let me answer the second question first, hoping that I don't forget the first one. Oh, no, I'll try the first question first; and then remind me if I forget the second.

In general, I am in favor of decentralization. I wouldn't want to make it an absolute principle, but the reason I would be in favor of it, even though there certainly is, I think, a wide margin of speculation here, is because I would imagine that in general a system of centralized power will operate very efficiently in the interest of the most powerful elements *within it*.

Now a system of decentralized power and free association will of course face the problem, the specific problem that you mention, of inequity—one region is richer than the other, etc. But my own guess is that we're safer in trusting to what I hope are the fundamental human emotions of sympathy and the search for justice, which may arise within a system of free association.

I think we're safer in hoping for progress on the basis of those human instincts than on the basis of the institutions of centralized power, which, I believe, will almost inevitably act in the interest of their most powerful components.

Now that's a little abstract and too general, and I wouldn't want to claim that it's a rule for all occasions, but I think it's a principle that's effective in a lot of occasions.

So, for example, I think that a democratic socialist libertarian United States would be more likely to give substantial aid to East Pakistani refugees than a system of centralized power which is basically operating in the interest of multinational corporations. And, you know, I think the same is true in a lot of other cases. But it seems to me that that principle, at least, deserves some thought.

As to the idea, which was perhaps lurking in your question anyway—it's an idea that's often expressed—that there is some technical imperative, some property of advanced technological society that requires centralized power and decision making—and a lot of people say that, from Robert McNamara on down—as far as I can see it's perfect nonsense, I've never seen any argument in favor of it.

It seems to me that modern technology, like the technology of data processing, or communication and so on, has precisely the opposite implications. It implies that relevant information and relevant understanding can be brought to everyone quickly. It doesn't have to be concentrated in the hands of a small group of managers who control all knowledge, all information and all decision making. So technology, I think, can be liberating, it has the property of being possibly liberating; it's converted, like everything else, like the system of justice, into an instrument of oppression because of the fact that power is badly distributed. I don't think there is anything in modern technology or modern technological society that leads away from decentralization of power, quite the contrary.

About the second point, there are two aspects to that: one is the question how MIT tolerates me, and the other question is how I tolerate MIT. *[Laughter.]*

Well, as to how MIT tolerates me, here again, I think, one shouldn't be overly schematic. It's true that MIT is a major institution of war research. But it's also true that it embodies very important libertarian values, which are, I think, quite deeply embedded in American society, fortunately for the world. They're not deeply embedded enough to save the Vietnamese, but they are deeply embedded enough to prevent far worse disasters.

And here, I think, one has to qualify a bit. There is imperial terror and aggression, there is exploitation, there is racism, lots of things like that. But there is also a real concern, coexisting with it, for individual rights of a sort which, for example, are embodied in the Bill of Rights, which is by no means simply an expression of class oppression. It is also an expression of the necessity to defend the individual against state power.

Now these things coexist. It's not that simple, it's not just all bad or all good. And it's the particular balance in which they coexist that makes an institute that produces weapons of war willing to tolerate, in fact, in many ways even encourage, a person who is involved in civil disobedience against the war.

Now as to how I tolerate MIT, that raises another question.

There are people who argue, and I have never understood the logic of this, that a radical ought to dissociate himself from oppressive institutions. The logic of that argument is that Karl Marx shouldn't have studied in the British Museum which, if anything, was the symbol of the most vicious imperialism in the world, the place where all the treasures an empire had gathered from the rape of the colonies, were brought together.

But I think Karl Marx was quite right in studying in the British Museum. He was right in using the resources and in fact the liberal values of the civilization that he was trying to overcome, against it. And I think the same applies in this case.

QUESTION: But aren't you afraid that your presence at MIT gives them a clean conscience?

CHOMSKY: I don't see how, really. I mean, I think my presence at MIT serves marginally to help, I don't know how much, to increase student activism against a lot of the things that MIT as an institution does. At least I *hope* that's what it does.

ELDERS: Is there another question?

QUESTION: I would like to get back to the question of centralization. You said that technology does not contradict decentralization. But the problem is, can technology criticize itself, its influences and so forth? Don't you think that it might be necessary to have a central organization that could criticize the influence of technology on the whole universe? And I don't see how that could be incorporated in a small technological institution.

CHOMSKY: Well, I have nothing against the interaction of federated free associations; and in that sense centralization, interaction, communication, argument, debate, can take place, and so on and so forth, and criticism, if you like. What I am talking about is the centralization of power.

QUESTION: But of course power is needed, for instance to forbid some technological institutions from doing work that will only benefit the corporation.

CHOMSKY: Yeah, but what I'm arguing is this: if we have the choice between trusting in centralized power to make the right decision in that matter, or trusting in free associations of libertarian communities to make that decision, I would rather trust the latter. And the reason is that I think that they can serve to maximize decent human instincts, whereas a system of centralized power will tend in a general way to maximize one of the worst of human instincts, namely the instinct of rapaciousness, of destructiveness, of accumulating power to oneself and destroying others. It's a kind of instinct which does arise and functions in certain historical circumstances, and I think we want to create the kind of society where it is likely to be repressed and replaced by other and more healthy instincts.

QUESTION: I hope you are right.

ELDERS: Well, ladies and gentlemen, I think this must be the end of the debate. Mr. Chomsky, Mr. Foucault, I thank you very much for your far-reaching discussion over the philosophical and theoretical, as well as the political questions of the debate, both for myself and also on behalf of the audience, here and at home.

Foucault Revolutionizes History

Paul Veyne

Translated by Catherine Porter

Michel Foucault's name is so well known that his work does not require a lengthy introduction. I prefer to begin with concrete examples in order to show the practical usefulness of Foucault's method and to try to dispel certain preconceived notions about the philosopher: that Foucault reifies an agency that defies human action and historical explanation; that he privileges breaks and structures over continuities and evolutions; that he has no interest in the social sphere. . . . In addition, the word *discourse* has created a great deal of confusion;[1] let us say, oversimplistically, that Foucault is not Lacan, nor can he be assimilated to semantics. Foucault uses the word *discourse* in his work in a special technical sense, one that specifically does not designate what is said. The very title of one of his books, *Les Mots et les choses*, is ironic.[2]

Once these doubtless inevitable errors have been dispelled,[3] we dis-

To Irène. Aix and London, April 1978.

1. Foucault's readers are not to blame. *The Archaeology of Knowledge*, an awkward and brilliant book in which the author achieved full awareness of what he was doing and took his theory to its logical conclusion ("What, in short, we wish to do is to dispense with 'things'" [Michel Foucault, *The Archaeology of Knowledge*, trans. A. M. Sheridan Smith (London, 1972), p. 47]; hereafter abbreviated *AK;* compare pp. 16–17 and the self-critical footnotes on *The History of Madness* and *The Birth of the Clinic*, p. 47 n. 1 and p. 54 n. 1), was written at the height of the structuralist and linguistic frenzy; moreover, as a historian Foucault began by paying more attention to discourse than to practice, studying practice by way of discourse. Nevertheless, the connection between Foucault's method and linguistics remains only partial, or accidental, or circumstantial.

2. See *AK*, p. 48 and, more generally, pp. 46–49. *Les Mots et les choses* is available in English translation as *The Order of Things: An Archaeology of the Human Sciences*, trans. pub. (New York, 1971).

3. Furthermore, "in *The Order of Things*, the absence of methodological signposting may have given the impression that my analyses were being conducted in terms of cultural

cover in this difficult body of thought something that is very simple and very new, something that cannot fail to gratify historians and make them feel at home from the outset. It is just what historians were hoping for, indeed, what they were already doing, though without clarity. Foucault is the consummate historian, the culmination of history. This philosopher is one of the great historians of our era, beyond any doubt; but he might also be the author of the scientific revolution around which all historians have been gravitating. If we are all positivists, nominalists, pluralists, and enemies of *-isms,* Foucault is the first to merit those designations fully. He is the first completely positivist historian.

My first obligation is thus to speak as a historian rather than as a philosopher—and for a very good reason. My second and final obligation is to speak through examples. The one I have selected—and it is not of my own devising—will be the source of all my arguments. I refer to the explanation for the end of gladiator fighting, as discovered by Georges Ville and described in his great posthumous book on Roman gladiatorship.

The term for Foucault's initial intuition is not structure, or break, or discourse: it is exceptionality, *rarity,* in the Latin sense of the word. Human phenomena are exceptional: they are not ensconced in the plenitude of reason; there is empty space around them for other phenomena that we in our wisdom do not grasp; what is could be otherwise. Human phenomena are arbitrary, in Mauss's sense. They cannot be taken for granted, although for contemporaries and even for historians they seem to be so self-evident that neither the former nor the latter notice them at all. But enough of this for the moment; let us move on to the facts. The story we are about to hear, thanks to my friend Georges Ville, is a long one: how gladiator fighting came to an end.

The fighting stopped gradually, or rather by fits and starts, in the course of the fourth century A.D., during the reign of the Christian emperors. Why did it stop, and why then? The answer seems obvious: the atrocities came to a halt because of Christianity. Yet, as it happens, this is not the case at all. Gladiatorship did not owe its disappearance to the Christians any more than slavery did. The Christians only condemned gladiatorship as part of their general condemnation of all public spectacles, which distracted souls from concentrating exclusively on their salvation. Among public spectacles, the theater, with all its improprieties, always struck Christians as more deserving of condemnation than gladiator fighting. While the pleasure of seeing blood flow brings intrinsic satisfaction, the pleasure of onstage indecency incites spectators to lascivious conduct in their daily lives. Is the explanation to be sought, then, in a

---

totality" (*AK,* p. 16). Even philosophers close to Foucault believed that his goal was to establish the existence of an *episteme* common to an entire era.

more broadly human—rather than narrowly Christian—humanitarian-ism, or in pagan wisdom? No, the answer does not lie here either. Hu-manitarianism is found only in a small minority of highly sensitive people (from time immemorial, crowds have flocked to witness torture, and Nietzsche, writing from the well-sheltered thinker's vantage point, de-scribed the healthy savagery of strong peoples). Such humanitarianism is too easily confused with a somewhat different sentiment, that of pru-dence. Before they adopted Roman gladiatorship with enthusiasm, the Greeks were wary of its cruelty, concerned that it might accustom the masses to violence, just as we worry today that violence on television may cause the crime rate to rise. This was not quite the same thing as deplor-ing the fate of the gladiators themselves. In the view of the sages, however, both pagan and Christian, the bloody spectacle of combats sullied the onlookers' souls (this is the real meaning of the excessively celebrated condemnations issued by Seneca and Saint Augustine). But it is one thing to condemn pornographic films because they are immoral and sully the viewer's soul; it is quite another to condemn them because they turn the human persons who are their actors into objects.

In ancient times, gladiators had the same ambivalent reputation as porno stars. When they were not exercising their fascination as stars in the arena, they aroused feelings of horror because these willing partici-pants in ludic death were at once assassins, victims, candidates for suicide, and walking future corpses. They were viewed as impure in exactly the same way prostitutes are. Both groups are sources of infection within communities; it is immoral to consort with them because they are unclean; they have to be handled with rubber gloves. This is under-standable: for the vast majority of the population, gladiators, like execu-tioners, aroused ambivalent feelings, both attraction and a prudent repulsion. On the one hand there was the taste for watching people suf-fer, the fascination with death, the pleasure of seeing corpses; on the other hand there was the anguish of seeing that within the very confines of public order it was legal to murder not only enemies or criminals but others as well. Society no longer provided a bulwark against the law of the jungle. In many civilizations, this political fear won out over the ele-ment of attraction; fear accounts for the cessation of human sacrifices. In Rome, on the other hand, attraction won out, and this is how the institu-tion of gladiatorship, unique in world history, came into being. The mix of horror and attraction led to the forceful repudiation of the very gladia-tors who were acclaimed as stars; they were deemed impure in the way blood, sperm, and corpses are impure. This allowed people to witness fighting and torture in the arena with a perfectly clear conscience. The most horrifying scenes from the ring were among the most popular mo-tifs of the "art objects" that adorned private homes.

But what is most astonishing is not the rather predictable lack of humanitarianism; it is the fact that this ingenuous attitude in the face of atrocity was legitimate, and even legal, orchestrated by public authorities; the sovereign himself, society's bulwark against the state of nature, organized these recreational murders for the entertainment of the public in peacetime, and it was he who presided and served as referee in the amphitheater. To flatter the master, court poets would congratulate him on the amusing ingeniousness of the tortures he had devised for everyone's pleasure *(voluptas, laetitia)*. Thus the horror itself, even legalized, is not the problem, for in other eras, too, crowds would flock to see public executions, autos-da-fé often presided over by Christian kings. The problem is that the public horror of gladiatorship was not veiled by any pretense whatsoever. Autos-da-fé were not intended to entertain; if a flatterer had congratulated a king of Spain or France for providing his subjects with that *voluptas,* he would have been infringing on the king's majesty and on the dignity of justice and its punishments.

Under these conditions, the cessation of gladiator fighting in the century of the Christian emperors looks like an impenetrable mystery. What was it that tipped the balance of ambivalence and allowed horror to win out over attraction? It cannot be pagan wisdom, or Christian doctrine, or humanitarianism. Could it be that political power was humanized or Christianized? But the Christian emperors were not professional humanitarians, and their pagan predecessors were not at all inhuman—they forbade human sacrifices among their Celtic and Carthaginian subjects, much as the English prohibited cremation among widows in India. Nero himself was not the sadist he is made out to be; Vespasian and Marcus Aurelius were no Hitlers. If the Christian emperors were inspired by their religion to bring gladiator fighting to a gradual halt, they went too far or not far enough. Christians did not clamor for such an outcome; they would have preferred to outlaw theater. Yet theater, for all its indecency, became more vigorous than ever, and it was to become very popular in Byzantium. Perhaps pagan Rome was a "society of spectacles" in which state power offered the people circuses and gladiators for political reasons? This bombastic tautology is not an explanation, especially since Christian Rome and the Byzantine Empire also turned out to be devoted to public spectacles. And yet an overbearing truth comes to the fore here: we simply cannot imagine a Byzantine emperor or a Christian king offering up gladiators to his people. With the end of antiquity, the state stopped killing for entertainment.

And for good reason. The real explanation for gladiatorship and its suppression lies in political power rather than in humanitarianism or in religion. However, this reason must be sought in the submerged base of the "political" iceberg, for this is the locus of the change that made gladiatorship unthinkable in the Byzantine Empire or in the Middle Ages. We need to turn away from standard "politics" to notice an *exceptional* form, a political period piece whose surprising convolutions constitute the key to the enigma. In other words, we must stop focusing our gaze on natural objects in order to notice a certain practice, a very specifically dated one, that objectified those objects in a respect that is as dated as the practice itself. For this is why there exists what I just referred to, in a popular expression, as the "concealed base of the iceberg"; we tend to overlook the practice and see only the objects that reify it in our eyes. So let us make the opposite move: by dint of a Copernican reversal, we shall no longer have to bisect the domain of natural objects with more and more ideological epicycles, without ever managing thereby to reach the level of real historical movements. This was the method Georges Ville followed spontaneously; it provides an excellent illustration of Foucault's thought and demonstrates its fruitfulness.

Rather than taking for granted the existence of a body called the governed, in relation to which a body of "governors" proceeds to act, let us consider the fact that practices for dealing with "the governed" may vary so widely over time that the so-called governed have little more in common than the name. They may be disciplined, that is, told what they must do (and if nothing is prescribed, they are not to budge); they may be treated as juridical subjects, which means that while certain things are forbidden, within those limits they may move about freely; or they may be exploited, and this is what happens in many monarchies: the prince takes control of a populated territory as if it were grazing land or a fish pond, and, in order to live and do his job as prince among princes, he claims for himself a portion of what is produced by the human fauna populating his domain (the prince's art lies in knowing how to avoid shaving too close to the scalp). Satirists accuse the prince of plunging this human fauna into political indifference; flatterers declare that he "makes" his people happy; neutral observers say that he allows his people to be happy and to put chickens in their own pots, provided the weather is propitious. In any event, the prince does not harass his subjects, does not aspire to force them into eternal salvation or to lead them into some great enterprise. He lets nature do its work and he lets his subjects do theirs, lets them reproduce and prosper, more in good years than in bad; he behaves like a gentleman farmer who does not force the hand of nature. It remains clearly understood that he is the owner and that his subjects are only a natural species in residence on his property.

Other practices are possible, for example "great enterprises," as suggested above; examples are not hard to come by. Or perhaps the natural object designated "the governed" is not human fauna, or some tribe being led more or less willingly toward a promised land, but a "population" to be managed the way the natural tendencies of water systems and plant life are managed by an agent of the conservation department, who controls and channels them in such a way that natural processes can continue and plant life will not die out. The agent-manager does not leave nature to its own devices: he meddles with it, but only in order to leave nature in better shape than before. He might be compared with a traffic cop who "channels" the spontaneous movement of traffic so it will flow smoothly: that is his job. As a result, drivers proceed in safety; this is called the welfare state, and it is the one we live in. It is not at all like the Old Regime, where a prince encountering traffic on the road would have imposed his own right of passage and left it at that. This is not to say that the management of fluctuation makes everything perfect for everyone, for the spontaneity of nature cannot be regulated according to whim; traffic flowing in one direction has to be stopped in order to allow the cross traffic to advance, with the result that some drivers who may be in more of a hurry than others still have to twiddle their thumbs at red lights.

Here we have quite different "attitudes" toward the natural object "the governed," many different ways of treating the governed "objectively"; or we may prefer to say that there are many different "ideologies" characterizing the relationship between governors and the governed. Let us put it this way: there are many different practices, some of which objectify a population, others a fauna, still others a tribe, and so on. While it may appear that we are dealing merely with figures of speech, modifications of the conventions governing word use, in reality, a scientific revolution is taking place in this shift in terminology. Appearances are reversed in just the same way as a shirtsleeve is turned inside out; in the process, the false problems are snuffed out and the true problem falls into place.

Let us apply this method to the gladiators. We shall ask in what political practice people are objectified in such a way that, if they want gladiators, they are cheerfully given their fill, and in what practice it would be unthinkable to give them what they want. The answer is not hard to find.

Suppose we are responsible for a flock of sheep that is being moved, that we have "taken on" this pastoral responsibility. We do not own the flock: the owner would be interested only in reaping the profits from shearing the sheep, would otherwise leave them to their own devices. Our job, however, is to supervise the flock's movements, for the sheep are not in a pasture but out on a highway. We have to keep the flock from dispersing, in its own interest of course. "Not that we are guides who know the destination, decide to lead the animals there, and herd them along," a Roman emperor might say. "The flock moves of its own accord, or rather its route shifts as it advances, for it is on the highway of History. Our job is to ensure its survival as a flock despite the dangers of the road and the animals' treacherous instincts, their weakness and inertia. We shall beat them with sticks; if we have to, with our own hands. We administer blows, not justice in all its majesty. Our flock is the Roman people and we are its senators. We are not its owners, since Rome has never been a territorial property endowed with human fauna: Rome came into being as a collectivity of men, as a city-state. For our part, we have assumed leadership of this human flock because we know better than it does what it needs. To carry out our mission we send 'lictors' on ahead carrying 'bundles' of knouts, so they can strike any animals who are creating disorder in the flock or wandering off. For sovereignty is not distinguished from menial police work by any measure of dignity.

"Our politics is limited to keeping the flock together as it moves along its historical trajectory; for the rest, we are well aware that animals are animals. We try not to abandon too many hungry ones along the way, for that would reduce the population of the flock; we feed them if we have to. Animals are neither moral nor immoral; they are what they are. We are no more concerned about denying gladiators' blood to the Roman people than a herder of sheep or cattle would be concerned about watching over his animals' mating behavior in order to prevent incestuous unions. We are intransigent on just one point, which is not the animals' morality but their energy: we do not want the flock to weaken, for that would be its loss and ours; so for example we do not let it have 'pantomime,' which the moderns would call opera, since this public spectacle has a softening effect. On the other hand, like Cicero and Pliny the senator, we see gladiators' combats as the best school for toughening up that any spectators can have. To be sure, there are those who cannot tolerate the spectacle, finding it cruel; but our sympathy as shepherds goes instinctively to the tough, strong, insensitive animals. It is thanks to them that the flock holds its own. Thus between the two poles of ambivalent feeling that gladiatorship arouses, we do not hesitate to endorse sadistic attraction rather than frightened repulsion, and we turn gladiatorship into a spectacle that is approved and organized by the State."

As I said, these words could have been spoken by a Roman senator or an emperor of the pagan era. Had I heard such talk earlier, of course, I would have written my big book on bread and circuses differently; I would have turned the argument around. But let us come back to our sheep. If we had been entrusted with children instead of sheep, if our practice had objectified a child-people and if we had objectified ourselves as paternal kings, our behavior would have been entirely different. We would have taken into account the sensitivity of the wretched population, and we would have gone along with their fearful rejection of gladiatorship; we would have commiserated with their terror at seeing unwarranted murder become an established institution within the confines of a peaceful state. "The Christian sect," we might have added, "would have liked us to go even further: it would have liked us to be priest-kings and not father-kings, so that, far from coddling children, we would view our subjects as souls to be led energetically down the path of virtue toward salvation, like it or not. The Christians would have liked us to ban theater as well as all other public spectacles. But we are well aware that children need to be entertained. For sectarians like the Christians, nudity is more offensive than gladiators' blood. We see things more imperially, however; and, like simple people in general and in keeping with public opinion everywhere, we view gratuitous murder as the most serious of matters."

What a gutting of rationalizing political philosophy! What a void surrounds those *exceptional* period pieces! What a lot of room lies between them for other as yet unimagined objectivizations! For, unlike the list of natural objects, that of objectivizations remains open. But let me hasten to reassure the reader, who must be wondering *why* the practice of "leading a flock" gave way to that of "coddling the children." It did so for the most positive, most historical, and almost the most materialist reasons in the world—for exactly the same kinds of reasons that explain any event whatsoever. One of these reasons, as it happens, was that in the fourth century A.D., when Roman emperors became Christians, they also ceased to govern via the senatorial class. Now it is fair to say that the Roman senate bore very little resemblance to today's senates, councils, or assemblies. It was a kind of thing with which we are completely unfamiliar: an academy, but of politics—a conservatory of the political arts. To understand what sort of transformation must have been involved in governing without the senate, we might imagine a literature that has always been subject to the dictates of an academy and that suddenly finds itself on its own; or we might imagine modern intellectual or scientific life without the university as its substructure or superstructure. The senate tended to preserve the gladiators the way the French Academy tends to preserve spelling: because its self-interest as a body lay in being conservative. Once the emperor is rid of the senate, once he begins to use a body of mere functionaries to run his empire, he ceases to play the role of head herdsman and takes on one of the roles available to true monarchs— father, priest, and so forth. And he becomes a Christian for just the same reason. It was not Christianity that led the emperors to adopt a paternalistic practice and made them ban gladiators; rather, it was history as a whole (the withering away of the senate, a new ethic according to which the body is not a toy, and so on) that brought about a change in political practice, with dual consequences: because they were paternalistic the emperors quite naturally adopted Christianity, and because they were paternalistic they put an end to gladiatorship.

The method followed here is self-evident. It consists in describing in quite objective terms what a paternalistic emperor does, what a head herdsman does, *without presupposing anything else at all*, without presupposing the existence of any goal, object, material cause (the governed masses, relations of production, an enduring State), or type of behavior (politics, depoliticization). It consists in judging people by their actions and in eliminating the eternal phantoms that language arouses in us. Practice is not some mysterious agency, some substratum of history, some hidden engine; it is what people do (the word says just what it means). If practices are, in one sense, "hidden" and if we may provisionally call them the "concealed base of the iceberg," it is quite simply because "practice" shares the fate of nearly all our behavior and that of universal history: we are often aware of it, but we have no concept for it. In the same way, when I speak, I am generally aware that I am speaking and am not in a hypnotic state; on the other hand, I do not have a conception of the grammar I am using instinctively. I think I am expressing myself naturally, in order to say what needs to be said; I am not aware that I am applying restrictive rules. Similarly, the governor who gives his flock free bread or who denies it gladiators believes he is doing what every governor has to do, when dealing with the governed, owing to the nature of politics itself; he is not aware that his practice, observed in and of itself, conforms to a specific grammar, that it embodies a specific politics, just as, while we believe we are speaking without presuppositions, in order to say what has to be said, what is on our minds, when we break the silence we can only speak a specific language, French or English or Latin.

Judging people according to their actions means not judging them according to their ideologies; it also means not judging them according to lofty eternal notions such as the governed, the State, freedom, or the essence of politics, notions that trivialize the originality of successive practices and render it anachronistic. If I make the mistake of saying, in effect, that "there was the emperor on the one hand, *the* governed on the other," as soon as I observe that the emperor gave the governed subjects bread and gladiators and then go on to ask why, I shall conclude that he did so for a no less eternal reason: to depoliticize them, or to get them to obey him, or love him.

Indeed we are used to reasoning in terms of targets, or from the starting point of a topic. For example, I once believed and wrote, wrongly, that bread and circuses were aimed at establishing a relation between the governed and the governors, or that they were a response to the objective challenge constituted by the governed. But if the governed are always and everywhere the same, if they all have the same natural reflexes, if they have a natural need for bread and circuses, or a need to be depoliticized, or to feel loved by their Master, why were they given bread and circuses only in Rome? Thus we need to reverse the terms of the proposition: in order for the governed to be perceived by the Master only as objects to be depoliticized, loved, or taken to the circus, they had to have been objectivized as a flock-people; in order for the Master to have been perceived only as needing to make himself popular with his flock, he had to have been objectivized as a guide rather than as a father-king or a priest-king. These objectivizations, correlatives of a certain political practice, are what account for bread and circuses; bread and circuses will never be explained by starting with an eternal governed, eternal governors, and an eternal relation of obedience or depoliticization that unites them. For while these keys will open any door, they will never provide access to understanding a phenomenon as particular and as precisely dated as bread and circuses—unless we allow specifications, historical accidents, and ideological influences to proliferate, at the price of endless verbiage.

Objects seem to determine our behavior, but our practice determines its own objects in the first place. Let us start, then, with that practice itself, so that the object to which it applies is what it is only in relation to that practice (in the sense that a "beneficiary" is a beneficiary inasmuch as I cause him or her to benefit from something, and that, if I guide someone, that person is the guided party). The relation determines the object, and only what is determined exists. The governed is too vague a term, and it does not exist as an entity; there exists only a flock-people, then a child-people to be coddled. This is simply another way of saying that at one time the observable practices entailed guiding and at another they entailed coddling (just as being guided is only a way of saying that someone is guiding you at the moment: one is not a guided party in the absence of a guide). The object is only the correlative of the practice; prior to the practice there exists no eternal governed that could be targeted more or less accurately and with respect to which one could modify one's aim so as to improve it. The prince who treats his people like children does not even conceive of the possibility of behaving differently: he does what goes without saying, things being as they are. The eternal governed does not *exceed* what one makes of it, it does not exist apart from the practice that is applied to it; its existence, if there is such a thing, is not indicated by any concrete aspect. (The flock-people did not have social security, and no one dreamed of providing it, nor did anyone feel guilty for failing to do so.) A notion that is connected to nothing in practice is only a word.

Such a word has only an ideological—or rather idealist—existence. Let us consider the leader of the flock, for instance. He gives the animals in his charge free bread because his mission is to lead the entire flock to its destination without leaving too many starved corpses behind; a thinned-out herd cannot defend itself against wolves. This is the actual practice, as it emerges from the facts (and from the following fact in particular: free bread was given not to destitute slaves but only to citizens). It is true that ideology offered a vaguely noble interpretation of that cruelly precise practice: the senate was exalted in proclamations declaring it to be the father of the people and affirming that it sought the good of the governed. But the same ideological platitude is repeated about very different practices: the sovereign who takes over a fish pond and exploits it for his own profit by levying a tax is also viewed as a father who makes his subjects happy, whereas in fact he lets them cope as best they can with nature and the seasons, for better or for worse. And the conservation agent is yet another benefactor of his subjects, someone who regulates natural fluctuations not for the fiscal benefits that he can draw from them, but for the proper management of nature itself, of which he has taken charge. We are beginning to see what ideology is: a noble and vague style, apt for idealizing practices while appearing to describe them. Ideology is an ample cloak that dissimulates the crooked and dissimilar contours of the real practices that succeed one another in history.

But where do these practices come from, each with its own inimitable contours? From historical changes, quite simply, from the countless transformations of historical reality, that is to say from the rest of history, like everything else. Foucault has not discovered a previously unknown new agency, called practice; he has made the effort to see people's practices *as they really are;* what he is talking about is the same thing every historian talks about, namely, what people do. The difference is simply that Foucault undertakes to speak about practice *precisely,* to describe its convoluted forms, instead of referring to it in vague and noble terms. He does not say: "I have discovered a sort of historical unconscious, a preconceptual agency, that I call practice or discourse, and that provides the real explanation for history. Ah yes! but how am I going to manage to explain this agency itself and its transformations?" No: he is talking about *the same thing we talk about,* for example, the practical conduct of a government; only he shows it as it really is, by stripping away the veils. Nothing could be stranger than to accuse Foucault of reducing our history to an intellectual process that is as implacable as it is irresponsible. Nevertheless, it is easy to understand why his philosophy is difficult for us to grasp: it does not look at all like Marx's or Freud's. Practice is not an agency (like the Freudian id) or a prime mover (like the relation of production), and moreover for Foucault there is no agency nor any prime mover (there is matter, however, as we shall see). That is why there is nothing wrong with calling practice, provisionally, the concealed base of the iceberg, in order to indicate that it presents itself to our spontaneous sight only heavily veiled, and that it is largely preconceptual; for the concealed base of an iceberg is not some agency that is different in nature from the exposed tip; it is made of ice, like the rest. Nor is it the motor that moves the iceberg along; it is below the line of visibility, that is all. It is accounted for in the same way as the rest of the iceberg. Foucault has only one thing to say to historians: "You may continue to explain history as you have always done. But be careful: if you look very closely, if you peel away the banalities, you will notice that there is more to explain than you thought; there are crooked contours that you haven't spotted."

For historians concerned not with what people do, but what they say, the method to follow is the same; the word *discourse* comes into play just as naturally to designate what is said as the word *practice* does to designate what is practiced. Foucault is not revealing a mysterious discourse different from the one we all understand; he is simply inviting us to observe exactly what is said. Now this observation proves that the realm of what is said presents biases, reticences, unexpected salient features and reflex angles of which the speakers are completely unaware. Underneath conscious discourse there is a grammar, as it were, a grammar that is determined by neighboring practices and grammars and that is revealed by attentive study of the discourse, provided that the student consents to lift off the heavy veils known as Science, Philosophy, and so on. In the same way, the prince thinks he governs or reigns; in fact, he manages fluctuations, or he coddles children, or he leads a flock. So it is clear what discourse is not: it is not semantics, not ideology, not the implicit. Far from inviting us to judge things on the basis of words, Foucault shows on the contrary that words mislead us, that they make us believe in the existence of things, in the existence of natural objects, of governed subjects, or of the State, whereas these things are only correlatives of the corresponding practices. For semantics is the incarnation of the idealist illusion. Nor is discourse ideology; it is almost the opposite. It is what is really said, unbeknownst to the speakers. The latter think they are speaking broadly and freely, whereas unwittingly what they are saying is narrow, limited by an incongruous grammar. Ideology, for its part, is much broader and freer, and for good reason: it is rationalization, idealization; it is an expansive veil. The prince wants to do all that is required and believes that he is doing just that, things being as they are; in reality, he behaves unwittingly like the owner of a fishpond, and ideology glorifies him as a good shepherd. Finally, discourse and its hidden grammar do not belong to the realm of the implicit; they are not logically contained in what is said or done, they are not axiomatic to or presupposed in what is said or done, for the good reason that what is said or done obeys a grammar of chance and not a logical, coherent, perfected grammar. If the political grammar of an era consists in coddling children or in managing fluctuations, it is owing to the hazards of history, to the salient features and reflex angles of neighboring practices and their transformations; it is not because Reason is constructing a coherent system. History is not utopia. Policies do not develop systematically from great principles (to each according to his needs, everything for the people and nothing by means of the people); they are the creations of history and not those of consciousness or reason.

So what exactly is that submerged grammar that Foucault wants us to notice? Why do we remain unconscious of it, as do the agents themselves? Because we repress it? No; because it is preconceptual. The role of consciousness is not to make us notice the world but to allow us to move within it. A king does not need to conceptualize what he is, or what his practice is; it suffices that they are what they are. The king needs to be conscious of the events occurring in his kingdom; that is all he needs in order to behave in terms of what he is without his knowledge. He does not need to be conceptually aware that he manages fluctuations; he will do so in any event. He simply needs to be aware that he is king, without further ado. A lion does not need to know he is a lion to behave like one, either; he needs only to know where to find his prey.

For a lion, being a lion goes so completely without saying that he is not aware that that is what he is; in the same way, kings who coddle peoples or who manage fluctuations do not know what they are. They are aware, of course, of what they are doing. They do not sign decrees in a sleepwalking state; they have the "mentality" that corresponds to their "material" acts. But it is absurd to make that distinction. When one behaves in a certain way one necessarily has the corresponding mentality; these two things go hand in hand and constitute a given practice, just like fear and trembling, or joy and hearty laughter. Representations and utterances constitute part of the practice, and that is why ideology does not exist, except for Flaubert's M. Homais, a celebrated materialist: to produce, one needs machines, one needs people, and these people need to be conscious of what they are doing. They must not be sleepwalkers; they must have their own representations of certain technical or social rules, and they have to have the requisite mentality or ideology. All of this constitutes a practice. But the people involved do not know what this practice is: it "goes without saying" for them, as for the king and for the lion, who do not know themselves what they are.

More precisely, they do not even know that they do not know (that is the meaning of the expression "to go without saying"), like an automobile driver *who does not see that he does not see,* if the dark of night is compounded by rain; for then not only does he see nothing beyond the range of his headlights, but he can no longer clearly make out where the lighted zone stops, so that he can no longer tell how far he can see and does not know that he is driving too fast for an unknown stopping distance. It is unquestionably an odd thing, well worth the attention of a philosopher, this capacity of human beings to remain unaware of their limits, their *exceptionality,* not to see that there is emptiness around them, to believe that at any given moment they are ensconced in the plenitude of reason. Perhaps this is the meaning of Nietzsche's idea (though I do not flatter myself that I understand that difficult thinker) that consciousness is merely reactive. By virtue of a "will to power," the king holds the job of king. He brings into material reality the potentialities of his historical period, and these potentialities tentatively mark out for him the practice of leading a flock or, if the senate fades away, that of coddling his people; for him, this goes without saying. He does not even suspect that he has any responsibility for it; he believes that his own behavior is dictated to him on a daily basis by things; he does not even suspect that things could be otherwise. While he remains unaware of his own will to power, which he perceives reified in natural objects, he is aware only of his own reactions, that is, he knows what he is doing, when he reacts to events by making decisions. But he does not understand that these particular decisions are a function of a certain royal practice, just as a lion's decisions are a function of being a lion.

The method thus consists, for Foucault, in understanding that things are only objectivizations of determined practices and that the determinations must be brought to light, since consciousness fails to conceptualize them. This bringing to light, at the end of an effort to visualize, is an original and even attractive experiment, one that might playfully be called "rarefaction." The product of this intellectual operation is abstract, and for good reason: it is not a picture in which one sees kings, peasants, or monuments, nor is it a received idea to which our consciousness is so accustomed that one is no longer sensitive to the idea's abstractness.

But what is most characteristic is the instant in which the rarefaction is produced. It does not take shape; on the contrary, it consists rather in a sort of unhooking. A moment before, there was nothing, nothing but a big flat thing so self-evident that it could hardly be seen, a thing called Power or the State. For our part, we were trying to grasp the coherence of a piece of history, one in which this big translucid kernel played a key role, along with common nouns and conjunctions; but it was not working, something was wrong, and false verbal problems such as "ideology" or "relations of production" were taking us around in circles. And then all at once we "realize" that the whole problem comes from the big kernel, with its falsely natural air; that we needed to stop believing in its self-evidence. We had to reduce it to ordinary experience, had to historicize it. And then, in the place that was previously occupied by the big thing-that-goes-without-saying, there appears a strange little "period" object, a rare, contorted object that has never been seen before. When we see it, we cannot help but take a moment to breathe a melancholy sigh over the human condition, over the poor unconscious and absurd things that we are, over the rationalizations that we fabricate for ourselves and whose object appears to be chortling.

In the time it takes to sigh, the bit of history has fallen into place all by itself. The false problems have fled; the joints all fit together; and, most important, the bit of history appears to have turned itself inside out like a sleeve. A moment before, we were like Blaise Pascal: we had the two ends of the historical chain (economy and society, the governors and the governed, interests and ideologies) firmly in hand, and it was in the middle that the muddle began: how could we make all that hold together? Now, it would be difficult for it not to. "Good form" is in the middle and is rapidly spreading to the edges of the picture. For, ever since the moment we historicized our false natural object, it has been an object only for a practice that objectivizes it. The practice, along with the object that it gives itself, is what comes first; it is this practice that is naturally unified. Infrastructure and superstructure, interest and ideology, and so on are no longer anything but useless patchworks imposed on a practice that functioned very well as it was and that is once again functioning very well: it is even on the basis of that practice that the edges of the picture are becoming intelligible. So why were we so furiously bent on chopping it into two slices? It is because we saw no other way to get out of the false situation we had gotten into by virtue of having grasped the problem by its two ends and not by the middle, as Deleuze says. The falseness lay in mistaking the object of a practice for a natural, well-known, unchanging, virtually material object: the collectivity, the State, the seed of madness.

This object was given at the outset (as befits matter), and practice reacted: it "took up the challenge," it built on that infrastructure. We did not realize that each practice, as determined by history as a whole, engenders its own corresponding object, just as pear trees produce pears and apple trees bear apples; there are no natural objects, there are no things. Things, objects, are only correlatives of practices. The illusion of a natural object ("the governed throughout history") conceals the hetero-geneous character of practices (coddling children is not managing fluc-tuations). Here is the source of all the dualist muddles; from here, too, stems the illusion of "reasonable choice." This last illusion exists, as we shall see, in two forms that at first glance look quite dissimilar. The first: "The history of sexuality is that of an eternal struggle between desire and repression." The second: "M. Foucault is against everything, he puts Damiens's frightful torture and the practice of incarceration in the same bag, as if a preference could not reasonably be declared." Our author is too much a positivist to nurture this dual illusion.

For "the governed" is neither a unity nor a multiplicity, any more than "repression" (or "its diverse forms") is, or "the State" (or "its forms in history"), for the simple reason that there is no such thing as "the governed." There are only multiple objectivizations ("population," "fauna," "subjects under law"), correlatives of heterogeneous practices. There are numerous objectivizations, and that is all: a relation between this multiplicity of practices and unity can be posited only if one attempts to credit the practices with a nonexistent unity; a gold watch, a zest of lemon, and a raccoon are also a multiplicity and do not seem to suffer for want of a common origin or object or principle. Only the illusion of dealing with natural objects creates a vague impression of unity. As one's vision becomes blurred, everything seems to look alike; a fauna, a popula-tion, and subjects under law seem to be the same thing, namely, the governed. The multiple practices disappear from view; they are the sub-merged base of the iceberg. This outlook does not allow for any uncon-scious, of course, or any ideological ruse or a politics of putting one's head in the sand. There is only the eternal teleological illusion, the Idea of the Good. From this perspective everything we do would be an attempt to reach an ideal goal.

Everything hinges on a paradox, one that is Foucault's central and most original thesis. *What is made,* the object, is explained by what went into its *making* at each moment of history; we are wrong to imagine that the *making*, the practice, is explained on the basis of what is made. I should like to try to show—in a first stage, rather too abstractly—how everything derives from this central thesis; then I shall do my utmost to clarify the matter.

The whole difficulty arises from the illusion that allows us to "reify" objectivizations as if they were natural objects. We mistake the end result for a goal; we take the place where a projectile happens to land as its intentionally chosen target. Instead of grasping the problem at its true center, which is the practice, we start from the periphery, which is the object, in such a way that successive practices resemble reactions to a single object, whether "material" or rational, that is taken as the starting point, as a given. Here is where the false dualist problems begin, along with the rationalisms. Since the practice is taken as a response to a given, we find ourselves with two links in a chain that we can no longer see how to solder back together. The practice is the response to a challenge, to be sure, but a given challenge does not always lead to the same response; the infrastructure determines the superstructure, to be sure, but the superstructure in turn reacts, and so on. For want of something better, we end up fastening the two ends of the chain together with a bit of string called ideology. And, more seriously still, we take the points of impact of successive practices to be preexisting objects that these practices were aiming for: their targets. Madness and the common good throughout the ages have been targeted differently by successive societies whose "attitudes" were not the same, so that they touched the target at different points. No matter: we can salvage our optimism and our rationalism, for these practices, however different they appear to be (or, rather, however unevenly they may have carried out the same attempt), still had a justification, namely, the target, which does not change (only the "attitude" of the marksman changes). If we are extremely optimistic, as few have been for at least a century, we shall conclude that humanity is making progress, that it is getting closer and closer to its goal. If our optimism is more retrospective indulgence than hope, we shall say that in the course of their history people gradually exhaust the totality of truth, that each society reaches one part of the goal and illustrates one potentiality of the human condition.

But we are most often optimists in spite of ourselves: we are well aware that indulgence is rarely called for and that societies are only what they are historically; for example, we understand that each society has its own list of what we call the tasks of the State: some societies want gladiators, others want social security; we know perfectly well that different civilizations have different attitudes toward "madness." In short, we believe both that no state resembles any other and also that the state is the State. Or, rather, we believe in the State only at the level of words: for, since we have become prudent, we would not dream of drawing up a complete list or an ideal list of the tasks of the State. We know all too well that history is more inventive than we are and we do not rule out the possibility that the State will one day be held responsible for unhappy love affairs. Thus we avoid drawing up a theoretical list, and we settle for an empirical, open list: we "record" what tasks the State has found itself asked to perform to date. In short, for us the State with its tasks is merely a word, and the optimistic faith that we have in this natural object must not be very sincere, since it does not act. The fact remains that the word continues to make us believe in a thing called the State. It makes no difference that we know that that State is not an object whose theoretical investigation we might undertake in advance or whose unfolding would allow us to discover it little by little; we continue nonetheless to fix our sights on it, instead of trying to discover, beneath the surface, the practice of which it is simply a projection.

Our mistake is not that we believe in the State, whereas only states exist: our mistake is that we believe in the State or in states, and we fail to study the practices that project the objectivizations we mistake for the State or its varieties. As history unfolds, various political practices spring up, taking the shape of social security in one case, gladiatorship in another. We tend to view this field of explosions, in which all sorts of different machines are blowing up in all directions, as a kind of firing range or shooting gallery, the site of a contest in marksmanship; thus we are greatly disturbed by the degree to which shots that hit the so-called target fall wide of the mark. This is known as the problem of Unity and Multiplicity. "The points of impact are so far apart! One projectile lands on gladiators, another on social security. Given such dispersal, how can we ever determine the exact position of the target? Do we even know for sure that all the shots were aimed at the same target? Ah! the problem of Multiplicity is a tough one; it may be insoluble!" Indeed—because it does not exist. The problem disappears when we stop mistaking extrinsic determinations for modalities of the State; it vanishes when we stop believing in the existence of a target, that is, natural objects.

We need to substitute a philosophy of relation, then, for a philosophy of objects taken as end or as cause; and we need to grasp the problem at its center, by way of practice or discourse. A practice gives rise to the objectivizations that correspond to it, and it is anchored in the realities of the moment, that is, in the objectivizations of neighboring practices. Or, to be more precise, a practice actively fills the void left by neighboring practices; it *actualizes* the potentialities that these neighboring practices prefigure in hollow form. If these practices are transformed, if the periphery of the hollow shifts, if the senate vanishes and if a new ethics of the human body comes to the fore, the practice will actualize these new potentialities, and it will no longer be the same practice as before. It is thus not by virtue of some personal conviction or caprice that the emperor is transformed from leader of a flock to father of a child-people; in a word, it is not through ideology.

Saint Augustine called this actualization love (the vocabulary of scholasticism comes in handy here), and he made it a teleology. Like Spinoza, Deleuze does nothing of the sort; he calls it desire, a word that has given rise to comic misunderstandings on the part of the "new philosophers" (Deleuze as drug pusher). Desire in Deleuze's sense is the most obvious thing in the world, so much so that it is virtually invisible. It is the correlative of reification: to walk is a desire; to coddle a child-people is a desire; to sleep and to die are desires. Desire is the fact that mechanisms function, that assemblages work, that potentialities, including that of sleeping, are realized rather than not; "every assemblage expresses and creates a desire by constructing the plane that makes it possible."[4] *L'amor che muove il sole e l'altre stelle.* It suffices, through the accident of birth, for a certain baby to be born in the king's chambers, as heir to the throne; he will automatically be interested in his job as king, he would not give it up for an empire, or, rather, he will not even ask himself whether or not he wants to be king. He is king, that is all; that is what desire is. Does man have such a need, then, to be king? A moot question: man has a "will to power," to actualization, which is indeterminate; it is not happiness that he is seeking. He does not have a list of specific needs to satisfy, after which he would remain quietly in a chair in his room; he is the actualizing animal, and he realizes the potentialities of all sorts that come his way: *non deficit ab actuatione potentiae suae,* as Saint Thomas put it.[5] Without which, of

4. Gilles Deleuze and Claire Parnet, *Dialogues,* trans. Hugh Tomlinson and Barbara Habberjam (New York, 1987), p. 96.

5. In other words, the notion of desire means that there is no such thing as human nature, or rather that human nature is a form with no content apart from what history provides. It means, too, that the opposition between individual and society is a false problem; if we conceive of the individual and society as two realities external to one another, then we can imagine that one causes the other: causality presupposes exteriority. But if we realize that what is called society already includes the participation of individuals, the problem disappears: the "objective reality" of society includes the fact that individuals are interested in it and make it function. To put it in somewhat different terms, the only potentialities an individual can realize are those that are tentatively sketched out in the surrounding world and that the individual actualizes by virtue of the fact that he or she is interested in them; the individual fills in the hollow forms that "society" (that is, other individuals or collectivities) outlines. The capitalist would not be an "objective reality" if he did not include a capitalist mind-set as his driving force; without that mind-set the capitalist would not exist at all. The notion of desire thus also means that the opposition between the material and the ideal, the infrastructure and the superstructure, is meaningless. The idea of efficient cause, as opposed to the idea of actualization, is a dualist idea, that is, an idea whose time is past. In his fine study of the notion of basic personality according to Kardiner, Claude Lefort does a good job of showing how the idea that the individual and society are two separate realities united by a causal relation leads to aporias; see Claude Lefort, *Les Formes de l'histoire: Essais d'anthropologie* (Paris, 1978), pp. 69ff. Why, then, should the term *desire* be used for the fact that people are interested in virtual arrangements and that they make these arrangements work? Because, it seems to me, affectivity is the mark of our

course, nothing would ever happen. For an unrealized potentiality, a potentiality "in the wild state," could have nothing but a phantom existence. What would madness be, "materially," apart from a practice that makes it madness? One does not say to oneself: "All right, so I'm an emperor's son, and the senate is gone, but let's set all that aside and ask rather how we ought to treat the governed. Say, now! there's one belief, Christian ideology, that strikes me as particularly convincing on this issue." No: one discovers that one is father-king without even having had time to think about it, one *is* father-king, and, that being the case, one behaves accordingly, "things being what they are."

Actualization and causality are two different things. That is why there is neither any such thing as ideology nor any such thing as belief. Belief in the paternal nature of royal power or the ideology of the welfare state cannot act on consciousness and thereby influence practice, since, on the contrary, practice itself is what objectivizes in the first place, objectivizes a father-king rather than a priest-king or a guide, objectivizes a child-people rather than a people to be led to eternal salvation or a herd. Now, a sovereign who "is" the father-king and who finds himself "objectively" matched with a child-people cannot fail to know what he is and what his people is; he has the ideas or the mind-set corresponding to his "objective" situation. For people do think about their own practice; they are more or less aware of what they are doing. Their practice, potentially coupled with their own awareness of it, fills the void left by neighboring practices and consequently is explained by the latter. People's consciousness does not explain their practice, nor is consciousness itself explained by neighboring conditions, either as ideology or as the result of belief or superstition.

> There [is] no need . . . to pass through the authority of an individual or collective consciousness in order to grasp the place of articulation of a political practice and theory; there [is] no need to try to discover to what extent this consciousness may, on the one hand, express silent conditions, and, on the other, show that it is susceptible to theo-

---

interest in things: desire is "the set of the affects which are transformed and circulate in an assemblage of symbiosis, defined by the cofunctioning of its heterogeneous parts" (Deleuze and Parnet, *Dialogues,* p. 70). In this light, desire, like *cupiditas* for Spinoza, is the origin of all the other affects. Affectivity—the body—is better acquainted with desire than consciousness is. The king thinks he sees his herd grazing because that is what imposes itself on his consciousness, things being what they are. His consciousness believes it sees a reified world; his affectivity alone proves that his world is actualized merely because the king is actualizing it, in other words, is interested in it. To be sure, people may also fail to be interested in a "thing"; but in that case the thing in question fails to exist objectively: thus capitalism does not succeed in existing in Third World countries where a feudal mentality prevails. The term "desiring-machine," found at the beginning of Deleuze's and Félix Guattari's *Anti-Oedipus: Capitalism and Schizophrenia,* trans. Robert Hurley, Mark Seem, and Helen R. Lane (1972; Minneapolis, 1983), is highly evocative of Spinoza (*automaton appetens*).

retical truths; one [does] not need to pose the psychological problem of an act of consciousness. [*AK*, p. 194]

The notion of ideology is merely a blunder deriving from two quite unnecessary operations, one that mangles and one that trivializes. In the name of materialism, practice is separated from consciousness; in the name of natural objects, what we see is no longer precisely a father-king, no longer precisely flow control but, more banally, the perennial governor or the perennial governed. From this point on we are reduced to designating ideology as the source of all the precision, all the *exceptional* and dated overornamentation characteristic of practice; a father-king will be nothing more than the eternal sovereign, but one influenced by a certain religious ideology, the ideology according to which royal power is paternalistic by nature. Natural objects are diversified by successive ideologies. The genesis of the notion of belief is substantially the same: people's behavior is imputed to some superstition when it is out of the ordinary, and the superstition itself becomes incomprehensible. And that is why we call some mentalities primitive. But, if a mentality or a belief accounts for a practice, we still need to explain the inexplicable, namely, the belief itself; we shall be reduced to noting pitifully that sometimes people believe and sometimes they do not, that they cannot be made to believe in any ideology that is presented to them simply because they are asked to believe, and, furthermore, that they are quite capable of believing in things that, on the level of belief, are mutually contradictory, however compatible they may be in practice. Roman emperors could simultaneously put on gladiator shows and use humanism as a reason to forbid human sacrifices, which the people were not demanding; this contradiction is not contradictory for the leader of a herd, who makes it his practice to give his animals what their instincts require. A father-king, for his part, will seem contradictory in another way: he will not let the bad children have the gladiators they want, and he will put the wicked seducers to death by way of the most fearful tortures.

In short, there is no such thing as ideology, the sacred texts notwithstanding, and we may as well resolve never to use the word again. The term sometimes designates an abstraction, namely, the meaning of a practice (it is in this sense that I have just used it), and sometimes more or less bookish realities, political doctrines, philosophies, even religions, that is, discursive practices. In the example we are considering, ideology is the meaning that can be attributed to the doctrine of the father-king, a doctrine that historians can make explicit on the basis of the king's actions: "Things being as they are," they will write, "and the people being merely a child, the people must be defended against itself, it must be dissuaded from blood lust and bad behavior through exemplary punishments, but only after it has been publicly chastened and threatened." (Naturally there is always the possibility that, if the king has a sense of humor and the gift of expression, he himself may have become aware of all this, like his future historians; but this is another matter.) Moreover, an ideology in the second sense of the word existed during the same period, namely, the Christian religion. That ideology too condemned evil thoughts, but it construed them somewhat differently: carnal temptations were deemed more dangerous than gladiators' blood.

The disappearance of gladiator fighting has long been credited to the influence of Christian doctrine on consciousness. In reality, that disappearance derives from the transformation of political practice, the meaning of which changed since things were no longer "objectively" what they had been.[6] This transformation, for its part, is not a conscious process. The king does not need to be persuaded that the people *is* a child: he sees that perfectly well all by himself; in his soul and consciousness, he will only deliberate about the means and timing he should use to coddle and chastise that child. It is easy to see the difference between ideology in the sense of doctrine and ideology in the sense of the meaning of a practice. (The doctrine in question, moreover, has its own concealed base and corresponds to a discursive practice, but that is another story.) Similarly, historians have disagreed about the increased severity of penal law at the time of the Christian emperors, particularly where sexual offenses were concerned: did this come about through the influence of Christianity? Did the law become more popular because the emperor was more paternalistic with his people, to such an extent that he applied the popular ideal of an eye for an eye in thoroughgoing fashion and even went beyond it? The second explanation has to be the correct one.

In any event, here we have two heterogeneous practices. The herd-people had a certain margin of sexual freedom and gladiators died; the child-people has a smaller margin and gladiators no longer die. If these transformations are measured on a scale of values, we may say that humanitarianism has progressed, that law has regressed, and that repression

6. Scientific revolutions have their precursors. The notion of "what goes without saying" broke through timidly, here and there, in phenomenology, and also elsewhere: Heinrich Wölfflin, *Principes fondamentaux de l'histoire de l'art: Le Problème de l'évolution du style dans l'art moderne*, trans. Claire and Marcel Raymond (Paris, 1952), pp. 17, 261, 276; trans. M. D. Hottinger, under the title *Principles of Art History: The Problem of the Development of Style in Later Art* (New York, 1932), seems to embody in advance pp. 193–94 of *The Archaeology of Knowledge*. To study what-goes-without-saying, we would need to trace the expressions *fraglos* or *taken for granted* among the sociologists who are disciples of Husserl, such as Felix Kaufmann (*Die philosophischen grundprobleme der lehre von der Strafrechtsschuld* [Leipzig, 1929]), Alfred Schutz (*Phenomenology of the Social World*), and even Max Scheler (*Die Wissensformen und die gesellschaft: Probleme einer soziologie des wissens* [Leipzig, 1926], p. 61). But phenomenology could not go any farther, no doubt, less because of the ego cogito (for phenomenology was subtle enough to think it could discern what-goes-without-saying in the very enticing subconscious "fringes" of the cogito) than because of its optimistic rationalism; we need only read Schutz's studies on the social distribution of knowledge, reprinted in his *Collected Papers*, ed. Maurice Natanson, 4 vols. (The Hague, 1962–66), 1:14 and 2:120, to see how an excess of rationalism can cause an admirable subject to be overlooked.

has increased, and these judgments will not be false. But we have done no more than take note of measures; we have not explained the transformations. History as a whole has substituted one misshapen period piece, the child-people, for another, differently misshapen one, the herd-people. This kaleidoscope bears little resemblance to the successive figures of a dialectical development; it cannot be explained by progress in consciousness, or by a decline, or by a struggle between two principles, desire and repression. Every period piece owes its odd shape to the place left vacant for it by the contemporary practices between which it was molded. The cutouts of the various pieces are in no way comparable; they are not robotlike creations, one of which may have more moving parts, more freedom, less repression, than the others. The sexuality of the ancients, if that is what we want to talk about, was not fundamentally more or less repressive than that of the Christians. It was simply based on a different principle: not the normality of reproduction, but activity as opposed to passivity. Thus it gave a different shape to homophilia, accepting active male homosexuality while condemning the passive form—along with female homosexuality—and encompassing the heterosexual search for female pleasure in its condemnation.

When Foucault seems to put on equal footing the unspeakable torture inflicted on Robert-François Damiens (he was quartered for attacking Louis XV with a penknife, though the king was wounded only slightly) and the improvements in prison conditions brought about by nineteenth-century philanthropists, he is not claiming that, if each of us could decide to live in some earlier century, we would not have varying preferences, for every epoch offers attractions and risks that differ according to individual taste. No, he is simply reminding us of four truths. (1) The succession of heterogeneities that has just been evoked does not trace a vector we can call progress. (2) The driving force behind the kaleidoscope is not reason, desire, or consciousness. (3) In order to make rational choices, preference is not enough—we need to be able to compare and thus to aggregate (but according to what conversion rate?) the heterogeneous and measured advantages and disadvantages according to our own subjective scale of values. (4) Finally, and most importantly, we must not fabricate rationalizing rationalisms; we must not hide heterogeneity behind reifications. In exercising the virtue of prudence, we must not compare two icebergs and calculate our preferences while neglecting the concealed base of one of them, nor must we distort the appreciation of the possible by maintaining that "things are as they are," for in fact there are no things: there are only practices. According to this new methodology of history, the truth of the matter is found here, rather than in "discourse" or epistemological breaks, although the latter have had more success in capturing the public's attention. Madness exists as an object only in and through a practice, but the practice in question is not itself madness.

This point of view has provoked outrage. Nevertheless, the idea that madness does not exist is plainly a positivist one: it is the idea of madness in itself that is purely metaphysical, although familiar to common sense. And yet . . . If I were to say that someone who eats human flesh really and truly does eat it, I would obviously be right; but I would also be right to claim that the eater is a cannibal only within a cultural context, within a practice that "valorizes" or objectivizes that mode of nutrition in such a way as to find it barbaric, or, on the contrary, sacred, and, in any case, in such a way as to make something of it. In neighboring practices, moreover, the same eater will be objectivized not as a cannibal but in some other way: he has two arms and is able to work, he has a king and is objectivized as a member of the child-people or as a beast belonging to the herd. We shall come back shortly to the discussion of this kind of problem, which stirred up heated discussion on an earlier occasion in Parisian circles, on the left bank of the Seine; to be sure, this happened in the fourteenth century. The fact that Foucault took such a decisive step, that of disqualifying the natural object, is what gives his work its philosophical stature, as far as I am able to judge.

A statement such as "attitudes toward *madmen* have varied considerably throughout history" is a metaphysical statement. Only through word play can one depict a madness "that exists materially" apart from a form that shapes it as madness; at most, there are neural molecules arranged in a certain way, sentences or gestures that an observer from Sirius might see as different from those of other humans, who are themselves different from each other. But what exist here are nothing but natural forms, trajectories in space, molecular structures or behaviors; these are *material for* a madness that does not yet exist at this stage. When one comes right down to it, the source of resistance in this polemic is the fact that, all too often, even when people think they are discussing the issue of the material or formal existence of madness, they have in mind another, more interesting problem: is it *correct* to attribute the shape of madness to the material for madness, or should one abandon all rationalist notions of mental health?

To say that madness does not exist is not to claim that madmen are victims of prejudice, nor is it to deny such an assertion, for that matter. The meaning of the proposition lies elsewhere. It neither affirms nor denies that madmen should not be excluded, or that madness exists because it is fabricated by society, or that madness is modified in its positivity by the attitudes various societies hold toward it, or that different societies have conceptualized madness in very different ways; the proposition does not deny, either, that madness has a behaviorist and perhaps a physiological component. But even if madness were to have such components, it would not yet be madness. A building stone becomes a keystone or a header only when it takes its place as part of a structure. The denial of madness is not situated at the level of attitudes toward the object, but at that of its objectivization; it does not mean that the only madmen are the people deemed mad. It means that at a level other than that of consciousness a certain practice is necessary for there even to be an object such as "the madman" to be judged to the best of one's knowledge and belief, or for society to be able to "drive someone mad." Denying the objectivity of madness is a matter of historical perspective and not of "openness to others." Modifications in the way madmen are treated are one thing; the disappearance of the objectivization "the madman" is another matter, one that does not depend on our will, however revolutionary, but one that obviously presupposes a metamorphosis of practices on such a scale that the word *revolution* pales in comparison. Animals do not exist any more than madmen do, though they may be treated well or badly; but, for an animal to begin to lose its objectivization, we need at a minimum the practices of an igloo full of Eskimos, during the long winter's nap, in the symbiosis of men and dogs mingling their warmth. The fact remains that through twenty-five centuries of history societies have objectivized in rather diverse ways the thing called dementia, madness, or insanity; thus we have the right to presume that no natural object is hidden behind the thing, and to doubt the rationalism of mental health. Moreover, it is undeniable that, for example, society can drive a person mad, and we are surely all familiar with examples of the phenomenon; but this kind of thing is not what is meant by the statement "madness does not exist." Whatever may be repeated or insinuated, the philosopher's phrase, whose meaning would have been instantly understood by the fourteenth-century Parisian masters,[7] does not translate its author's choices or obses-

---

7. For example, see Duns Scotus: "It is necessary to know in this connection that matter is in act, but that it is the act of nothing *[materia est in actu, sed nullius est actus]*; it is something in act, since it is a thing rather than nothing *[est quoddam in actu, ut est res quaedam extra nihil]*, an effectuation of God, a creation arrived at full term. But it is the act of nothing, if only because it serves as the basis for all actualizations" (Duns Scotus, *De rerum principio,* q. VII, art. 1, schol. 4, *Opera Omnia,* 26 vols. [Paris, 1891–95], 3:38B).

I have just amused myself translating into Scotist terms what is perhaps the fundamental problem of philosophy-history according to Foucault: as soon as one goes beyond the problematics of Marxist materialism, which is where many historians stop (but unless he had "convictions," a trained philosopher could not take that problematics seriously for long), one must both deny the transhistorical reality of natural objects and also grant those objects enough objective reality so that they remain something to be explained, and not simply subjective phantoms to be described; it is necessary for natural objects not to exist and for history to remain a reality to be explained. Thus, for Duns Scotus, matter is neither a being of reason nor a physically separable reality. For Foucault (who read Nietzsche in 1954–55, if I remember correctly), phenomenology offered an initial way out of this difficulty. For Husserl, "things" are not extramental *res,* but neither are they simple psychological contents; phenomenology is not a form of idealism. However, essences thus understood were immediate givens to be described, and not pseudo-objects to be explained scientifically or historically. Phenomenology describes a layer of beings that predates science; as soon as one moves on to explain these beings, phenomenology yields deliberately to science, while the essences turn back into things. Foucault ultimately resolved the difficulty through a Nietzschean philosophy of the primacy of relations: *things exist only through relation,* as we

sions. If a reader concludes triumphantly from all this that madness really does exist, except perhaps speculatively, as he had always supposed, that is his business. For Foucault as for Duns Scotus, the material for madness (behavior, neuromicrobiology) really exists, but not as madness; to be mad only materially is precisely not yet to be mad. A man must be objectivized as a madman for the prediscursive referent to appear retrospectively as material for *madness;* for why consider behavior and nerve cells rather than fingerprints?

Thus it would be wrong to accuse Foucault, a philosopher who believes that matter exists in act, of being an idealist (in the popular sense of the word). When I showed the present text to Foucault, he responded roughly as follows: "I personally have never written that *madness does not exist,* but it can be written; for phenomenology, madness exists, but it is not a thing, whereas one has to say on the contrary that madness does not exist, but that it is not therefore nothing." One may even say that nothing exists in history, since in history everything depends on everything else, as we shall see—which is to say that things exist only materially: they have a faceless, not yet objectivized existence. The claim that sexuality, for example, is practice and "discourse" does not mean that sex organs do not exist, or that what was called the sex drive before Freud came along does not exist; "'prediscursive'" referents (*AK*, p. 47) such as these are the footings of a practice, on the same basis as the importance or the disappearance of the Roman senate. But they are not pretexts for rationalism, and that is the point here. The prediscursive referent *is not* a natural object, a target for teleology: there is no return of the repressed. There exists no "eternal problem" of madness, considered as a natural object constituting a challenge that elicits varied responses through the ages. Molecular differences no more constitute madness than do differences between fingerprints; differences in behavior and reasoning are no more madness than are our differences in handwriting or differences of opinion.

What we see as the stuff of madness will be material for something entirely different in another practice. Since madness is not a natural object, we cannot have a "reasonable" discussion of the "correct" attitude to be "adopted" towards it. For what is called reason (and what philosophers have been concerned with) does not stand out against a neutral background, and it does not make pronouncements about realities. It speaks,

---

shall see further on, *and the determination of this relation is precisely what explains things.* In short, everything is historical, everything depends on everything else (and not on relations of production alone), nothing exists transhistorically, and to explain a so-called object amounts to showing on what *historical* context it depends. The only difference between this conception and Marxism is that, in sum, Marxism has a naive view of causality (one thing depends on *an* other, smoke depends on fire). However, the notion of a single determining cause is prescientific.

on the basis of "discourses" of which it is unaware, about objectivizations of which it is unaware (and with which those who have been called historians might do well to be concerned). All this displaces the borders of philosophy and history because in both cases it transforms their content. Their content is transformed because what was meant by truth is transformed. For some time now, nature and convention have been cast in opposition to one another; more recently, nature has been pitted against culture. There has been a good deal of talk about historical relativism and the arbitrariness of culture. History and truth. It had to break down sooner or later. History has become the story of what men have called truths and of their struggles over those truths.

Here, then, is a wholly *material* universe, made up of prediscursive referents that remain faceless potentialities; in this universe practices that are never the same engender, at varying points, objectivizations that are never the same, ever-changing faces. Each practice depends on all the others and on their transformations. Everything is historical, and everything depends on everything else. Nothing is inert, nothing is indeterminate, and, as we shall see, nothing is inexplicable. Far from being dependent upon our consciousness, this world determines our consciousness. A first consequence is that a given referent is not charged with becoming one particular changeless face; it does not have to become a particular objectivization: state, madness, or religion. This is the celebrated theory of discontinuities: there is no such thing as "madness through the ages," or religion through the ages, or medicine through the ages. Preclinical medicine had nothing in common with nineteenth-century medicine but the name; conversely, if we are looking for a seventeenth-century phenomenon that has something in common with what we mean by nineteenth-century historical science, we will find it not in the historical genre but in controversy (in other words, what resembles what we call History is the book called *Histoire des variations,* a book that is still admirable and, moreover, highly readable, rather than the unreadable *Discours sur l'histoire universelle*). In short, in a given era the set of practices gives rise, on a given material point, to a unique historical countenance in which we think we recognize what is called, in vague terms, historical science or religion; but what takes shape at that same point in another era will have its own unique and very different countenance and, conversely, a countenance vaguely similar to the earlier one will take shape at a some other point. This is what denying the existence of natural objects means: across the ages we do not encounter the evolution or modification of a single object that always appears in the same place. We are dealing with a kaleidoscope, not a tree nursery. Foucault does not say: "For my part, I prefer discontinuity, breaks," but: "Beware of false continuities." A false natural object such as religion or a certain religion aggregates very dissimilar elements (ritualism, sacred books, a sense of security, disparate emotions, and so on) that, in other eras, will be expressed in very different practices and objectivized through these practices in very different guises. As Deleuze would say, trees do not exist; only rhizomes exist.

As accessory consequences, we find that there is no such thing as functionalism or institutionalism. History is an amorphous terrain, not a firing range: through the centuries, the institution we know as the prison is not a function that meets a continuing need, and the transformations of that institution cannot be explained by the successes or failures of such a function. We have to begin with a global viewpoint, that is, with successive practices, for, according to the historical period, the same institution will fulfill different functions and vice versa. Moreover, a given function exists only by virtue of a practice, and it is not the practice that responds to the "challenge" of the function (the function "bread and circuses" exists only in and through the practice of "leading the herd"; there is not a timeless function of redistribution or depoliticization spanning the centuries).

As a result, the opposition between diachrony and synchrony, between genesis and structure, is a false problem. Genesis is nothing more than the actualization of a structure;[8] in order for us to be able to contrast the structure known as medicine with its slow genesis, there would have to be continuity, medicine would have had to grow like a thousand- year-old tree. Genesis does not go from beginning to end; origins do not exist, or, if they do, they are rarely beautiful, as others have noted. Nineteenth-century medicine cannot be explained by starting with Hippocrates and moving forward through time, which does not exist; there were only successive structures (medicine in Molière's day, the clinic), *each* of which had its own genesis, a genesis that is explained in part by the transformations of the preceding medical structure and in part by the transformations of the rest of the world, in all probability; for why should a structure be entirely explicable in terms of the preceding structure? Why, on the contrary, should the successor structure be completely foreign to its predecessor? Once again, our author clears away metaphysical fictions and false problems, positivist that he is. It is odd that this enemy of trees should have been taken for a creationist. Foucault is a historian of the purest sort: everything is historical, history is entirely explicable, and *all words ending in -ism have to be rooted out.*

In history only individual or even singular constellations exist, and each one can be fully explained on the sole basis of the means available. Without recourse to the social sciences? Since every discourse, every practice has its anchor-points and its objectivizations, it seems difficult to speak of the former and the latter without drawing to some extent, for example, on linguistics or economics, if we are talking about linguistic or

8. See Deleuze, *Difference and Repetition,* trans. Paul Patton (New York, 1994), pp. 183–84.

economic anchor-points; this is something Foucault scarcely mentions, either because it is more or less self-evident, or because he does not much believe in it, or because it is not what interests him. Unless I am blinded by my own egotism here—for in my inaugural lecture at the Collège de France I contended that history had to be written with the help of the social sciences and that it implied invariants. Be that as it may, it seems to me that the crucial issue for Foucault is the following: even if history were subject to scientific explanation, would the science in question be situated at the level of our rationalisms? Are the invariants of historical explanation the same thing as "natural objects"?

This, I believe, is the real nub of the question for Foucault. It is of little importance to him that the inevitable invariants are organized, at least here and there, in a system of scientific truths, or that one cannot go beyond a simple typology of historical conjunctures, or that the invariants can be reduced to formal propositions, to a philosophical anthropology like that of Spinoza's Book II or *The Genealogy of Morals*. The main point is that the social sciences, if sciences there must be, cannot be a rationalization of natural objects, a body of knowledge for the elite. They presuppose first and foremost a historical analysis of natural objects, that is, a genealogy, a bringing to light of the practice or discourse in question.

After the historian has done his work with them, can the invariants be organized in a hypothetico-deductive system? This is a factual question of minor interest: science does not refer to a constitutive activity of the mind, to a harmony between being and thought, to Reason, but more modestly to the fact that, in certain sectors, the movements of the kaleidoscope, the throw of the dice, the concurrence of historical moments, turn out to form relatively isolated systems, servo-mechanisms that, as such, are repetitive; this is often the case with physical phenomena. As for knowing whether the same thing holds true, at least here and there, in human history, the question is an interesting one, but it is limited in scope, indeed doubly so. It consists in asking oneself what phenomena are like, and not what the demands of Reason are; in no way can it lead to devaluing historical explanation as unscientific. Science is not a higher form of knowledge; it is knowledge that is applied to "models in series," whereas historical explanation deals with "prototypes," one case at a time. Owing to the very nature of the phenomena under investigation, science has formal models as invariants; historical explanation has truths that are more formal still. Although wholly caught up in the circumstantial, historical explanation is not a whit less rigorous than science. *Positivisme oblige.*

To be sure, positivism is only a relative program and a negative one. One is always a positivist with respect to someone else, someone whose rationalizations one denies; after the metaphysical fictions have been swept away, positive knowledge still has to be reconstructed. Historical analysis begins by establishing that there is no such thing as a State, not even a Roman State, but only correlatives (a herd to guide, a flow to man-age) of dated practices each of which, in its own time, seemed to be self-evident, seemed to be politics itself. Now, since only the determinate exists, the historian does not account for politics itself, but rather for the herd, the flow, and other determinations; for politics, the State and Power do not exist.

But then how can one explain without banking on mainsprings, on invariants? Otherwise explanation would give way to intuition (one does not explain the color blue, one takes note of it) or to the illusion of under-standing. Of course: except that the formal requirement of invariants does not prejudge the level at which these same invariants will be situ-ated. If the explanation discovers relatively isolable subsystems in history (a given economic process, a given organizational structure), the explana-tion will settle for applying a model to them or at least relating them to a principle ("a door must be either open or closed; the algebraic sum of the stakes of a game of international security must be zero, whether the interested parties know it or not; if they did not know it, or if they pre-ferred another outcome, that explains their fate"). If, on the contrary, the historical event is entirely circumstantial, the search for the invariant will not stop until the seeker arrives at anthropological propositions.

Except that these anthropological propositions themselves are for-mal, and history alone gives them content. There is no concrete transhis-torical truth, no material human nature, no return of the repressed. For the idea of a repressed nature has no meaning except in the case of an individual, who has had his own history; in the case of societies, what is repressed in one era is in reality the different practice of another, and the eventual return of this so-called repressed is in reality the genesis of a new practice. Foucault is not the French Marcuse. I referred earlier to the horror inspired in the Romans by the very gladiator they perceived simultaneously as a star; was that horror, which did not succeed in bring-ing gladiatorship to an end before the time of the Byzantine Empire, a repressed fear of murder during a state of civil peace? Would fear of murder be a transhistorical requirement stemming from human nature, a requirement that governing authorities in all eras would do well to take into account, on the grounds that if the front door is shut it will come in through the back? No; for in the first place this fear was not repressed but rather modified through reactivity (the reactivity discussed in *The Genealogy of Morals*—here is an invariant mainspring with a philosophical flavor). It was a pharisaical disgust at the sight of death's prostitute, the gladiator. Secondly, the so-called transhistorical fear of murder is not transhistorical at all. It is material; it is concrete; it has to do with a spe-cific governmental practice; it is the fear of seeing an innocent citizen die, within the secure space of civil peace, which implies a certain politico-cultural discourse, a certain practice of the city-state. This so-called natu-ral fear cannot be enunciated in purely formal terms, even in a truism. It does not exist formally; it is not fear of death or murder (for it allows the murder of criminals).

For Foucault, the interest of history does not lie in the elaboration of invariants, whether these remain in the realm of philosophy or organize themselves into social sciences; it lies in using the invariants, whatever they are, to dissolve the rationalisms that keep on springing up. History is a Nietzschean genealogy. That is why history according to Foucault passes itself off as philosophy (which is neither true nor false); it is very far, in any case, from the empiricist vocation traditionally attributed to history. "Let no one enter here unless he is or becomes a philosopher." Foucault's is a history written in abstract terms rather than in the semantics of a specific period still invested with local color; it is a history that seems to find partial analogies everywhere, to sketch out typologies—for a history written in a web of abstract words offers less picturesque diversity than anecdotal narration.

This history of a humorous or ironic bent dissolves appearances, and thus it has created the impression that Foucault is a relativist ("what was true a thousand years ago is an error today"). As a history that rejects natural objects and ratifies the kaleidoscope, it has created the impression that Foucault is a skeptic. He is neither. For a relativist judges that men have held different views, over the centuries, of the *same* object: "About Man, about Beauty, some have thought one thing at one moment whereas others, in another era, have thought something else; how can anyone figure out what is true?" For our author, this is much ado about nothing, because the point at issue is precisely *not* the same from one era to another; as for the point that demonstrably belongs to a given era, the truth is perfectly explicable, devoid of any wobbly indeterminacy. Foucault would undoubtedly subscribe to statements affirming that humanity only sets itself tasks it can accomplish:[9] at any given moment, human practices are what all of history makes them, so that at any given moment humanity is adequate to itself—which is not very flattering for humanity. Nor does the denial of natural objects lead to skepticism; no one doubts that rockets aimed at Mars will, thanks to Newton's calculations, reach their target, and Foucault does not doubt, I hope, that Foucault is right. He simply reminds us that the objects of a science and the very notion of science are not eternal truths. And Man, quite clearly, is a false object: the human sciences do not thereby become impossible, but they are obliged to change their object, an enterprise undertaken by the physical sciences as well.

In reality, the problem lies elsewhere. If I am not mistaken, the notion of truth is disrupted because philosophical truth, having to confront

9. Nietzsche, *The Gay Science*, trans. Walter Kaufmann (New York, 1974), no. 196: "One hears only those questions for which one is able to find answers." Marx says that humanity solves all the problems it sets itself; Nietzsche says that it sets itself only problems it can solve; compare *AK*, pp. 44–45, and Deleuze, *Difference and Repetition*, p. 158.

the truths of scientific inquiry, has been replaced by history. Before, all science was provisional and philosophy was aware of this; now, all science is provisional and historical analysis demonstrates this, over and over. Analyses such as those of medicine, modern sexuality, or Roman power are perfectly valid or at least they may be. What cannot be valid, on the other hand, are claims to knowledge of the nature of sexuality "in general" or power "in general": not because the truth about these grandiose objects cannot be reached, but because there is no place for truth or for error either, since these grandiose objects do not exist. Big trees do not grow in kaleidoscopes. Men believe they do, they may be made to believe this, and they may even fight over their belief, but that is another story. The fact remains that so far as sexuality is concerned, or Power, or the State, or madness, or a lot of other things, there can be no truth and no error, since these "things" do not exist; one cannot make true or erroneous statements about the digestive or reproductive processes of centaurs.

At every moment, the world is what it is: the fact that its practices and objects are *exceptional,* that they are surrounded by emptiness, does not mean that they are surrounded by some truth which no one has grasped to date. The figures the kaleidoscope will produce in the future will be neither more nor less true than earlier ones. There is, in Foucault, no repressed and no return of the repressed; there is nothing unsaid clamoring to be heard:

> the positivities that I have tried to establish must not be understood as a set of determinations imposed from the outside on the thought of individuals, or inhabiting it from the inside, in advance as it were; they constitute rather the set of conditions in accordance with which a practice is exercised. . . . These positivities are not so much limitations imposed on the initiative of subjects as the field in which that initiative is articulated. [*AK,* pp. 208–9]

Consciousness cannot balk at the conditions of history, since consciousness is not constitutive but constituted. To be sure, it rebels continually, rejecting gladiators, discovering or inventing the Poor. These rebellions signify the establishment of a new practice, not an eruption of the absolute.

> The existence of systems of rarefaction does not imply that, over and beyond them lie great vistas of limitless discourse, continuous and silent, repressed and driven back by them, making it our task to abolish them and at last to restore it to speech. Whether talking in terms of speaking or thinking, we must not imagine some unsaid thing, or

an unthought, floating about the world, interlacing with all its forms and events.[10]

Foucault is no more an unwitting Malebranche than he is the Lacan of history. Let me go even further and declare that he is not a humanist. For what is a humanist if not someone who believes in semantics? Now "discourse," for humanists, is the negation of semantics. But this cannot be! Language does not reveal reality, and Marxists ought to be the first to understand this and to keep the history of words in its proper place. No, language is not born against a background of silence; it is born against a background of discourse. A humanist is someone who interrogates texts and people *at the level of what they are saying,* or rather who does not even suspect that there could be any other level.

Foucault's philosophy is not a philosophy of "discourse" but a philosophy of relation. For relation is the name of what has been called structure. Instead of a world made up of subjects, or objects, or the dialectic between them, a world in which consciousness knows its objects in advance, targets them, or is itself what the objects make of it, we have a world in which relation is primary. Structures are what give to matter their own objective faces. In this world, one does not play chess with eternal figures, the king or the fool; the chessmen are what the successive configurations of the chessboard make of them. Thus

> we should try to study power, not starting from the primitive terms of relation, civil subject, State, law, sovereign, and so on, but starting from relation itself, insofar as it is relation that determines the elements on which it bears; rather than asking ideal subjects what they may have yielded of themselves or of their powers in order to allow themselves to be subjected, we have to try to find out how relations of subjection can manufacture subjects.[11]

Foucault is a philosopher of relation who does not ontologize Power or anything at all; if anyone does, it is those who speak only of the State, whether to bless it or curse it or define it "scientifically," whereas the State is the simple correlative of a certain specifically dated practice.

Madness does not exist; only its relation to the rest of the world exists. To find out how a philosophy of relation plays itself out, we have to see it at work on a well-known problem, that of the enrichment of the past and its works in terms of the interpretations that the future will give it through the centuries. In a well-known passage in *The Creative Mind,* Henri Bergson studies this apparent action of the future on the past.

10. Foucault, "The Discourse on Language," trans. Rupert Swyer, appendix to Foucault, *The Archaeology of Knowledge,* trans. Sheridan Smith (New York, 1982), p. 229.
11. Foucault, "Il faut défendre la société," *Annuaire du Collège de France* (Paris, 1976), p. 361.

Concerning the notion of preromanticism, he writes:

> If there had not been a Rousseau, a Chateaubriand, a Vigny, a Victor Hugo, not only should we never have perceived, but also *there would never really have existed,* any romanticism in the earlier classical writers, for this romanticism of theirs only materialises by lifting out of their work a certain aspect, and this slice (découpure), with its particular form, no more existed in classical literature before romanticism appeared on the scene than there exists, in the cloud floating by, the amusing design that an artist perceives in shaping to his fancy the amorphous mass.[12]

The paradox of selective cutouts is known today as the paradox of multiple "readings" of a given work. Here we have the problem of relation in a nutshell, and it is especially the problem of the individual.

Leibniz writes about a traveler in India who does not know that, back home, his wife has died.[13] The traveler nevertheless is truly transformed: he becomes a widower. To be sure, "being a widower" is only a relation (the same person may be at the same time a widower with respect to his late wife, a father with respect to his son, and a son with respect to his father); the fact remains that the relation resides in the individual who bears it *(omne praedicatum inest subjecto):* to have a relation of widowerhood is to *be* a widower. It must be one thing or the other, we will be told. The husband's status may be determined from without, just as the preromantic cutout is only, according to some, an interpretation inflicted from without on classical works that are helpless to defend themselves; in this case, the truth of a text will be what is said about it and the individual—father, son, spouse and widower—is what the rest of the world makes of him. Alternatively, the relation may be internal, emerging from within the interested party itself; it was inscribed from time immemorial, in the traveler-monad, that he would be a widower and God could read his future widowerhood in that monad (which obviously presupposes that, through a preestablished harmony, the monad married to the traveler dies for her part at the appropriate moment, just as two well-synchronized clocks mark the fatal hour at the same moment); in this case, everything that is said about a text will be true. In the first case, nothing is true of an individuality, traveler, or work; in the second case, everything is true, and the text, stuffed to the bursting point, contains in

---

12. Henri Bergson, *The Creative Mind,* trans. Mabelle L. Andison (New York, 1946), p. 24. The Bergsonian idea of the enrichment of the past by the future is also found in Nietzsche, *The Gay Science,* no. 94, "Growth after Death"; see also Nietzsche, *Human, All Too Human: A Book for Free Spirits,* trans. R. J. Hollingdale, 2 vols. (Cambridge, 1986), 2:217, no. 12 and *The Will to Power,* trans. Kaufmann and Hollingdale (New York, 1967), no. 974.

13. See Gottfried Wilhelm Leibniz, *Philosophische Schriften,* trans. and ed. Hans Heinz Holz, 3 vols. in 5 (Darmstadt, 1965–85), 5:129. Cited by Yvon Belaval, *Leibniz critique de Descartes* (Paris, 1960), p. 112.

advance the most contradictory interpretations. This is what Russell calls the problem of external and internal relations.[14] In fact, it is the problem of individuality.

Does a work have only the import that is attributed to it? Does it have all the imports that may be discovered in it? And what becomes of the import given it by the chief interested party, the author? For the problem to arise, the work has to exist, has to have been erected like a monument; it has to be a full-fledged individuality, complete with meaning, with import. Only then can one be astonished that this work in which nothing is lacking, neither text (in print or manuscript) nor meaning, is additionally capable of receiving new meanings from the future, or that it perhaps already contains all other meanings imaginable. But what if the work did not exist? What if it received its meaning only through relation? What if its meaning, which can be declared authentic, were quite simply the import that it had in relation to its author or to the period in which it had been written? What if, similarly, the imports to come were not enrichments of the work but other imports, different but not competing ones? What if all these imports, past and future, were different individuations of a matter that received them indifferently? In this case, the problem of relation vanishes, along with the work's individuality. The work, as an individuality that supposedly retains its physiognomy through time, *does not exist* (only its relation to each of its interpreters exists), but it *is not nothing:* it is determined in each relation; the meaning it had in its time, for example, may be the object of positive discussions. What exists, on the other hand, is the *matter* of the work, but that matter is nothing, so long as the relation has not made one thing or another of it. As Duns Scotus said, matter is in act, without being the act of any thing. This matter is the manuscript or printed text, insofar as that text is *capable of* taking on *a* meaning, is made to have *a* meaning and is not some gobbledygook typed out at random by a monkey at a keyboard. Relation comes first. That is why Foucault's method very probably grew out of a reaction against the wave of phenomenology that came along immediately after the Liberation in France. Perhaps Foucault's problem was the following: how can one do better than a philosophy of consciousness and still avoid falling into the aporias of Marxism? Or perhaps it was the inverse: how can one escape a philosophy of the subject without falling into a philosophy of the object?

Phenomenology is not guilty of being an "idealism," but it can be faulted for being a philosophy of the cogito. Husserl does not bracket off the existence of God and the devil into parentheses only in order to open the brackets back up surreptitiously, as Lukács claimed; when Husserl describes the centaur's essence, he leaves pronouncements about its exis-

---

14. See Bertrand Russell, *Principles of Mathematics* (London, 1937), pars. 214–16, and Jean Claude Pariente, *Le Langage et l'individuel* (Paris, 1973), p. 139.

tence or nonexistence and its physiological functions to the sciences. Phenomenology goes awry not when it fails to explain things (since it never promised to explain them) but when it describes them on the basis of consciousness, taken as constitutive and not as constituted. Every explanation of madness presupposes first of all an accurate description of madness. For such a description, can we rely on what our consciousness allows us to see? Yes, if consciousness is constitutive, if, as the saying goes, it knows reality "as well as if it had made it itself." No, if consciousness is constituted without its own knowledge, if it is the unwitting dupe of a constituting historical practice. And our consciousness is indeed duped. It believes that madness exists, although it hastens to add that madness is not a thing, since our consciousness finds itself so much at home there—provided that it shows enough subtlety in its descriptions to slip into that familiar place. And we have to acknowledge that the subtlety of phenomenological description does elicit admiring exclamations.

Now it is curious that Marxists share the same belief in the object (and the same belief in consciousness: the consciousness of agents is the medium through which ideology acts on reality). The explanation starts from a given object, the relation of production, and moves on to other objects. We hardly need to recall here for the hundredth time the inconsistencies to which this approach leads: that in no case can a historical object, an event, such as the relation of production, explain "in the final analysis"; in no case can it be a prime mover, since the object itself is a conditioned event. If the use of water-powered mills causes serfdom, then we need to ask for what historical reasons water-powered mills were used rather than whatever method had been customary before; thus our prime mover is no such thing. There can be no *event in the final analysis;* that is a contradiction in terms. The Scholastics explained this in their own way by saying that a prime mover cannot have any force: if it belongs to the order of the virtual before it exists, if it is an event, it must have causes in order to be actualized, and thus it is no longer a last resort. Let us skip over the subsequent muddles, which do not elicit admiring exclamations; the relation of production ultimately becomes the label for everything that is useful for explaining how the world works, including symbolic property—which amounts to jumping into the pond to get out of the rain. What the relation of production is supposed to explain is now part of the relation of production. Consciousness itself is part of the object that is supposed to determine it. What is most important lies elsewhere, however: it is the fact that objects continue to exist; people continue to speak of the State, power, the economy, and so on. Not only do the spontaneous teleologies thus remain in place, but the object to be explained is taken as an explanation, and that explanation moves on from one object to another. We have seen the difficulties to which this has led; we have also seen that it perpetuated the teleological illusion, idealism in Nietzsche's sense, the "history and truth" aporia. In contrast, Foucault proposes a positivism in which he invites us to eliminate the last unhistoricized objects, the last traces of metaphysics; and he proposes a materialism according to which explanation no longer proceeds from one object to another, but from everything to everything, and this objectivizes specifically dated objects on faceless matter. For the mill even to be perceived as a means of production and for its use to disrupt the world, it must first be objectivized owing to a step-by-step disruption of the surrounding practices, a disruption that itself . . . and so on ad infinitum. To tell the truth, this is what we historians, like Molière's M. Jourdain, had always believed *at heart.*

The Foucault-style genealogy-history thus completely fulfills the project of traditional history; it does not ignore society, the economy, and so on, but it structures this material differently—not by centuries, peoples, or civilizations, but by practices. The plots it relates are the history of the practices in which men have seen truths and of their struggles over these truths.[15] This new model history, this "archaeology," as its inventor calls it, "is deployed in the dimension of a general history" (*AK*, p. 164); it does not specialize in practice, discourse, the concealed part of the iceberg—or, rather, the concealed part of discourse and practice is not separable from the exposed part. In this regard there is no evolution in Foucault, and the *History of Sexuality* did not innovate when it linked the analysis of a discursive practice to the social history of the bourgeoisie; *The Birth of the Clinic* had already anchored a transformation of medical discourse in institutions, political practice, hospitals; and so on. Every history is archaeological by nature and not by choice. Explaining history and making it explicit consists in first perceiving it whole, in relating the so-called natural objects to the specifically dated and exceptional practices that objectivized the objects, and in explaining the practices not on the basis of a unique motive force but on the basis of all the neighboring practices in which they are anchored. This pictorial method produces strange paintings, in which relations replace objects. To be sure, the paintings are indeed those of the world we know. Foucault is no more an

15. Foucault's method may well be derived from a meditation on section 12 of the second essay of Nietzsche, *On the Genealogy of Morals*, trans. Kaufmann and Hollingdale (New York, 1967), pp. 76–79. More generally speaking, the primacy of relation implies an ontology of the will to power; Foucault's work could have as its epigraph two texts from Nietzsche's *The Will to Power*. First: "Against the doctrine of the influence of the milieu and external causes: the force within is infinitely superior; much that looks like external influence is merely its adaptation from within. The very same milieus can be interpreted and exploited in opposite ways: there are no facts *[es gibt keine Tatsachen]*" (no. 70). As we can see, facts do not exist, not only on the level of the interpreting consciousness, but also on the level of reality where they are exploited. Which leads to a critique of the idea of truth, in a second text: "'Interpretation,' the introduction of meaning—not 'explanation.'. . . There are no facts *[es gibt keinen Tatbestand]*" (no. 604). Here the word *interpretation* designates not only the meaning one *finds* in a thing, its interpretation, but also the fact of interpreting it, that is, the meaning one *gives* it.

abstract painter than Cézanne. The landscape around Aix is recognizable, only it is endowed with a violent emotional charge; it seems to be emerging from an earthquake. All the objects, human beings included, are transcribed here in an abstract spectrum of colored relations in which the painter's touch obscures their practical identity[16] and in which their individuality and their limits are blurred. After these thirty-seven pages of positivism, let us reflect a moment on this world in which a faceless and perpetually agitated matter brings into being on its surface, at constantly shifting points, faces that are always different and that do not exist, in which everything is individual, so much so that nothing is.

Foucault is not seeking to reveal that a "discourse," or even a practice, exists: he says that no rationality exists. As long as we believe that "discourse" is an authority or an infrastructure, as long as we ask what relation of causality that authority may have to social or economic evolution, and whether Foucault does not do "idealist" history, we have not yet understood. Foucault's importance is precisely that he is not "doing" Marx or Freud: he is not a dualist, he does not claim to be contrasting reality with appearance, as rationalism does when all else fails, with the return of the repressed as the reward. Foucault, for his part, strips away the reassuring banalities, the natural objects in their horizon of promising rationality in order to restore to reality—the only reality, the unique reality, our reality—its irrational, "exceptional," uncanny historical originality. It is one thing to undress reality in this way in order to dissect it and explain it; it is something else again, something more naive, to think that one is discovering a second reality underneath, a second reality that explains the first and operates it by remote control. Is Foucault still a historian? There is no right or wrong answer to this question, since history is itself one of those false natural objects. History is what one makes of it. It has never stopped changing; it does keep its eye fixed on an eternal horizon. What Foucault does will be called history and, by the same token, will belong to history, if historians avail themselves of the gift he is offering and do not find it too unripe; in any event, the windfall will not remain unclaimed, for natural elasticity (also called will to power, but that expression is so equivocal . . .) abhors a vacuum.

---

16. See Kurt Badt, *Die Kunst Cézannes* (Munich, 1956), pp. 38, 121, 126, 129, 173; trans. Sheila Ann Ogilvie, under the title *The Art of Cézanne* (London, 1965).

Desire and Pleasure

Gilles Deleuze

Translated by Daniel W. Smith

A

One of the essential theses of *D. and P.*[1] concerned *dispositifs* of power.[2] It seems essential to me in three respects:

1) In itself and in relation to "leftism": the profound political novelty of this conception of power, which is opposed to every theory of the State.

2) In relation to Michel: since it allowed him to go beyond the duality of discursive formations and nondiscursive formations, which was still

---

This text was first published as Gilles Deleuze, "Désir et plaisir," *Magazine littéraire*, no. 325 (Oct. 1994): 57–65. All notes are added by the French editor and the translator.

1. See Michel Foucault, *Discipline and Punish: The Birth of the Prison*, trans. Alan Sheridan (New York, 1977).

2. I have left the terms *dispositif* (Foucault) and *agencement* (Deleuze) untranslated in the text, since neither has a suitable English equivalent. Brian Massumi has translated them, respectively, as *apparatus* and *assemblage;* see Gilles Deleuze and Félix Guattari, *A Thousand Plateaus: Capitalism and Schizophrenia*, trans. Brian Massumi (Minneapolis, 1987). *Agencement,* from the verb *agencer* (to put together, organize, order, lay out, arrange), is used to describe processes as diverse as the ordering of elements, the organization of a novel, the construction of a sentence, the arrangement of a collection, or the layout of an office or apartment. *Dispositif,* from the verb *disposer* (to arrange [flowers], to set [the table], to range [troops], and so on), is generally used to describe a mechanical device or apparatus, such as an alarm or a safety mechanism, and more particularly to describe a military plan of action (for example, *dispositif d'attaque*, "attack force"; *dispositif de défense*, "defense system"; *dispositif de combat*, "fighting plan"). Deleuze here compares his conception of *agencements* of desire to Foucault's conception of *dispositifs* of power, seeing the latter as a stratification of the former. In an important article written in 1988, Deleuze provides a more complete analysis of Foucault's concept of a *dispositif,* assigning it a greater extension than that allotted to it here; see Deleuze, "What Is a *Dispositif*?" in *Michel Foucault: Philosopher*, trans. Timothy J. Armstrong (New York, 1992), pp. 159–68.—TRANS.

present in *A. K.*, and to explain how the two types of formations are distributed or articulated segment by segment (without the one being reduced to the other or their resembling each other . . . etc.).[3] It is not a matter of suppressing the distinction but of finding a reason for their relations.

3) For a precise consequence: *dispositifs* of power operate neither through repression nor through ideology. Hence a rupture with an alternative that everyone had more or less accepted. In place of repression or ideology, *D. and P.* formulated a conception of normalization, and of disciplines.

B

This thesis concerning *dispostifs* of power seemed to me to move in two directions, in no way contradictory, but distinct. In both cases, these *dispositifs* were irreducible to a State apparatus. But according to one direction, they consisted of a diffuse and heterogenous multiplicity, "micro-*dispositifs*." According to another direction, they referred to a diagram, a kind of abstract machine immanent to the entire social field (hence panopticism, defined by the general function of seeing without being seen and applicable to any multiplicity). These were, so to speak, the two directions of microanalysis, both equally important, since the second showed that Michel was not satisfied with a "dissemination."

C

H. S. took a new step forward in relation to *D. and P.*[4] The point of view remains, precisely, neither repression nor ideology. But, to move quickly, *dispositifs* of power are no longer content to be normalized; they tend to be constitutive (of sexuality). They are no longer content to form knowledges; they are constitutive of truth (the truth of power). They no longer refer to "categories" that are, despite everything, negative (madness, delinquency as the object of confinement) but to a category that is said to be positive (sexuality). This latter point is confirmed by the interview in *La Quinzaine littéraire*.[5] In this respect, I believe there is a new move forward in the analyses of *H. S.* The danger is, Is Michel reverting

3. See Foucault, *The Archaeology of Knowledge*, trans. A. M. Sheridan Smith (New York, 1972).

4. See Foucault, *The History of Sexuality: An Introduction*, trans. Robert Hurley (New York, 1978).

5. See Lucette Finas, "Les Rapports de pouvoir passent à l'intérieur des corps," interview with Foucault, *La Quinzaine littéraire*, no. 247 (1–15 Jan. 1977): 5; rpt. in Foucault, *Dits et écrits*, ed. Daniel Defert and François Ewald, 4 vols. (Paris, 1994), 3:228–36.

to an analogue of the "constituting subject," and why does he feel the need to resurrect the truth, even if he creates a new concept for it? These are not my own questions, but I think these two false questions will be asked as long as Michel has not explained himself further.

D

For myself, a first question concerns the nature of the microanalysis that Michel worked out in *D. and P.* The difference between *micro* and *macro* was obviously not one of size, in the sense that micro-*dispositifs* would concern small groups (the family is no less extended than any other formation). Nor is it a question of an extrinsic dualism, since there are micro-*dispositifs* immanent to the State apparatus, and the segments of the State apparatus also penetrate the micro-*dispositifs*—a complete immanence of the two dimensions. Must we understand the difference, then, to be one of scale? One paragraph of *H. S.* explicitly refuses this interpretation.[6] But this paragraph seems to make the macro refer to the strategic model, and the micro to the tactical model. This makes me uncomfortable, since micro-*dispositifs* seem to me to have an entirely strategic dimension in Michel's work (especially if one takes into account the diagram from which they are inseparable). Another direction would be that of "relations of force" as determining the micro; see in particular the interview in *La Quinzaine.* But Michel, I believe, has not yet developed this point: his original conception of relations of force, what he calls a *rapport de force,* must be a concept as new as the others.

In any case, there is a difference in kind, a heterogeneity, between the micro and the macro. This in no way excludes the immanence of the two. But in the end, my question would be this: Does this difference in kind still allow us to talk about *dispositifs* of power? The notion of the State is not applicable at the level of a microanalysis, since, as Michel says, it is not a matter of miniaturizing the State. But is the notion of power still applicable? Is it not itself the miniaturization of a global concept?

Here I come to my first difference with Michel. If I speak, with Félix,[7] of the *agencement* of desire, it is because I am not sure that micro-*dispositifs* can be described in terms of power. For myself, an *agencement* of desire implies that desire is never either a "natural" or a "spontaneous" determination. For example, feudalism is an *agencement* that brings about new relations with the animal (the horse), with the earth, with deterritorialization (the knight's journey, the Crusades), with women (courtly love), . . . etc. Completely mad *agencements,* but always historically attributable. For my part, I would say that desire circulates in this *agencement* of

6. See Foucault, *The History of Sexuality,* pp. 99–100.
7. The reference is obviously to Félix Guattari.

heterogenous elements, in this type of "symbiosis": desire is one and the same thing as a determined *agencement,* a cofunctioning. Of course an *agencement* of desire will include *dispositifs* of power (for example, feudal powers), but they must be situated among the different components of the *agencement.* On a first axis, one can distinguish within *agencements* of desire states of things and enunciations (which would conform to the two types of formations or multiplicities according to Michel). On another axis, one could distinguish the territorialities or reterritorializations and the movements of deterritorialization that an *agencement* entails (for example, all the movements of deterritorialization that the Church brings about, knighthood, peasantry). *Dispositifs* of power would emerge wherever reterritorializations, even abstract ones, are brought about. *Dispositifs* of power would then be a component of *agencements.* But the *agencements* would also be composed of points of deterritorialization. In short, it is not the *dispositifs* of power that assemble *[agenceraient],* nor would they be constitutive; it is rather the *agencements* of desire that would spread throughout the formations of power following one of their dimensions. This is what allows me to respond to the question, necessary for myself, not necessary for Michel: How can power be desired? The first difference, for me, would thus be that power is an affection of desire (it being given that desire is never a "natural reality"). All this is very approximate; there are more complicated relationships between the two movements of deterritorialization and reterritorialization than those I am giving here. But it is in this sense that desire seems to me to be primary and to be the element of a microanalysis.

E

I continue to follow Michel on a point that seems to me to be fundamental: neither ideology nor repression (for example, statements, or rather enunciations, have nothing to do with ideology). The *agencements* of desire have nothing to do with repression. But obviously, for *dispositifs* of power, I do not have Michel's firmness; I become rather vague, given the ambiguous status they have for me. In *D. and P.,* Michel says that they normalize and discipline; I would say that they recode and reterritorialize (I suppose that, here again, there is more than a distinction of words). But given my primacy of desire over power, or the secondary character that *dispositifs* of power have for me, their operations retain a repressive effect, since they crush not desire as a natural given but the cutting edges of *agencements* of desire. I take one of the most beautiful theses of *H. S.:* the *dispositif* of sexuality reduces sexuality to sex (to the difference between the sexes . . . etc., and psychoanalysis is full of this reductionism). I see there an effect of repression, precisely at the frontier of the micro and the macro: sexuality, as a historically variable and determinable *agencement* of desire, with its cutting edges of deterritorialization, flux, and combinations, will be reduced to a molar instance, "sex," and even if the methods of this reduction are not repressive, the (nonideological) effect is repressive, insofar as the *agencements* are broken not only in their potentialities but in their microreality. Then they can no longer exist except as phantasms, which change and divert them completely, or as shameful things, . . . etc. A small problem that greatly interests me: why certain "disturbed" people are more susceptible to shame, and even dependent on shame, than others (the enuretic or the anoretic, for example, are hardly susceptible to shame at all). I thus have need of a certain concept of repression, not in the sense that repression would be brought to bear on a spontaneity, but because collective *agencements* would have many dimensions, and *dispositifs* of power would be only one of these dimensions.

F

Another fundamental point: I believe that the thesis "neither repression—nor ideology" has a correlate, and perhaps itself depends upon this correlate. A social field is not defined by its contradictions. The notion of contradiction is a global and inadequate one that already implies a strong complicity among the "contradictories" in *dispositifs* of power (for example, the two classes, the bourgeoisie and the proletariat). In fact, it seems to me that another great novelty of Michel's conception of power would be: a society does not contradict itself, or rarely. But his response is: it is strategized, it strategizes. I find that very beautiful; I see clearly the immense difference (strategy versus contradiction); I would have to reread Clausewitz in this regard. But I am not completely at ease with this idea.

I would say, for my part, that a society, a social field, does not contradict itself, but what is primary is that it takes flight; it first of all flees in every direction; it is lines of flight that are primary (even if *primary* is not chronological). Far from lying outside the social field or emerging from it, lines of flight constitute its rhizome or cartography. Lines of flight are the same thing as movements of deterritorialization: they imply no return to nature; they are points of deterritorialization in *agencements* of desire. What is primary in feudalism are the lines of flight it presupposes; the same holds for the tenth through twelfth centuries; the same for capitalism. Lines of flight are not necessarily "revolutionary"; on the contrary, they are what the *dispositifs* of power will seal off, tie up. Around the eleventh century, numerous lines of deterritorialization began to move at the same time: the last invasions; the bands of pillagers; the deterritorialization of the Church; the emigrations of the peasants; the transformation of chivalry; the transformation of cities, which increasingly abandon territorial models; the transformation of money, which is injected into new circuits; the change of the feminine condition with the themes of courtly love, which even deterritorializes chivalrous love, . . . etc. Strategy will only be secondary in relation to lines of flight, to their conjunctions, their orientations, their convergences or divergences. Here again I come back to the primacy of desire, since desire is precisely in the lines of flight, the conjunction and dissociation of flows. It merges with them.

It seems to me, then, that Michel confronts a problem that does not have the same status for me. For if *dispositifs* of power are in some way constitutive, there can only be phenomena of "resistance" against them, and the question bears on the status of these phenomena. In effect, they themselves will neither be ideological nor antirepressive. Hence the importance of the two pages in *H. S.* where Michel says, don't make me say that these phenomena are a struggle. . . . But what status is he going to give to them? Here, several directions: (1) That of *H. S.*, in which the phenomena of resistance would be like the inverse image of the *dispositifs;* they would have the same characters, diffusion, heterogeneity, . . . etc.; they would be "vis-à-vis."[8] But this direction appears to me to block the exits as much as it opens one up. (2) The direction of the interview in *Politique-Hebdo:* if *dispositifs* of power are constitutive of truth, if there is a truth of power, it must have as a counterstrategy a kind of power of truth, against powers.[9] Hence the problem of the role of the intellectual in Michel and his manner of reintroducing the category of truth. Since he rejuvenates it completely by making it depend on power, will he find in this rejuvenation a material that can be turned against power? But here I do not see how. We must wait for Michel to explain this new conception of truth, at the level of his microanalysis. (3) A third direction would be pleasures, the body and its pleasures. Here again, the same wait for me. How do pleasures animate counterpowers, and how does he conceive of this notion of pleasure?

It seems to me that there are three notions that Michel takes in a completely new direction, but without having yet developed them: relations of force, truths, pleasures.

There are certain problems I face that Michel does not because they are resolved in advance by his own research. Conversely, I tell myself, for some encouragement, that there are other problems I do not face, which of necessity he must confront because of his theses and sentiments. Lines of flight and movements of deterritorialization, as collective historical determinations, do not seem to me to have any equivalent in Michel. For myself, the status of phenomena of resistance is not a problem; since lines of flight are primary determinations, since desire assembles the social

8. See Foucault, *The History of Sexuality,* pp. 95–97.
9. See Foucault, "La Fonction politique de l'intellectuel," *Politique-Hebdo,* 29 Nov.–5 Dec. 1976, pp. 31–33; rpt. in *Dits et écrits,* 3:109–14.

field, it is rather the *dispositifs* of power that are both produced by these *agencements* and crushed or sealed off by them. I share Michel's distaste for those who consider themselves marginals; the romanticism of madness, delinquency, perversion, and drugs is less and less bearable for me. But for me, lines of flight, that is, *agencements* of desire, are not created by marginals. On the contrary, they are objective lines that cut across a society, and on which marginals install themselves here and there in order to create a buckle, a whirl, a recoding. I therefore have no need for the status of phenomena of resistance; if the first given of a society is that everything takes flight, then everything in it is deterritorialized. Hence the status of the intellectual, and the political problem will not be the same theoretically for Michel and for myself (I will try to say below how I view this difference).

G

The last time we saw each other, Michel told me, with much kindness and affection, something like, I cannot bear the word *desire;* even if you use it differently, I cannot keep myself from thinking or living that desire = lack, or that desire is repressed. Michel added, whereas myself, what I call pleasure is perhaps what you call desire; but in any case I need another word than *desire*.

Obviously, once again, this is more than a question of words. Because for my part I can scarcely tolerate the word *pleasure*. But why? For me, desire implies no lack; neither is it a natural given. It is an *agencement* of heterogenous elements that function; it is process as opposed to structure or genesis; it is affect as opposed to sentiment; it is "*haec*-eity" (the individuality of a day, a season, a life) as opposed to subjectivity; it is an event as opposed to a thing or person. And above all, it implies the constitution of a plane of immanence or a "body without organs," which is defined solely by zones of intensity, thresholds, gradients, flows. This body is as much biological as it is collective and political; the *agencements* of desire are made and unmade upon it, and it supports the cutting edges of deterritorialization or the lines of flight of the *agencements*. It varies (the body without organs of feudalism is not the same as that of capitalism). If I call it the body without organs, it is because it is opposed to all the strata of organization—those of the organism, but also the organization of power. It is the totality of the organizations of the body that will break apart the plane or the field of immanence and impose another type of "plane" on desire, in each case stratifying the body without organs.

If I say all this rather confusedly, it is because there are several problems that arise for me in relation to Michel: (1) I cannot give any positive value to pleasure because pleasure seems to me to interrupt the immanent process of desire; pleasure seems to me to be on the side of strata and organization; and it is in one and the same movement that desire is subject to the law from within and scanned by pleasures from without; in both cases, there is the negation of the field of immanence proper to desire. I tell myself that it is not by chance that Michel attaches a certain importance to Sade, and myself on the contrary to Masoch. It would not be enough to say that I am masochistic, and Michel sadistic. That would be nice, but it's not true. What interests me in Masoch are not the pains but the idea that pleasure interrupts the positivity of desire and the constitution of its field of immanence (just as, or rather in a different manner, in courtly love there is the constitution of a field of immanence or a body without organs in which desire lacks nothing and refrains as long as possible from the pleasures that would interrupt its processes). Pleasure seems to me to be the only means for a person or a subject to "find itself again" in a process that surpasses it. It is a reterritorialization. And from my point of view, desire is related to the law of lack and to the norm of pleasure in the same manner.

2) On the other hand, Michel's idea that *dispositifs* of power have an immediate and direct relationship is essential. But, for me, this is because they impose an organization on the body. Whereas the body without organs is the locus or agent of deterritorialization (and hence the plane of immanence or desire), every organization—the entire system of what Michel calls biopower—brings about reterritorializations of bodies.

3) Could I think of equivalences of this type: what for me is the body without organs corresponds to what for Michel is "body-pleasures"? Can I relate the "body-flesh" distinction, of which Michel spoke to me, to the "body without organs–organization" distinction? Very important paragraph in *H. S.,* on life as giving a possible status to forces of resistance.[10] For me, this life, of which Lawrence spoke, is not at all nature; it is exactly the variable plane of immanence of desire, which passes through every determined *agencement.* Conception of desire in Lawrence, in relationship to positive lines of flight. (Small detail: the way Michel makes use of Lawrence at the end of *H. S.* is the opposite of the way I make use of him.)

H

Has Michel advanced the problem that concerned us: to maintain the rights of a microanalysis (diffusion, heterogeneity, fragmentary character) but at the same time to maintain a kind of principle of unification that is not of the "State," "party," totalization, or representation type?

First of all, on the side of power itself, I return to the two directions of *D. and P.*: on the one hand, the diffuse and fragmentary character of micro-*dispositifs,* but also, on the other hand, the diagram or abstract ma-

10. See Foucault, *The History of Sexuality,* pp. 144–45.

chine that covers the whole of the social field. There is a problem that still remains in *D. and P.*, it seems to me: the relationship between these two instances of microanalysis. I believe that the question changes slightly in *H. S.:* here, the two directions of microanalysis are microdisciplines on the one hand and biopolitical processes on the other.[11] This is what I meant in point C of these notes. Now the point of view in *D. and P.* suggested that the diagram, which is irreducible to the global instance of the State, perhaps brings about a micro-unification of the small *dispositifs*. Must we understand now that it is biopolitical processes that would assume this function? I confess that the notion of the diagram appears to me to be very rich; will Michel meet up with it again on this new terrain?

But on the side of lines of resistance, or what I call lines of flight: How should we conceive of the relations or conjugations, the conjunctions, the processes of unification? I would say that the collective field of immanence in which *agencements* are made at a given moment, and where they trace their lines of flight, also have a veritable diagram. It is necessary then to find the complex *agencement* capable of actualizing this diagram, by bringing about the conjunction of lines or points of deterritorialization. It is in this sense that I spoke of a war machine, which is completely different from a State apparatus and from military institutions, but also from *dispositifs* of power. We would thus have, on the one hand, a State-diagram of power (the State being the molar apparatus that actualizes the microelements of the diagram as a plane of organization); on the other hand, the war machine–diagram of lines of flight (the war machine being the *agencement* that actualizes the microelements of the diagram as the plane of immanence). I will stop at this point, since this would bring into play two types of very different planes—a kind of transcendent plane of organization over against the immanent plane of *agencements*—and we would fall once again into the preceding problems. And here I do not know how to situate myself in relation to Michel's present research.

(Addition: what interests me in the two opposed states of the plane or diagram is their historical confrontation, and the very diverse forms under which it takes place. In one case, we have a plane of organization and development, which is hidden by nature, but which brings into view everything that is visible; in the other case, we have a plane of immanence, where there is no longer anything but speeds and slownesses, no development, and where everything is seen, heard, . . . etc. The first plane should not be confused with the State, but is linked to it; the second on the contrary is linked to a war machine, to a reverie of the war machine. At the level of nature, for example, Cuvier, but also Goethe, conceived of the first type of plane. Hölderlin, in *Hypérion,* but even more so Kleist, conceived of the second type. Suddenly, here are two types of intellectuals, and what Michel says in this respect should be compared

11. See ibid., pp. 139–41.

with what he says on the position of the intellectual. Or in music, the two conceptions of the sonorous plane confront each other. The power-knowledge link, as Michel has analyzed it, could be explained in this way: powers imply a plane-diagram of the first type [for example, the Greek city and Euclidean geometry]. But conversely, on the side of counterpowers and more or less in relation with the war machines, there is the other type of plane, and kinds of "minor" knowledges [Archimedean geometry, or the geometry of the cathedrals that the State will fight against]. Is this a form of knowledge characteristic of the lines of resistance, which does not have the same form as the other form of knowledge?)

FOUCAULT AND THE ANCIENTS

Introductory Remarks to Pierre Hadot

Arnold I. Davidson

Pierre Hadot's "Forms of Life and Forms of Discourse in Ancient Philosophy," his inaugural lecture to the chair of the History of Hellenistic and Roman Thought at the Collège de France, gives an overview of the major themes and preoccupations of his many writings and gives some indication of the historical scope of his work. This lecture also illuminates the methodological problems one faces in studying the history of thought, especially problems concerning the evolution, reinterpretation, and even misunderstanding of the meaning and significance of philosophical terminology. In this brief introduction, I can do no more than attempt to provide a context for Hadot's inaugural lecture, by way of summary of his major work, *Exercices spirituels et philosophie antique,*[1] and, more specifically, to sketch the profound importance that Hadot's writings had for the last works of Michel Foucault.

Hadot's focus on the notion of spiritual exercises in ancient philosophy is meant to emphasize, in the first place, that in the ancient schools of thought philosophy was a way of life. Philosophy presented itself as a "mode of life, as an act of living, as a way of being" (*ES,* p. 221). The lesson of ancient philosophy consisted in "an invitation for each man to transform himself. Philosophy is conversion, transformation of the way of being and the way of living, the quest for wisdom" (*ES,* p. 227). Philosophy, so understood to be a form of life, required exercises that were nei-

1. See Pierre Hadot, *Exercices spirituels et philosophie antique,* 2d ed. (Paris, 1987); hereafter abbreviated *ES;* all translations are my own. A shorter, first edition of this book was published in 1981. A much expanded English language edition of this book has been published as *Philosophy as a Way of Life,* trans. Michael Chase, ed. Arnold I. Davidson (Oxford, 1995).

ther simply exercises of thought nor even moral exercises, but rather, in the full sense of this term, *spiritual* exercises. Since they aimed at realizing a transformation of one's vision of the world and a metamorphosis of one's personality, these exercises had an existential value, not only a moral one. They did not attempt only to insure behavior in accordance with a code of good conduct but involved all aspects of one's being—intellect, imagination, sensibility, and will (see *ES*, pp. 13–15, 59–61). Spiritual exercises were thus exercises in learning how to live the philosophical life.

The figure of Socrates provides Hadot with the first clear illustration of the practice of spiritual exercises. A master of dialogue with others and of dialogue with himself, Socrates should be seen as a master of this practice of spiritual exercises. According to Hadot, a Socratic dialogue is a spiritual exercise practiced in common, and it incites one to give attention to oneself, to take care of oneself, through inner spiritual exercises. The Socratic maxim "know thyself" requires a relationship of the self to itself that "constitutes the basis of all spiritual exercise" (*ES*, p. 31). Every spiritual exercise is "dialogical" insofar as it is an "exercise of authentic presence," of the self to itself and of the self to others (*ES*, p. 34). Hadot quotes Victor Goldschmidt's remark, characterizing Platonic dialogues, that "'the dialogue intends to form more than to inform,'" to form the interlocutor and reader so as to lead him to conversion, to a transformation of his way of life (*ES*, pp. 35–36). In these Socratic and Platonic dialogues, what is most important is not the solution to a particular problem but the path traversed in arriving at this solution (see *ES*, p. 35). Hence, we understand the crucial significance of the dimension of the interlocutor. This essential dimension

> prevents the dialogue from being a theoretical and dogmatic account and forces it to be a concrete and practical exercise, because, to be precise, it is not concerned with the exposition of a doctrine, but with guiding an interlocutor to a certain settled mental attitude: it is a combat, amicable but real. We should note that this is what takes place in every spiritual exercise; it is necessary to make oneself change one's own point of view, attitude, set of convictions, therefore to dialogue with oneself, therefore to struggle with oneself. [*ES*, p. 34]

Hadot proceeds to show, in great detail, the central role of this spiritual combat with oneself, aimed at a total transformation of one's way of being, in both Stoicism and Epicureanism. For both of these philosophical schools, the principal cause of human suffering is the passions, for example, disorderly desires and exaggerated fears; and, therefore, philosophy is, in the first place, a therapeutics for the passions (see *ES,* pp. 16–17). In Stoicism, the fundamental spiritual attitude is that of attention *(prosochè),* which is a "continual vigilance . . . an always alert consciousness of oneself, a constant tension of spirit" (*ES,* p. 19). This vigilance allows the Stoic to keep the fundamental rule of life—the distinction between that which depends on us and that which does not depend on us—always ready to hand *(procheiron).* Stoic exercises of memorization and meditation are intended to insure that all of the events of one's life are viewed in the light of this attention to, this spiritual concentration on, the fundamental rule, which, as a result, will deliver us from the passions that do not depend on us. This accounts for the Stoic attention to the present moment, to his transformed attitude to the past and the future, which are not within our control.[2] Epicureanism also gives a very large place to the practice of spiritual exercises. But for the Epicurean, the therapeutics of the soul consists in "bringing the soul back from the worries of life to the simple joy of existing" (*ES,* p. 25). Along with exercises of meditation similar to those in Stoicism, the Epicurean must exercise, not the continual tension and vigilance of the Stoic, but a form of relaxation that detaches his thought from the vision of painful things and fixes his attention on pleasures. He must make "a deliberate choice, always renewed, for relaxation and serenity and for a profound gratitude towards nature and life, which, if we know how to find it, offers us unceasing pleasure and joy" (*ES,* p. 28). In Epicureanism, this pleasure itself is a spiritual exercise. According to Hadot, Stoicism and Epicureanism can be taken to correspond to two opposed, but inseparable, poles of our inner life— "tension and relaxation, duty and serenity, moral consciousness and the joy of existing" (*ES,* p. 57; see also p. 225). In antiquity, true philosophy is a spiritual exercise, and philosophical theories, either explicitly or implicitly, are placed in the service of a spiritual practice that expresses a particular existential attitude (see *ES,* pp. 51–52). The plurality of ancient schools allows us to compare the consequences of different possible fundamental rational attitudes (see *ES,* p. 225).

Throughout his studies, Hadot emphasizes further that, beginning with Plato, philosophy is also represented as an exercise and training for death. In the conflict between the universal rationality of the Logos and the changing appetites of the corporeal individual, the person who remains faithful to the Logos risks losing his life. The story of Socrates, writes Hadot, is one of death through fidelity to the immutable norms of the Logos (see *ES,* p. 37). Tracing this theme of the presentation of phil-

2. For a detailed discussion of the significance of the present moment in Stoic and Epicurean thought, as well as in Goethe, see Hadot, "'The Present Alone Is Our Joy': The Meaning of the Present Instant in Goethe and in Ancient Philosophy," *Diogenes,* no. 133 (1986): 60–82.

osophy as an "exercise for death" through Stoicism, Epicureanism, Plotinus, Neoplatonism, and early Christianity, Hadot shows that each philosophy, in its own way, linked this exercise to "the contemplation of the totality, to the elevation of thought, passing from individual and impassioned subjectivity to the objectivity of the universal perspective, that is to say, to the exercise of pure thought" (*ES*, pp. 41–42). It is in this perspective, moreover, that one must place ancient physics, itself a spiritual exercise that allowed one to see the human world "from above" (see *ES*, pp. 42–44).[3] Hadot concludes that "all of the contemplative and speculative work of the philosopher thus becomes a spiritual exercise in the degree to which, elevating thought to the perspective of the Whole, it liberates it from the illusions of individuality" (*ES*, p. 42).

The spiritual progress of philosophy towards wisdom brings about tranquility of the soul, self-sufficiency, and cosmic consciousness. These three essential aspects of the philosophical way of life all require the practice of spiritual exercises of self-transformation in order to be attained. Tranquility of the soul *(ataraxia)* results from the philosophical therapeutics intended to cure anxiety; self-sufficiency *(autarkeia)*, the state in which the self depends only on itself, demands a methodical transformation of oneself; cosmic consciousness is a kind of spiritual surpassing of oneself that requires a consciousness of being part of the cosmic whole (see *ES*, pp. 218–19, 231). Hadot repeatedly reminds us that each of these three goals is part of the philosophical way of life; they are not merely the objects of philosophical speculation and theory but must be exhibited directly in one's very mode of being. Hadot insists on the distinction, formulated by the Stoics but admitted implicitly by the majority of philosophers, between philosophical discourse (or the discourse on philosophy) and philosophy itself:

> According to the Stoics, the parts of philosophy, that is to say, physics, ethics, and logic, were in fact not the parts of philosophy itself, but the parts of philosophical discourse. They meant by that that, since it was a question of teaching philosophy, it was necessary to propose a theory of logic, a theory of physics, a theory of ethics. The requirements of discourse, both logical and pedagogical, obliged one to make these distinctions. But philosophy itself, that is to say, the mode of philosophical life is no longer a theory divided into parts, but a unique act that consists in *living* logic, physics, and ethics. One no longer then produces the theory of logic, that is, of speaking and of thinking properly, but one thinks and speaks properly; one no longer produces the theory of the physical world, but one contemplates the

3. For further development of this theme, see Hadot, "Histoire de la pensée hellénistique et romaine: La Physique comme exercice spirituel et le regard d'en haut," in *Annuaire du Collège de France, 1987–1988: Résumé des cours et travaux* (Paris, 1988), pp. 401–5.

cosmos; one no longer produces the theory of moral action, but one acts in a virtuous and just manner. [*ES,* pp. 219–20]

Hadot, furthermore, traces the reduction of philosophy to philosophical discourse beginning in the Middle Ages. He argues that, apart from the monastic use of the word *philosophia,* during the Middle Ages philosophy becomes a purely theoretical and abstract activity, no longer a way of life. Moreover, beside the absorption of philosophy by Christian theology, the teaching of philosophy in the modern university further obscures the distinction between philosophical discourse and philosophy as a way of life, to the extent that philosophy is evidently no longer a kind of life, "unless it is the kind of life of the professor of philosophy" (*ES,* pp. 56–57, 222–24). Of course, Hadot also notes certain aspects of the work of Descartes, Spinoza, Schopenhauer, Bergson, Nietzsche, Heidegger, and the existentialists that recover, by different means, some of the existential dimensions of the spiritual exercises of ancient philosophy (see *ES,* pp. 57, 223–24, 232). But it is clear that, in modern times, philosophical discourse has all but overtaken philosophy as a way of life. And this shift has had deep consequences for the conception and representation of philosophy. In ancient philosophy, it was "not only Chrysippus or Epicurus who are considered philosophers because they developed a philosophical discourse, but also every man who lives according to the precepts of Chrysippus or Epicurus" (*ES,* p. 225). Even someone who neither wrote nor taught anything was considered a philosopher, if his life was, for instance, perfectly Stoic. There were men who lived all of Stoicism, who spoke like Stoics and who saw the world like Stoics. They attempted to realize the ideal of Stoic wisdom, a certain way of being a man; their whole being, and not only their moral behavior, was involved in trying to live a particular kind of philosophical life. Such a way of life was the ancient embodiment of philosophy. "Ancient philosophy proposes an art of living to man; modern philosophy, on the contrary, presents itself above all as the construction of a technical language reserved for specialists" (*ES,* p. 225).

By focusing on the *askesis* of philosophy, on the practice of spiritual exercises, and by linking this practice to a specific representation of the goals and motivations of philosophy, Hadot forces us to rethink our own modern presumptions in reading ancient texts (see *ES,* pp. 52, 56–57, 222). But Hadot's interest in ancient spiritual exercises is not merely a literary or historical one, since he recognizes in this work of the self on itself an essential aspect of the philosophical life: "philosophy is an art of life, a style of life that engages the whole of existence" (*ES,* p. 230). This combination of overarching philosophical interest with the detailed historical and literary study of ancient philosophy also aptly characterizes the last published works of Michel Foucault, not only his last two books,

The Use of Pleasure and *The Care of the Self,* but a series of related essays that deal with both ancient philosophy and early Christianity.[4] Indeed, in order fully to understand Foucault's motivations and his object of study, one must take into account the way in which Hadot's work on ancient spiritual exercises helped to form his entire project. I do not think that it is an exaggeration to claim that Foucault's study of ancient sexual behavior is guided or framed in terms of Hadot's notion of spiritual exercises, that Foucault's aim is to link the practices of the self exhibited in the domain of sexual behavior to the spiritual training and exercise that govern the whole of one's existence.[5] In ancient thought, governing one's sexual practices was one aspect of that governing of oneself that was a goal of spiritual *askesis.*

We know that Foucault first approached Hadot at the end of 1980 and recommended that Hadot present his candidacy for election to the Collège de France. By this time, Foucault had already been a careful reader of Hadot's work, including his major essay on spiritual exercises originally published in 1977 and reprinted as the first chapter of *Exercices spirituels et philosophie antique* (see *ES,* p. 229). Although there are important differences of interpretation and emphasis, both philosophical and historical, between Hadot and Foucault, differences that deserve their own separate study, I want here simply to indicate the basic convergence of interest that links their work. By understanding Foucault's debt to Hadot, one is, in my opinion, better able to understand the point of his last works. The introduction to *The Use of Pleasure,* which effectively serves as an introduction to both this volume and *The Care of the Self,* sets forth Foucault's intentions in undertaking his study of ancient sexual practices. Foucault wanted to isolate the component of morality that he called "ethics" or the self's relationship to itself. Distinct from the study of codes of moral behavior, Foucault wanted to write a history of "ethics," which he also regularly called "ascetics," "understood as a history of the forms of moral subjectivation and of the practices of the self that are meant to insure it."[6] Foucault thought of the self's relationship to itself as having four main aspects: the ethical substance, that part of oneself that is taken to be the relevant domain for ethical judgment; the mode of subjection, the way in which the individual establishes his relation to moral obligations and rules; the self-forming activity or ethical work that

4. See Michel Foucault, *The Use of Pleasure* and *The Care of the Self,* vols. 2 and 3 of *The History of Sexuality,* trans. Robert Hurley (New York, 1985 and 1986) and *Résumé des cours, 1970–82* (Paris, 1989). The relevant courses are from 1979–80, 1980–81, and 1981–82; "The Battle for Chastity," in *Western Sexuality: Practice and Precept in Past and Present Times,* ed. Philippe Ariès and André Béjin (Oxford, 1985); "L'Écriture de soi," *Corps écrit,* no. 3 (1983): 3–23; and *Technologies of the Self: A Seminar with Michel Foucault,* ed. Luther H. Martin, Huck Gutman, and Patrick H. Hutton (Amherst, Mass., 1988).

5. See Foucault, "Subjectivité et vérité, 1980–81," *Résumé des cours, 1970–82,* pp. 136–39.

6. Foucault, *The Use of Pleasure,* p. 29; hereafter abbreviated *UP.*

one performs on oneself in order to transform oneself into an ethical subject; and, finally, the telos, the mode of being at which one aims in behaving ethically.[7] As Foucault summarizes his intention, it is to study

> a process in which the individual delimits that part of himself that will form the object of his moral practice, defines his position relative to the precept he will follow, and decides on a certain mode of being that will serve as his goal. And this requires him to act upon himself, to undertake to know himself, to monitor, test, improve, and transform himself. [*UP,* p. 28; translation slightly modified]

We can recognize here Foucault's appropriation of Hadot's framework for interpreting ancient thought. In Hadot's terminology, Foucault's aim is to isolate those spiritual exercises, which cannot be reduced to a code of good conduct, whose aim is the exercise of wisdom, the philosophical way of life. And parallel to Hadot's argument that these spiritual exercises gradually became almost eclipsed by a conception of philosophy as an abstract, theoretical activity, so Foucault, on a different level, argued that codes of behavior gradually came to be emphasized at the expense of forms of subjectivation. Foucault singled out classical Greek, Hellenistic, and Roman philosophy as places where these elements of *askesis* were most emphasized, were strongest and most dynamic (see *UP,* pp. 29–30). Hadot's notion of spiritual exercises makes it possible to see how the history of ethics can be, in certain historical periods, a history of *askesis,* and how the occlusion of this dimension of the philosophical life is tied to changing representations of philosophy itself. Foucault, like all original and creative thinkers, developed his thought within a very specific context of filiation. If, as is now widely recognized, the work of Georges Canguilhem is indispensable to understanding the early Foucault, the work of Pierre Hadot is crucial to understanding his last writings.[8] But what Hadot has done, beyond his influence on any particular thinkers, is to open up dimensions of ancient philosophy we have typically overlooked or forgotten. Thus, he has rediscovered and reconceptualized the sig-

7. See *UP,* pp. 26–28. See also Foucault, "On the Genealogy of Ethics: An Overview of Work in Progress," *The Foucault Reader,* ed. Paul Rabinow (New York, 1984), pp. 340–72. I have discussed Foucault's conception of ethics at greater length in my "Archaeology, Genealogy, Ethics," in *Foucault: A Critical Reader,* ed. David Couzens Hoy (Oxford, 1986), pp. 221–33.

8. On Foucault's relation to Canguilhem, see Gary Gutting, *Michel Foucault's Archaeology of Scientific Reason* (Cambridge, 1989). Of course, I do not want to underestimate other profound influences on Foucault's last works, especially the writings of Paul Veyne. But Hadot's relation to Foucault has been much less appreciated, and never, to my knowledge, discussed in detail. Furthermore, his influence on Foucault seems to me no less significant than the influence, frequently acknowledged, of Veyne. I have examined the relationship among Hadot, Foucault, Veyne, and Georges Dumézil at greater length in Davidson, "Ethics as Ascetics: Foucault, the History of Ethics, and Ancient Thought," in *Foucault and the Writing of History,* ed. Jan Goldstein (Oxford, 1994), pp. 63–80.

nificance of ancient philosophy for our present moment in philosophy's unfolding history. As he has written:

> And I consider as a sign of the times the fact, to my eyes unexpected and bewildering, that at the close of the twentieth century, Foucault, myself, and certainly many others at the same time as us, at the end of totally different itineraries, would have encountered each other in this living rediscovery of ancient experience. [*ES*, p. 233]

Forms of Life and Forms of Discourse in Ancient Philosophy

Pierre Hadot

Translated by Arnold I. Davidson and Paula Wissing

Mr. Administrator,
Dear colleagues,
Ladies and Gentlemen,

"Each one of you expects two things from me on the occasion of this inaugural lecture: first of all, that I express my thanks to those who made my presence here possible and second, that I present the method that I will use to carry out the task entrusted to me."[1] Petrus Ramus, who held the chair in rhetoric and philosophy at the Collège Royal, opened his inaugural lecture, delivered in Latin, with words to this effect on 24 August 1551, only twenty years after the founding of this institution. We see that the practice of giving this lecture dates back more than four hundred years and that even at that time its major themes were already set. And I in turn will remain faithful to this venerable tradition today.

More than a year has gone by already, dear colleagues, since you decided to create a chair in the History of Hellenistic and Roman Thought. Shortly thereafter you honored me by entrusting it to me. How, without being awkward or superficial, can I express the extent of my gratitude and my joy at the confidence you have shown toward me?

I am able to see in your decision a reflection of that freedom and

Delivered as the inaugural lecture to the chair of the History of Hellenistic and Roman Thought, Collège de France, Friday, 18 February 1983. © 1983 by The Collège de France.

1. Petrus Ramus, *Regii Eloquentiae Philosophiaeque Professoris, Oratio Initio Suae Professionis Habita* (Paris, 1551). See Walter J. Ong, *Ramus and Talon Inventory: A Short-Title Inventory of the Published Works of Peter Ramus (1515–1572) and of Omer Talon (ca. 1510–1562) in Their Original and in Their Variously Altered Forms* (Cambridge, Mass., 1958), p. 158.

independence of mind that have traditionally characterized the great institution into which you have welcomed me. For, despite my election, I
possess few of the qualities that would usually attract notice, and the discipline I represent is not among those in fashion today. In a way I am what
the Romans called a *homo nouus,* as I do not belong to that intellectual
nobility one of whose principal titles is traditionally that of "former student of the École Normale Supérieure." Moreover, you certainly noticed
during my visits to you that I lack that tranquil authority conferred by
the use and mastery of the idioms currently spoken in the Republic of
Letters. My language, as you will again ascertain today, is not graced with
those mannerisms that now seem to be required when one ventures to
speak of the human sciences. However, several of you encouraged me to
present my candidacy, and during the traditional visits, which so enriched
me, I was extremely touched to find so much sympathy and interest, particularly among those of you who are specialists in the exact sciences, for
the field of research I have come before you to defend. In other words, I
believe I did not have to convince you—you were persuaded already—
of the need for the Collège to ensure a way to maintain the close bonds
between areas of teaching and research that are too often artificially separated: Latin and Greek, philology and philosophy, Hellenism and Christianity. I thus marveled to discover that at the end of the twentieth
century, when many of you on a daily basis employ technical procedures,
modes of reasoning, and representations of the universe of almost super-
human complexity that open a future to humanity we could not even
conceive of earlier, the ideal of humanism, which inspired the foundation
of the Collège de France, continues to retain for you, undoubtedly in a
more conscious and critical but also more vast, intense, and profound
form, all of its value and significance.

I spoke of a close connection between Greek and Latin, philology
and philosophy, Hellenism and Christianity. I believe that this formula-
tion corresponds exactly to the inspiration found in the teaching of Pierre
Courcelle, who was my colleague at the Fifth Section of the École Pratique des Hautes Études and to whom I wish to render homage today,
indeed, whom I succeed, if I may say so, in an indirect line, via the ap-
pointment of Rolf Stein. I believe that Pierre Courcelle, who was so bru-
tally taken from us, is intensely present in the hearts of many of us
tonight. For me he was a teacher who taught me much, but he was also a
friend who showed great concern for me. I will speak now only of the
scholar, to recall his immense output of truly great books, innumerable
articles, and hundreds of reviews. I do not know if the scope of this gigantic labor has been sufficiently measured. The first lines of his great work
Les Lettres grecques en Occident de Macrobe à Cassiodore give a clear idea of
the revolutionary direction his work had for his time. "A substantial book
on Hellenistic literature in the West from the death of Theodosius up to

the time of the Justinian reconquest may seem surprising," wrote Courcelle. First of all, it was surprising for a Latinist to be interested in Greek literature. However, as Courcelle noted, this Greek literature made possible the flowering of Latin literature and produced Cicero, who represented the most complete development of Greco-Roman culture at its apex, and it was this literature that nearly became a substitute for Latin when during the second century A.D. Latin was overshadowed by Greek as a literary language. However, it still must be stated and deplored that, despite Courcelle's initiative and example and owing to a prejudice that has not been totally overcome and that maintains the disastrous break made in French scholarship between Greek and Latin, what he had to say in 1943, forty years ago, is unfortunately still true today: "I know of no synthetic work that examines the Greek influence on the thought and culture of the Roman Empire." Once again it was surprising to see a Latinist devote such an important study to a later period and show that in the fifth and sixth centuries, a time of so-called decadence, Greek literature had undergone a remarkable renaissance, which, thanks to Augustine, Macrobius, Boethius, Martianus Capella, and Cassiodorus, was to make it possible for the European Middle Ages to maintain contact with Greek thought until the Arab translations made possible its rediscovery in richer sources. Again, it was surprising to see a philologist attack problems in the history of philosophy, showing the key influence exercised on Latin Christian thought by Greek and pagan Neoplatonism, not only by Plotinus but—this was an important detail—by his disciple Porphyry as well. Even more surprising, this philologist based his conclusions on a rigorously philological method. I mean that he was not content merely to reveal vague analogies between Neoplatonic and Christian doctrines or to evaluate influences and originalities in a purely subjective way—in a word, to rely on rhetoric and inspiration to establish his conclusions. No, following the example of Paul Henry, the learned editor of Plotinus who has also been a model of scientific method for me, Courcelle compared the texts. He discovered what anyone could have seen but no one had seen before him, that a certain text of Ambrose had been literally translated from Plotinus, that one of Boethius had been literally translated from a Greek Neoplatonic commentator on Aristotle. This method made it possible to establish indisputable facts, to bring the history of thought out of the vagueness and artistic indistinctness into which certain historians, even contemporaries of Courcelle, tended to relegate it.

If *Les Lettres grecques en Occident* provoked surprise, the *Recherches sur les "Confessions" de saint Augustin,* the first edition of which appeared in 1950, almost caused a scandal, particularly because of the interpretation Courcelle proposed for Augustine's account of his own conversion. Augustine recounts that as he was weeping beneath a fig tree, overcome with pressing questions and heaping bitter reproaches upon himself for his indecision, he heard a child's voice repeating, "Take it up and read." He then opened Paul's Epistles at random, as if he were drawing a lot, and read the passage that converted him. Alerted by his profound knowledge of Augustine's literary procedures and the traditions of Christian allegory, Courcelle dared to write that the fig tree could well have a purely symbolic value, representing the "mortal shadow of sin," and that the child's voice could also have been introduced in a purely literary way to indicate allegorically the divine response to Augustine's questioning. Courcelle did not suspect the uproar his interpretation would unleash. It lasted almost twenty years. The greatest names in international patristics entered the fray. Obviously I do not wish to rekindle the flames here. But I would like to stress how interesting his position was from a methodological point of view. Indeed it began with the very simple principle that a text should be interpreted in light of the literary genre to which it belongs. Most of Courcelle's opponents were victims of the modern, anachronistic prejudice that consists in believing that Augustine's *Confessions* is primarily an autobiographical account. Courcelle on the contrary had understood that the *Confessions* is essentially a theological work, in which each scene may take on a symbolic meaning. One is always surprised, for example, by the length of Augustine's account of his stealing pears while he was an adolescent. But this is explained by the fact that these fruits stolen from a garden become symbolically, for Augustine, the forbidden fruit stolen from the Garden of Eden, and the episode gives him the opportunity to develop a theological reflection on the nature of sin. In this literary genre, then, it is extremely difficult to distinguish between a symbolic enactment and an account of a historical event.

A very large part of Courcelle's work was devoted to tracing the fortunes of great themes such as "Know thyself" or great works such as Augustine's *Confessions* or Boethius's *Consolation of Philosophy* in the history of Western thought. Not the least original of his contributions, appearing in several of the major works he wrote from this perspective, was his association of literary study and iconographical inquiry, pertaining, for example, to illustrations produced throughout the ages for the *Confessions* or the *Consolation*. These iconographical studies, which are fundamental in reconstructing the history of religious mentalities and imagination, were all undertaken in collaboration with Mrs. Jeanne Courcelle, whose great knowledge of the techniques of art history and iconographic description greatly enriched her husband's work.

This all-too-brief recollection permits a glimpse, I hope, of the general development, the itinerary, of Courcelle's research. Starting from late antiquity, he was led to go back in time, especially in his book on the theme of "Know thyself," toward the philosophy of the imperial and Hellenistic period, and, on the other hand, to follow, across the years, ancient works, themes, and images as they evolved in the Western tradition. Finally, it is my hope that this history of Hellenistic and Roman thought I am now going to present to you reflects the spirit and the profound orientation of Courcelle's teaching and work.

According to the scheme given by Petrus Ramus, I have just spoken of what he himself called the *ratio muneris officiique nostri:* the object and method of the teaching entrusted to me. In the title of my chair, the word *thought* can seem very vague; indeed it can be applied to an immense and undefined domain ranging from politics to art, from poetry to science and philosophy, or religion and magic. In any event, the term invites one to make breathtaking excursions into the vast world of wondrous and fascinating works produced during the great period of the history of humanity that I propose to study. Perhaps we will accept this invitation from time to time, but our intention is to turn to the essential, to recognize the typical or the significant, to attempt to grasp the *Urphänomene,* as Goethe would say. And specifically, *philosophia,* the way the term was understood then, is one of the typical and significant phenomena of the Greco-Roman world. It is this above all which engages our attention. Nevertheless, we have preferred to speak of "Hellenistic and Roman thought" to reserve the right to follow this *philosophia* in its most varied manifestations and above all to eliminate the preconceptions the word *philosophy* may evoke in the modern mind.

"Hellenistic and Roman": these words themselves open an immense period before us. Our history begins with the highly symbolic event represented by Alexander's fantastic expedition and with the emergence of the world called Hellenistic, that is, with the emergence of this new form of Greek civilization beginning from the moment when Alexander's conquests and, in their wake, the rise of kingdoms extended this civilization into the barbarian world from Egypt to the borders of India, and then brought it into contact with the most diverse nations and civilizations. The result is a kind of distance, a historical distance, between Hellenistic thought and the Greek tradition preceding it. Our history then covers the rise of Rome, which will lead to the destruction of the Hellenistic kingdoms, brought to completion in 30 B.C. with Cleopatra's death. After that will come the expansion of the Roman empire, the rise and triumph of Christianity, the barbarian invasions, and the end of the Western empire.

We have just traversed a millennium. But from the standpoint of the history of thought, this long period must be treated as a whole. Indeed it is impossible to know Hellenistic thought without recourse to later documents, those of the imperial era and late antiquity, which reveal it to us; and it is equally impossible to understand Roman thought without taking its Greek background into account.

We need to recognize from the outset that almost all of Hellenistic literature, principally its philosophical productions, has disappeared. The

Stoic philosopher Chrysippus, to cite only one example among many, wrote seven hundred works, all of which are lost; only a few fragments have come down to us. We would undoubtedly have a very different idea of Hellenistic philosophy if this gigantic catastrophe had not occurred. How can we hope to compensate in some way for this irreparable loss? Obviously, there is the chance that discoveries might sometimes bring unknown texts to light. For example, in the mid–eighteenth century, an Epicurean library was found at Herculaneum. It contained texts of remarkable interest, not only for the knowledge it provided of that school but also regarding Stoicism and Platonism. Even today the Institute of Papyrology in Naples continues to mine, in an exemplary manner, these precious documents, endlessly improving both the texts and the commentaries. Another example: during the excavations, led for fifteen years by our colleague Paul Bernard in Aï Khanoun, near the border between Afghanistan and the U.S.S.R., to find the remains of a Hellenistic town of the kingdom of Bactrian, a philosophical text, unfortunately terribly mutilated, was discovered. The presence of such a document in such a place suffices, furthermore, to make one recognize the extraordinary expansion of Hellenism brought on by the Alexandrian conquests. Most likely it dates from the third or second century B.C. and represents a fragment, unfortunately very difficult to read, of a dialogue in which it is possible to recognize a passage inspired by the Aristotelian tradition.[2]

Except for finds of this type, which are extremely rare, one is obliged to exploit existing texts to their fullest, which often are of a much later date, in order to find information about the Hellenistic period. Obviously, it is necessary to begin with the Greek texts. Despite many excellent studies, much remains to be done in this area. For example, the collections of philosophical fragments that have come down to us need to be completed or updated. Hans von Arnim's collection of fragments from the earliest Stoics is exactly eighty years old and requires serious revision. Moreover, there exists no collection of fragments for the Academicians from the period that runs from Arcesilas to Philo of Larissa. On the other hand, mines of information, such as the works of Philo of Alexandria, Galen, Athenaeus, and Lucian or the commentaries on Plato and Aristotle written at the end of antiquity, have never been systematically made use of. But the Latin writers are also indispensable to this line of inquiry. For although the Latinists do not always agree, one has to admit that Latin literature, except for the historians (and even there!), is comprised largely of either translations, paraphrases, or imitations of Greek texts. Sometimes this is completely evident, for one can compare line by line and word for word the Greek originals that were translated or paraphrased by the Latin writers; sometimes the Latin writers themselves also quote

2. See Pierre Hadot and Claude Rapin, "Les Textes littéraires grecs de la Trésorerie d'Aï Khanoun," pt. I, *Études, Bulletin de Correspondance Héllenique* 111 (1987): 225–66.

their Greek sources; sometimes, finally, one can legitimately speculate about these influences with the help of reliable evidence. Thanks to the Latin writers, a large part of Hellenistic thought was preserved. Without Cicero, Lucretius, Seneca, or Aulus Gellius, many aspects of the philosophy of the Epicureans, Stoics, and Academicians would be irretrievably lost. The Latins of the Christian period are moreover just as precious: without Marius Victorinus, Augustine, Ambrose of Milan, Macrobius, Boethius, or Martianus Capella, how many Greek sources would be completely unknown to us! Two projects are thus inseparable: on the one hand, to explain Latin thought in light of its Greek background, and, on the other hand, to rediscover Greek thought, which has been lost to us, in the works of Latin writers. If both these tasks are to be carried out, any separation of Greek and Latin scholarship is totally impossible.

Here we are witness to the great cultural event of the West, the emergence of a Latin philosophical language translated from the Greek. Once again, it would be necessary to make a systematic study of the formation of this technical vocabulary that, thanks to Cicero, Seneca, Tertullian, Victorinus, Calcidius, Augustine, and Boethius, would leave its mark, by way of the Middle Ages, on the birth of modern thought. Can it be hoped that one day, with current technical means, it will be possible to compile a complete lexicon of the correspondences of philosophical terminology in Greek and Latin? Furthermore, lengthy commentaries would be needed, for the most interesting task would be to analyze the shifts in meaning that take place in the movement from one language to another. In the case of the ontological vocabulary the translation of *ousia* by *substantia,* for example, is justly famous and has again recently inspired some remarkable studies. This brings us once more to a phenomenon we discreetly alluded to earlier with the word *philosophia,* and which we will encounter throughout the present discussion: the misunderstandings, shifts or losses in meaning, the reinterpretations, sometimes even to the point of misreadings, that arise once tradition, translation, and exegesis coexist. So our history of Hellenistic and Roman thought will consist above all of recognizing and analyzing the evolution of meanings and significance.

It is precisely the need to explain this evolution that justifies our intention to study this period as a whole. Translations from the Greek into Latin are indeed only a particular aspect of this vast process of unification, that is, of hellenization, of the different cultures of the Mediterranean world, Europe, and Asia Minor that took place progressively from the fourth century B.C. up until the end of the ancient world. Hellenic thought had the strange capacity to absorb the most diverse mythical and conceptual themes. All the cultures of the Mediterranean world thus eventually expressed themselves in the categories of Hellenic thought, but at the price of important shifts in meaning that distorted the content of the myths, the values, and the wisdom of each culture, as well as the content of the Hellenic tradition itself. First the Romans, who were able to retain their language, then the Jews, and then the Christians fell into this sort of trap. Such was the price for the creation of the remarkable linguistic and cultural community that characterizes the Greco-Roman world. This process of unification also ensured a surprising continuity at the heart of philosophical and religious literary traditions.

This evolutionary continuity and progressive unification can be seen most remarkably in the area of philosophy. At the beginning of the Hellenistic period an extraordinary proliferation of schools emerged in the wake of the Sophist movement and the Socratic experience. But beginning with the third century B.C. a kind of sorting out occurred. In Athens the only schools to survive were those whose founders had thought to establish them as well-organized institutions: the school of Plato, the school of Aristotle and Theophrastus, the school of Epicurus, and that of Zeno and Chrysippus. In addition to these four schools there were two movements that are primarily spiritual traditions: skepticism and cynicism. After the institutional foundations of the schools in Athens collapsed at the end of the Hellenistic period, private schools and even officially subsidized teaching posts continued to be established throughout the Empire, and here the spiritual traditions of their founders were their reference points. Thus, for six centuries, from the third century B.C. until the third century A.D., we witness a surprising stability among the six traditions we have just mentioned. However, beginning with the third century A.D., Platonism, in the culmination of a movement underway since the first century, yet again at the price of subtle shifts in meaning and numerous reinterpretations, came to absorb both Stoicism and Aristotelianism in an original synthesis, while all the other traditions would become marginal. This unifying phenomenon is of major historical importance. Thanks to the writers of lesser antiquity but also to the Arab translations and the Byzantine tradition, this Neoplatonist synthesis will dominate all the thought of the Middle Ages and Renaissance and will provide, in some fashion, the common denominator among Jewish, Christian, and Moslem theologies and mysticisms.

We have just given a very brief outline of the main paths of the history of the philosophical schools of antiquity. But as a history of ancient *philosophia*, our history of Hellenistic and Roman thought is less focused on studying the doctrinal diversities and particularities of these different schools than it is on attempting to describe the very essence of the phenomenon of *philosophia* and finding the traits shared by the "philosopher" or by "philosophizing" in antiquity. We must try to recognize in some way the strangeness of this phenomenon, in order then to try to understand better the strangeness of its permanence throughout the whole history of Western thought. Why, you may ask, speak of strangeness when *philosophia* is a very general and common thing? Doesn't a philosophical quality color all of Hellenistic and Roman thought? Weren't generalization and popularization of philosophy characteristics of the time? Philosophy is found everywhere—in speeches, novels, poetry, science, art. However, we must not be deceived. These general ideas, these commonplaces that may adorn a literary work, and true "philosophizing" are separated by an abyss. Indeed, to be a philosopher implies a rupture with what the skeptics called *bios*, that is, daily life, when they criticized other philosophers for not observing the common conduct of life, the usual manner of seeing and acting, which for the skeptics consisted in respecting customs and laws, practicing a craft or plying a trade, satisfying bodily needs, and having the faith in appearances indispensable to action. It is true that even while the skeptics chose to conform to the common conduct of life, they remained philosophers, since they practiced an exercise demanding something rather strange, the suspension of judgment, and aiming at a goal, uninterrupted tranquillity and serenity of the soul, that the common conduct of life hardly knew.

This very rupture between the philosopher and the conduct of everyday life is strongly felt by nonphilosophers. In the works of comic and satiric authors, philosophers were portrayed as bizarre, if not dangerous characters. It is true, moreover, that throughout all of antiquity the number of charlatans who passed themselves off as philosophers must have been considerable, and Lucian, for example, freely exercised his wit at their expense. Jurists too considered philosophers a race apart. According to Ulpian, in the litigation between professors and their debtors the authorities did not need to concern themselves with philosophers, for these people professed to despise money. A regulation made by the emperor Antonin the Pious on salaries and compensations notes that if a philosopher haggles over his possessions, he shows he is no philosopher. Thus philosophers are strange, a race apart. Strange indeed are those Epicureans, who lead a frugal life, practicing a total equality between the men and women inside their philosophical circle—and even between married women and courtesans; strange, too, those Roman Stoics who disinterestedly administer the provinces of the Empire entrusted to them and are the only ones to take seriously the laws promulgated against excess; strange as well this Roman Platonist, the Senator Rogatianus, a disciple of Plotinus, who on the very day he is to assume his functions as praetor gives up his responsibilities, abandons all his possessions, frees his slaves, and eats only every other day. Strange indeed all those philosophers whose behavior, without being inspired by religion, nonetheless completely breaks with the customs and habits of most mortals.

By the time of the Platonic dialogues Socrates was called *atopos*, that is, "unclassifiable." What makes him *atopos* is precisely the fact that he is a "philo-sopher" in the etymological sense of the word; that is, he is in love with wisdom. For wisdom, says Diotima in Plato's *Symposium*, is not a human state, it is a state of perfection of being and knowledge that can only be divine. It is the love of this wisdom, which is foreign to the world, that makes the philosopher a stranger in it.

So each school will elaborate its rational depiction of this state of perfection in the person of the sage, and each will make an effort to portray him. It is true that this transcendent ideal will be deemed almost inaccessible; according to some schools there never was a wise man, while others say that perhaps there were one or two of them, such as Epicurus, this god among men, and still others maintain that man can only attain this state during rare, fleeting moments. In this transcendent norm established by reason, each school will express its own vision of the world, its own style of life, and its idea of the perfect man. This is why in every school the description of this transcendent norm ultimately coincides with the rational idea of God. Michelet remarked very profoundly, "Greek religion culminated with its true god, the sage." We can interpret this remark, which Michelet does not develop, by noting that the moment philosophers achieve a rational conception of God based on the model of the sage, Greece surpasses its mythical representation of its gods. Of course, classical descriptions of the sage depict the circumstances of human life and take pleasure in describing how the sage would respond to this or that situation, but the beatitude the wise man resolutely maintains throughout his difficulties is that of God himself. Seneca asks what the sage's life would be in solitude, if he were in prison or exile, or cast upon the shores of a desert island. And he answers that it would be the life of Zeus (that is, for the Stoics, the life of universal Reason), when, at the end of each cosmic period, after the activity of nature has ceased, he devotes himself freely to his thoughts; like Zeus the sage would enjoy the happiness of being self-sufficient. Thus the thoughts and will of the Stoic wise man completely coincide with the thoughts, will, and development of Reason immanent to the evolution of the Cosmos. As for the Epicurean sage, he, like the gods, watches the infinity of worlds arising out of atoms in the infinite void; nature is sufficient for his needs, and nothing ever disturbs the peace of his soul. For their part, the Platonic and Aristotelian sages raise themselves in subtly different ways, by their life of the mind, to the realm of the divine Mind itself.

Now we have a better understanding of *atopia,* the strangeness of the philosopher in the human world. One does not know how to classify him, for he is neither a sage nor a man like other men. He knows that the normal, natural state of men should be wisdom, for wisdom is nothing more than the vision of things as they are, the vision of the cosmos as it is in the light of reason, and wisdom is also nothing more than the mode of being and living that should correspond to this vision. But the philosopher also knows that this wisdom is an ideal state, almost inaccessible. For such a man, daily life, as it is organized and lived by other men, must necessarily appear abnormal, like a state of madness, unconsciousness, and ignorance of reality. And nonetheless he must live this life every day, in this world in which he feels himself a stranger and in which others perceive him to be one as well. And it is precisely in this daily life that he must seek to attain that way of life which is utterly foreign to the everyday world. The result is a perpetual conflict between the philosopher's effort to see things as they are from the standpoint of universal nature and the conventional vision of things underlying human society, a conflict between the life one should live and the customs and conventions of daily life. This conflict can never be totally resolved. The cynics, in their refusal of the world of social convention, opt for a total break. On the contrary, others, such as the skeptics, fully accept social convention, while keeping their inner peace. Others, the Epicureans for example, attempt to re-create among themselves a daily life that conforms to the ideal of wisdom. Others still, such as the Platonists and the Stoics, strive, at the cost of the greatest difficulties, to live their everyday and even their public lives in a "philosophical" manner. In any event, for all of them, the philosophical life will be an effort to live and think according to the norm of wisdom, it will be a movement, a progression, though a never-ending one, toward this transcendent state.

Each school, then, represents a form of life defined by an ideal of wisdom. The result is that each one has its corresponding fundamental inner attitude—for example, tension for the Stoics or relaxation for the Epicureans—and its own manner of speaking, such as the Stoic use of percussive dialectic or the abundant rhetoric of the Academicians. But above all every school practices exercises designed to ensure spiritual progress toward the ideal state of wisdom, exercises of reason that will be, for the soul, analogous to the athlete's training or to the application of a medical cure. Generally, they consist, above all, of self-control and meditation. Self-control is fundamentally being attentive to oneself: an unrelaxing vigilance for the Stoics, the renunciation of unnecessary desires for the Epicureans. It always involves an effort of will, thus faith in moral freedom and the possibility of self-improvement; an acute moral consciousness honed by spiritual direction and the practice of examining one's conscience; and lastly, the kind of practical exercises described with such remarkable precision particularly by Plutarch: controlling one's anger, curiosity, speech, or love of riches, beginning by working on what is easiest in order gradually to acquire a firm and stable character.

Of first importance is "meditation," which is the "exercise" of reason; moreover, the two words are synonymous from an etymological point of view. Unlike Buddhist meditation practices of the Far East, Greco-Roman philosophical meditation is not linked to a corporeal attitude but is a purely rational, imaginative, or intuitive exercise that can take extremely varied forms. First of all it is the memorization and assimilation of the fundamental dogmas and rules of life of the school. Thanks to this exercise, the vision of the world of the person who strives for spiritual progress will be completely transformed. In particular, philosophical meditation on the essential dogmas of physics, for example the Epicurean contemplation of the genesis of worlds in the infinite void or the Stoic contemplation of the rational and necessary unfolding of cosmic events, can lead to an exercise of the imagination in which human things appear of little importance in the immensity of space and time. It is necessary to try to have these dogmas and rules for living "ready to hand" if one is to be able to conduct oneself like a philosopher under all of life's circumstances. Moreover, one has to be able to imagine these circumstances in advance in order to be ready for the shock of events. In all the schools, for various reasons, philosophy will be especially a meditation upon death and an attentive concentration on the present moment in order to enjoy it or live it in full consciousness. In all these exercises, all the means obtainable by dialectic and rhetoric will be utilized to obtain the maximum effect. In particular, this consciously willed application of rhetoric explains the impression of pessimism that some readers believe they discern in the *Meditations* of Marcus Aurelius. All images are suitable for him if they strike the imagination and make the reader conscious of the illusions and conventions of mankind.

The relationship between theory and practice in the philosophy of this period must be understood from the perspective of these exercises of meditation. Theory is never considered an end in itself; it is clearly and decidedly put in the service of practice. Epicurus is explicit on this point: the goal of the science of nature is to obtain the soul's serenity. Or else, as among the Aristotelians, one is more attached to theoretical activity considered as a way of life that brings an almost divine pleasure and happiness than to the theories themselves. Or, as in the Academicians' school or for the skeptics, theoretical activity is a critical activity. Or, as among the Platonists, abstract theory is not considered to be true knowledge: as Porphyry says, "Beatific contemplation does not consist of the accumulation of arguments or a storehouse of learned knowledge, but in us theory must become nature and life itself." And, according to Plotinus, one cannot know the soul if one does not purify oneself of one's passions in order to experience in oneself the transcendence of the soul with respect to the body, and one cannot know the principle of all things if one has not had the experience of union with it.

To make possible these exercises in meditation, beginners are exposed to maxims or summaries of the principal dogmas of the school. Epicurus's *Letters*, which Diogenes Laertius preserved for us, are intended to play this role. To ensure that these dogmas have a great spiritual effectiveness, they must be presented in the form of short, striking formulae, as in Epicurus's *Principal Doctrines*, or in a rigorously systematic form, such as the *Letter to Herodotus* by the same author, which permitted the disciple to grasp in a kind of single intuition the essentials of the doctrine in order to have it more easily at hand. In this case the concern for systematic coherence was subordinated to spiritual effectiveness.

The dogmas and methodological principles of each school are not open to discussion. In this period, to philosophize is to choose a school, convert to its way of life, and accept its dogmas. This is why the core of the fundamental dogmas and rules of life for Platonism, Aristotelianism, Stoicism, and Epicureanism remained unchanged throughout antiquity. Even the scientists of antiquity always were affiliated with a philosophical school: the development of their mathematical and astronomical theorems changed nothing of the fundamental principles of the school to which they claimed allegiance.

This does not mean that theoretical reflection and elaboration are absent from the philosophical life. However, this activity never extended to the dogmas themselves or the methodological principles but rather to the ways of demonstrating and systematizing these dogmas and to secondary, doctrinal points issuing from them on which there was not unanimity in the school. This type of investigation is always reserved for the more advanced students, for whom it is an exercise of reason that strengthens them in their philosophical life. Chrysippus, for example, felt himself capable of finding the arguments justifying the Stoic dogmas established by Zeno and Cleanthes, which led him, moreover, to disagree with them not concerning these dogmas but on the way of establishing them. Epicurus, too, leaves the discussion and study of points of detail to the more advanced students, and much later the same attitude will be found in Origen, who assigns the "spiritual ones" the task of seeking, as he himself says, by way of exercise, the "hows" and "whys" and of discussing these obscure and secondary questions. This effort of theoretical reflection can result in the composition of enormous works.

Obviously, these systematic treatises and scholarly commentaries, such as Origen's treatise on *Principles* or Proclus's *Elements of Theology*, very legitimately attract the attention of the historian of philosophy. The study of the progress of thought in these great texts must be one of the principal tasks in a reflection on the phenomenon of philosophy. However, it must be recognized that generally speaking the philosophical works of Greco-Roman antiquity almost always perplex the contemporary reader. I do not refer only to the general public, but even to specialists in the field. One could compile a whole anthology of complaints made against ancient authors by modern commentators who reproach them for their bad writing, contradictions, and lack of rigor and coherence. Indeed, it is my astonishment both at these critics and at the universality and persistence of the phenomenon they condemn that inspires the reflections I have just presented, as well as those I wish to turn to now.

It seems to me, indeed, that in order to understand the works of the philosophers of antiquity we must take account of all the concrete conditions in which they wrote, all the constraints that weighed upon them: the framework of the school, the very nature of *philosophia,* literary genres, rhetorical rules, dogmatic imperatives, and traditional modes of reasoning. One cannot read an ancient author the way one does a contemporary author (which does not mean that contemporary authors are easier to understand than those of antiquity). In fact, the works of antiquity are produced under entirely different conditions than those of their modern counterparts. I will not discuss the problem of material support: the *volumen* or *codex,* each of which has its own constraints. But I do want to stress the fact that written works in the period we study are never completely free of the constraints imposed by oral transmission. In fact, it is an exaggeration to assert, as has still been done recently, that Greco-Roman civilization early on became a civilization of writing and that one can thus treat, methodologically, the philosophical works of antiquity like any other written work.

For the written works of this period remain closely tied to oral conduct. Often they were dictated to a scribe. And they were intended to be read aloud, either by a slave reading to his master or by the reader himself, since in antiquity reading customarily meant reading aloud, emphasizing the rhythm of the phrase and the sounds of the words, which the author himself had already experienced when he dictated his work. The ancients were extremely sensitive to these effects of sound. Few philosophers of the period we study resisted this magic of the spoken word, not even the Stoics, not even Plotinus. So if oral literature before the practice of writing imposed rigorous constraints on expression and obliged one to use certain rhythmic, stereotypic, and traditional formulas conveying images and thoughts independent, if one may say so, of the author's will, this phenomenon is not foreign to written literature to the degree that it too must concern itself with rhythm and sound. To take an extreme but very revealing example, the use of poetic meter in *De rerum natura* dictates the recourse to certain somewhat stereotypical formulas and keeps Lucretius from freely using the technical vocabulary of Epicureanism that he should have employed.

This relationship between the written and the spoken word thus explains certain aspects of the works of antiquity. Quite often the work proceeds by the associations of ideas, without systematic rigor. The work retains the starts and stops, the hesitations, and the repetitions of spoken discourse. Or else, after rereading what he has written, the author introduces a somewhat forced systematization by adding transitions, introductions, or conclusions to different parts of the work.

More than other literature, philosophical works are linked to oral transmission because ancient philosophy itself is above all oral in character. Doubtless there are occasions when someone was converted by reading a book, but one would then hasten to the philosopher to hear him speak, question him, and carry on discussions with him and other disciples in a community that always serves as a place of discussion. In matters of philosophical teaching, writing is only an aid to memory, a last resort that will never replace the living word.

True education is always oral because only the spoken word makes dialogue possible, that is, it makes it possible for the disciple to discover the truth himself amid the interplay of questions and answers and also for the master to adapt his teaching to the needs of the disciple. A number of philosophers, and not the least among them, did not wish to write, thinking, as did Plato and without doubt correctly, that what is inscribed in the soul by the spoken word is more real and lasting than letters drawn on papyrus or parchment.

Thus for the most part the literary productions of the philosophers are a preparation, extension, or echo of their spoken lessons and are marked by the limitations and constraints imposed by such a situation.

Some of these works, moreover, are directly related to the activity of teaching. They may be either a summary the teacher drafted in preparing his course or notes taken by students during the course, or else they may be texts written with care but intended to be read during the course by the professor or a student. In all these cases, the general movement of thought, its unfolding, what could be called its own temporality, is regulated by the temporality of speech. It is a very heavy constraint, whose full rigor I am experiencing today.

Even texts that were written in and for themselves are closely linked to the activity of teaching, and their literary genre reflects the methods of the schools. One of the exercises esteemed in the schools consists of discussing, either dialectically, that is, in the form of questions and answers, or rhetorically, that is, in a continuous discourse, what were called "theses," that is, theoretical positions presented in the form of questions: Is death an evil? Is the wise man ever angry? This provides both training in the mastery of the spoken word and a properly philosophical exercise. The largest portion of the philosophical works of antiquity, for example those of Cicero, Plutarch, Seneca, Plotinus, and more generally those classified by the moderns as belonging to what they called the genre of diatribe, correspond to this exercise. They discuss a specific question, which is posed at the outset of the work and which normally requires a yes or no answer. In these works, the course of thought consists in going back to general principles that have been accepted in the school and are capable of resolving the problem in question. This search to find principles to solve a given problem thus encloses thought within narrowly defined limits. Different works written by the same author and guided according to this "zetetic" method, "one that seeks," will not necessarily be coherent on all points because the details of the argument in each work will be a function of the question asked.

Another school exercise is the reading and exegesis of the authoritative texts of each school. Many literary works, particularly the long commentaries from the end of antiquity, are the result of this exercise. More generally, a large number of the philosophical works from that time utilize a mode of exegetical thinking. Most of the time, discussing a "thesis" does not consist in discussing the problem in itself but the meaning that one should give to Plato's or Aristotle's statements concerning this problem. Once this convention has been taken into account, one does in fact· discuss the question in some depth, but this is done by skillfully giving Platonic or Aristotelian statements the meanings that support the very solution one wishes to give to the problem under consideration. Any possible meaning is true provided it coheres with the truth one believes one has discovered in the text. In this way there slowly emerges, in the spiritual tradition of each school, but in Platonism above all, a scholasticism which, relying on argument from authority, builds up gigantic doctrinal edifices by means of an extraordinary rational reflection on the fundamental dogmas. It is precisely the third philosophical literary genre, the systematic treatise, that proposes a rational ordering of the whole of doctrine, which sometimes is presented, as in the case of Proclus, as a *more geometrico*, that is, according to the model of Euclid's *Elements*. In this case one no longer returns to the principles necessary to resolve a specific question but sets down the principles directly and deduces their consequences. These works are, so to speak, "more written" than the others. They often comprise a long sequence of books and are marked by a vast overarching design. But, like the *Summae theologicae* of the Middle Ages that they prefigure, these works must themselves also be understood from the perspective of dialectical and exegetical scholarly exercises.

Unlike their modern counterparts, none of these philosophical productions, even the systematic works, are addressed to everyone, to a general audience, but are intended first of all for the group formed by the members of the school; often they echo problems raised by the oral teaching. Only works of propaganda are addressed to a wider audience.

Moreover, while he writes the philosopher often extends his activity as spiritual director that he exercises in his school. In such cases the work may be addressed to a particular disciple who needs encouragement or who finds himself in a special difficulty. Or else the work may be adapted to the spiritual level of the addressees. Not all the details of the system can be explained to beginners; many details can be revealed only to those further along the path. Above all, the work, even if it is apparently theoretical and systematic, is written not so much to inform the reader of a doctrinal content but to form him, to make him traverse a certain itinerary in the course of which he will make spiritual progress. This procedure is clear in the works of Plotinus and Augustine, in which all the detours, starts and stops, and digressions of the work are formative elements. One must always approach a philosophical work of antiquity with this idea of spiritual progress in mind. For the Platonists, for example, even mathematics is used to train the soul to raise itself from the sensible to the intelligible. The overall organization of a work and its mode of exposition may always answer to such preoccupations.

Such then are the many constraints that are exercised on the ancient author and that often perplex the modern reader both with respect to what is said and the way in which it is said. Understanding a work of antiquity requires placing it in the group from which it emanates, in the tradition of its dogmas, its literary genre, and requires understanding its goals. One must attempt to distinguish what the author was required to say, what he could or could not say, and, above all, what he meant to say. For the ancient author's art consists in his skillfully using, in order to arrive at his goals, all of the constraints that weigh upon him as well as the models furnished by the tradition. Most of the time, furthermore, he uses not only ideas, images, and patterns of argument in this way but also texts or at least preexisting formulas. From plagiarism pure and simple to quotation or paraphrase, this practice includes—and this is the most characteristic example—the literal use of formulas or words employed by the earlier tradition to which the author often gives a new meaning adapted to what he wants to say. This is the way that Philo, a Jew, uses Platonic formulas to comment on the Bible, or Ambrose, a Christian, translates Philo's text to present Christian doctrines, the way that Plotinus uses words and whole sentences from Plato to convey his experience. What matters first of all is the prestige of the ancient and traditional formula, and not the exact meaning it originally had. The idea itself holds less interest than the prefabricated elements in which the writer believes he recognizes his own thought, elements that take on an unexpected meaning and purpose when they are integrated into a literary whole. This sometimes brilliant reuse of prefabricated elements gives an impression of "bricolage," to take up a word currently in fashion, not only among anthropologists but among biologists. Thought evolves by incorporating prefabricated and preexisting elements, which are given new meaning as they become integrated into a rational system. It is difficult to say what is most extraordinary about this process of integration: contingency, chance, irrationality, the very absurdity resulting from the elements used, or, on the contrary, the strange power of reason to integrate and systematize these disparate elements and to give them a new meaning.

An extremely significant example of this conferring of a new meaning can be seen in the final lines of Edmund Husserl's *Cartesian Meditations*. Summing up his own theory, Husserl writes, "The Delphic oracle γνῶθι σεαυτόν [know thyself] has acquired a new meaning. . . . One must first lose the world by the ἐποχή [for Husserl, the 'phenomenological bracketing' of the world], in order to regain it in a universal self-consciousness. *Noli foras ire*, says saint Augustine, *in te redi, in interiore hom-*

ine habitat veritas." This sentence of Augustine's, "Do not lose your way from without, return to yourself, it is in the inner man that truth dwells," offers Husserl a convenient formula for expressing and summarizing his own conception of consciousness. It is true that Husserl gives this sentence a new meaning. Augustine's "inner man" becomes the "transcendental ego" for Husserl, a knowing subject who regains the world in "a universal self-consciousness." Augustine never could have conceived of his "inner man" in these terms. And nonetheless one understands why Husserl was tempted to use this formula. For Augustine's sentence admirably summarizes the whole spirit of Greco-Roman philosophy that prepares the way for both Descartes's *Meditations* and Husserl's *Cartesian Meditations.* And by the same procedure of taking up such a formula again, we ourselves can apply to ancient philosophy what Husserl says of his own philosophy: the Delphic oracle "Know thyself" has acquired a new meaning. For all the philosophy of which we have spoken also gives a new meaning to the Delphic formula. This new meaning already appeared among the Stoics, for whom the philosopher recognizes the presence of divine Reason in the human self and who opposes his moral consciousness, which depends on him alone, to the rest of the universe. This new meaning appeared even more clearly among the Neoplatonists, who identify what they call the true self with the founding intellect of the world and even with the transcendent Unity that founds all thought and all reality. In Hellenistic and Roman thought this movement, of which Husserl speaks, is thus already outlined, according to which one loses the world in order to find it again in universal self-consciousness. Thus Husserl consciously and explicitly presents himself as the heir to the tradition of "Know thyself" that runs from Socrates to Augustine to Descartes. But that is not all. This example, borrowed from Husserl, better enables us to understand concretely how these conferrals of new meaning can be realized in antiquity as well. Indeed, the expression *in interiore homine habitat veritas,* as my friend and colleague Goulven Madec has pointed out to me, is an allusion to a group of words borrowed from chapter 3, verses 16 and 17, of Paul's letter to the Ephesians, from an ancient Latin version, to be exact, in which the text appears as *in interiore homine Christum habitare.* But these words are merely a purely material conjunction that exists only in this Latin version and do not correspond to the contents of Paul's thought, for they belong to two different clauses of the sentence. On the one hand, Paul wishes for *Christ to dwell in the heart* of his disciples through faith, and, on the other hand, in the preceding clause, he wishes for God to allow his disciples *to be strengthened* by the divine Spirit *in the inner man, in interiorem hominem,* as the Vulgate has it. So the earlier Latin version, by combining *in interiore homine* and *Christum habitare,* was either a mistranslation or was miscopied. The Augustinian formula, *in interiore homine habitat veritas,* is thus created from a group of words that do not represent a unified meaning in Saint Paul's text; but taken in itself, this group of words has a meaning for Augustine, and he explains it in the context of *De vera religione* where he uses it: the inner man, that is, the human spirit, discovers that what permits him to think and reason is the Truth, that is, divine Reason—that is, for Augustine, Christ, who dwells in, who is present within, the human spirit. In this way the formula takes on a Platonic meaning. We see how, from Saint Paul to Husserl, by way of Augustine, a group of words whose unity was originally only purely material, or which was a misunderstanding of the Latin translator, was given a new meaning by Augustine, and then by Husserl, thus taking its place in the vast tradition of the deepening of the idea of self-consciousness.

This example borrowed from Husserl allows us to touch on the importance of what in Western thought is called the *topos*. Literary theories use the term to refer to the formulas, images, and metaphors that forcibly impose themselves on the writer and the thinker in such a way that the use of these prefabricated models seems indispensable to them in order to be able to express their own thoughts.

Our Western thought has been nourished in this way and still lives off a relatively limited number of formulas and metaphors borrowed from the various traditions of which it is the result. For example, there are maxims that encourage a certain inner attitude such as "Know thyself"; those which have long guided our view of nature: "Nature makes no leaps," "Nature delights in diversity." There are metaphors such as "The force of truth," "The world as a book" (which is perhaps extended in the conception of the genetic code as a text). There are biblical formulas such as "I am who I am," which have profoundly marked the idea of God. The point I strongly wish to emphasize here is the following: These prefabricated models, of which I have just given some examples, were known during the Renaissance and in the modern world in the very form that they had in the Hellenistic and Roman tradition, and they were originally understood during the Renaissance and in the modern world with the very meaning these models of thought had during the Greco-Roman period, especially at the end of antiquity. So these models continue to explain many aspects of our contemporary thought and even the very significance, sometimes unexpected, that we find in antiquity. For example, the classical prejudice, which has done so much damage to the study of late Greek and Latin literatures, is an invention of the Greco-Roman period, which created the model of a canon of classical authors as a reaction against mannerism and the baroque, which, at that time, were called "Asianism." But if the classical prejudice already existed during the Hellenistic and especially imperial eras, this is precisely because the distance we feel with respect to classical Greece also appeared at that time. It is precisely this Hellenistic spirit, this distance, in some ways modern, through which, for example, the traditional myths become the objects of scholarship or of philosophical and moral interpretations. It is through Hellenistic and Roman thought, particularly of late antiquity, that the Renaissance will perceive Greek tradition. This fact will be of decisive importance for the birth of modern European thought and art. In another respect contemporary hermeneutic theories that, proclaiming the autonomy of the written text, have constructed a veritable tower of Babel of interpretations where all meanings become possible, come straight out of the practices of ancient exegesis, about which I spoke earlier. Another example: for our late colleague Roland Barthes, "many features of our literature, of our teaching, of our institutions of language . . . would be elucidated and understood differently if we fully knew . . . the rhetorical code that gave its language to our culture." This is completely true, and we could add that this knowledge would perhaps enable us to be conscious of the fact that in their methods and modes of expression our human sciences often operate in a way completely analogous to the models of ancient rhetoric.

Our history of Hellenistic and Roman thought should therefore not only analyze the movement of thought in philosophical works, but it should also be a historical topics that will study the evolution of the meaning of the *topoi,* the models of which we have spoken, and the role they have played in the formation of Western thought. This historical topics should work hard at discerning the original meanings of the formulas and models and the different significances that successive reinterpretations have given them.

At first, this historical topics will take for its object of study those works that were founding models and the literary genres that they created. Euclid's *Elements,* for example, served as a model for Proclus's *Elements of Theology* but also for Spinoza's *Ethics.* Plato's *Timaeus,* itself inspired by pre-Socratic cosmic poems, served as a model for Lucretius's *De rerum natura,* and the eighteenth century, in turn, will dream of a new cosmic poem that would exhibit the latest discoveries of science. Augustine's *Confessions,* as it was misinterpreted, moreover, inspired an enormous literature up to Rousseau and the romantics.

This topics could also be a topics of aphorisms: for example, of the maxims about nature that dominated the scientific imagination until the nineteenth century. This year [at the Collège de France], we will study in this way the aphorism of Heraclitus that is usually phrased as "Nature loves to hide herself," although this is certainly not the original meaning of the three Greek words so translated. We will examine the significance this formula takes on throughout antiquity and later on, as a function of the evolution of the idea of Nature, the very interpretation proposed by Martin Heidegger.

Above all, this historical topics will be a topics about the themes of meditations, of which we spoke a few minutes ago, which have dominated and still dominate our Western thought. Plato, for example, had defined philosophy as an exercise for death, understood as the separation of the soul from the body. For Epicurus this exercise for death takes on a new meaning; it becomes the consciousness of the finitude of existence that gives an infinite value to each instant: "Persuade yourself that every new day that dawns will be your last one. And then you will receive each un-hoped for hour with gratitude." In the perspective of Stoicism, the exercise for death takes on a different character; it invites immediate conversion and makes inner freedom possible: "Let death be before your eyes each day and you will not have any base thoughts or excessive desires." A mosaic at the Roman National Museum is inspired, perhaps ironically, by this meditation, as it depicts a skeleton with a scythe accompanied by the inscription, *Gnothi seauton,* "Know thyself." Be that as it may, Christianity will make abundant use of this theme of meditation. There it can be treated in a manner close to Stoicism, as in this monk's reflection: "Since the beginning of our conversation, we have come closer to death. Let us be vigilant while we still have the time." But it changes radically when it is combined with the properly Christian theme of participation in Christ's death. Leaving aside all of the rich Western literary tradition, so well illustrated by Montaigne's chapter, "That to philosophize is to learn to die," we can go straight to Heidegger in order to rediscover this fundamental philosophical exercise in his definition of the authenticity of existence as a lucid anticipation of death.

Linked to the meditation upon death, the theme of the value of the present instant plays a fundamental role in all the philosophical schools. In short it is a consciousness of inner freedom. It can be summarized in a formula of this kind: You need only yourself in order immediately to find inner peace by ceasing to worry about the past and the future. You can be happy right now, or you will never be happy. Stoicism will insist on the effort needed to pay attention to oneself, the joyous acceptance of the present moment imposed on us by fate. The Epicurean will conceive of this liberation from cares about the past and the future as a relaxation, a pure joy of existing: "While we are speaking, jealous time has flown; seize today without placing your trust in tomorrow." This is Horace's famous *laetus in praesens,* this "enjoyment of the pure present," to use André Chastel's fine expression about Marsilio Ficino who had taken this very formula of Horace's for his motto. Here again the history of this theme in Western thought is fascinating. I cannot resist the pleasure of evoking the dialogue between Faust and Helena, the climax of part two of Goethe's *Faust:* "Nun schaut der Geist nicht vorwärts, nicht zurück, / Die Gegenwart allein ist unser Glück" ["And so the spirit looks neither ahead nor behind. The present alone is our joy . . . Do not think about your destiny. Being here is a duty, even though it only be an instant"].

I have come to the end of this inaugural address, which means that I have just completed what in antiquity was called an *epideixis,* a set speech. It is in a direct line with those that professors in the time of Libanius, for example, had to give in order to recruit an audience while at the same time trying to demonstrate the incomparable worth of their special-

ity and to display their eloquence. It would be interesting to investigate
the historic paths by which this ancient practice was transmitted to the
first professors at the Collège de France. In any case, at this very moment,
we are in the process of fully living a Greco-Roman tradition. Philo of
Alexandria said of these set speeches that the lecturer "brought into
broad daylight the fruit of long efforts pursued in private, as painters and
sculptors seek, in realizing their works, the applause of the public." And
he opposed this behavior to the true philosophical instruction in which
the teacher adapts his speech to the state of his listeners and brings them
the cures they need in order to be healed.

The concern with individual destiny and spiritual progress, the in-
transigeant assertion of moral requirements, the call for meditation, the
invitation to seek this inner peace that all the schools, even those of the
skeptics, propose as the aim of philosophy, the feeling for the seriousness
and grandeur of existence—this seems to me to be what has never been
surpassed in ancient philosophy and what always remains alive. Perhaps
some people will see in these attitudes an escape or evasion that is incompatible with the consciousness we should have of human suffering and
misery, and they will think that the philosopher thereby shows himself to
be irremediably foreign to the world. I would answer simply by quoting
this beautiful text by Georges Friedmann, from 1942, which offers a
glimpse of the possibility of reconciling the concern for justice and spiritual effort; it could have been written by a Stoic of antiquity:

> Take flight each day! At least for a moment, however brief, as long
> as it is intense. Every day a "spiritual exercise," alone or in the com-
> pany of a man who also wishes to better himself. . . . Leave ordinary
> time behind. Make an effort to rid yourself of your own passions. . . .
> Become eternal by surpassing yourself. This inner effort is necessary,
> this ambition, just. Many are those who are entirely absorbed in mili-
> tant politics, in the preparation for the social revolution. Rare, very
> rare, are those who, in order to prepare for the revolution, wish to
> become worthy of it.[3]

3. Georges Friedmann, *La Puissance et la sagesse* (Paris, 1970), p. 359.

The Final Foucault and His Ethics

Paul Veyne

Translated by Catherine Porter and Arnold I. Davidson

Paul Veyne's essays on Michel Foucault have long been recognized as among the most important discussions of Foucault's work. "Le Dernier Foucault et sa morale" was first published in Critique *in 1986. However, it appeared there without Veyne's remarks on Foucault and AIDS, which Veyne had intended to publish with the original essay. At his request, we have restored these passages in our translation.*
—Arnold I. Davidson

Foucault was as strongly attracted to Greco-Roman antiquity, in the end, as was Nietzsche, his intellectual master. Admiration entails an element of candor and a dissymmetry that intellectuals, a resentful, lot, ordinarily find repugnant; thus I was surprised one day to see Foucault get up from his worktable and ask me naively: "Don't you find certain masterpieces overwhelmingly superior to others? For me, the appearance of Oedipus, blind, at the end of Sophocles' play . . ." We had never spoken of *Oedipus Rex*—we did not talk much about literature—and Foucault's rhetorical question expressed a sudden emotion that did not require a response. Similarly, when we took turns extolling the work of René Char, we discreetly limited ourselves to a couple of sentences. But when he had to delve into ancient literature to write his last two books, Foucault did so with palpable pleasure, which he succeeded in prolonging, and I can still hear him say, in the obligatory laconic manner, that Seneca's letters were superb. And indeed there is an affinity between Foucault's elegance as an individual and the elegance that characterized Greco-Roman civilization. In short, classical elegance privately served as Foucault's image of an art of living, a possible ethics. During his last years, while he was working on the Stoics, he thought a great deal about suicide ("but I'm not

225

gong to talk about it; if I kill myself, it will be obvious enough"); his death was more or less tantamount to suicide, as we shall see. However, Foucault constructed for himself such a singular conception of morality that there is a real problem: within his philosophy, was an ethics for Foucault even possible?

Clearly no one will charge him with aspiring to renew the Stoic ethics of the Greeks. In the last interview he was able to give in his life, he expressed himself quite clearly: the solution to a contemporary problem will never be found in a problem raised in another era, which is not the same problem except through a false resemblance. Foucault never thought he saw an alternative to the Christian ethic in the Greeks' sexual ethic, quite the contrary. From one age to another, problems are not similar, any more than is nature or reason; the eternal return is also an eternal departure (he had been fond of this expression of Char's); only successive valorizations exist. In a sempiternal new deal, time endlessly redistributes the cards. Foucault's affinity with ancient morality is reduced to the modern reappearance of a single card in a completely new hand: the card of the self working on the self, an aestheticization of the subject, in two very different moralities and two very different societies.

Morality with no claim to universality. Foucault was a warrior in the trenches, Jean-Claude Passeron used to say to me; a warrior is a man who can get along without truth, who only knows the sides taken, his and that of his adversary, and who has enough energy to fight without having to justify himself in order to reassure himself. "Each breath drawn proposes a reign," Char also writes. The course of history does not include eternal problems, problems of essences or of dialectics; it only offers valorizations that differ from one culture to another and even from one individual to another, valorizations that, as Foucault was fond of saying, are neither true nor false: they are, that's all, and each individual is the patriot of his or her own values. This is more or less the opposite of collective fatalism à la Spengler. The future will eradicate our values; the past of their dynastyless genealogy has already called them into question, but no matter: they are our flesh and blood, as long as they are our own present. In his first lecture in 1983 at the Collège de France, Foucault contrasted an "analytic philosophy of truth in general" with his own preference "for critical thought that would take the form of an ontology of ourselves, of an ontology of the present"; he went so far, that day, as to relate his own work to "the form of reflection that extends from Hegel to the Frankfurt School via Nietzsche and Max Weber." We must be careful not push that rather excessively circumstantial analogy too far, but it does suggest two things. Foucault's books are, strictly speaking, the works of a historian, at least in the eyes of those who have acknowledged that all history is interpretative; but Foucault would not have written all the historians' books. For the interpretation that is history has as its second agenda the project of being a complete inventory, whereas Foucault played the part of historian only with respect to points where the past masks the geneal-ogy of our present. This last word remains the crucial one. There is no more relativism as soon as one has stopped opposing truth to time or even identifying Being with time: what is opposed to time as well as eter-nity is our own valorization of the present. What does it matter that time passes and that its frontier wipes out our valorizations? No warrior has been shaken in his patriotism by the idea that, had he been born on the other side of the border, his heart would have beaten for the other side.

Nietzsche's philosophy, Foucault was fond of saying, is not a philoso-phy of truth, but of speaking-truly. For a warrior, truths are useless, and it is still saying too much to claim that they are inaccessible; if they were dictated by resemblance or by analogy with things, one might despair of attaining them, as Heidegger did at one point in his journey. But in think-ing they are seeking the truth of things, people succeed only in establish-ing the rules according to which they will be said to be speaking truly or falsely. In this sense, knowledge is not only linked to the powers that be, it is not only a weapon of power, it is not even power at the same time that it is knowledge; knowledge is only power, radically, for one can only speak truly by virtue of the force of the rules imposed at one time or another by a history whose individuals are at once, and mutually, actors and victims. Thus by truths we do not mean true propositions to be dis-covered or accepted but the set of rules that make it possible to utter and to recognize those propositions held as true.

It will be agreed that a warrior's philosophy is much closer to the philosophy of an actor in history than to any fatalism. Around 1977, Fou-cault, in circumstances I prefer to forget, wrote in *Le Monde* something less forgettable: human freedoms and rights are based more surely on the actions of men and women committed to putting themselves into power and to defending themselves than on the doctrinal affirmation of reason or on the Kantian imperative. Here Foucault was of course de-nouncing the overvaluation of philosophy: he hardly believed that the discursive practice of an era expressed its characteristic choices in the forms it repeated, in its canonical texts, or that the emergence of nuclear terror could be traced back to an unfortunate proposition by Descartes. But there was more to it than this: there was a conviction—a well-founded one, moreover—of the futility of rationalizations and ratioci-nations. In 1982 or 1983, in Foucault's apartment, we were watching a televised report on the Palestinian-Israeli conflict; at one point one of the combatants (which side he was on is utterly unimportant) was invited to speak. Now this man spoke in terms quite different from the ones ordi-narily encountered in political discussions: "I know only one thing," this partisan said, "I want to win back the lands of my forefathers. This is what I have wanted since my teens; I don't know where this passion comes from, but there it is." "There we have it at last," Foucault said to me, "everything has been said, there's nothing more to say."

Each valorization of the will to power, or each discursive practice (more scholarly types will spell out the relation between Nietzsche and Foucault on this point), is a prisoner of itself, and universal history is woven of nothing but such threads. The Greek valorization of pleasure rather than sex meant that the Greeks encountered no other object than that pleasure; the sex of the partner remained indifferent. We can guess to what extent such a philosophy, which, as they say, takes away man's reasons to fight because this philosophy itself fights without recourse to reason, ought to have been unpopular. It was not, thanks to two misunderstandings: the failure to recognize the transcendental level of Foucault's critique and the interpolation of a negativity that finally allowed one to believe what one wished to believe and to situate oneself on the right side.

To be sure, what is called a culture has no unity of style; it is a mishmash of rigorously interpretable discursive practices, it is a chaos of precision. But all these practices have in common the fact that they are both empirical and transcendental: empirical and thus always surpassable, transcendental and thus constitutive as long as they are not effaced (and only the devil knows with what force these "discourses" then impose themselves, since they are the *conditions of possibility* of all action). Foucault did not object to being made to say that the transcendental was historical. These *conditions of possibility* inscribe all reality within a two-horned polygon whose bizarre limits never match with the ample folds of a well-rounded rationality; these unrecognized limits are taken for reason itself and seem to be inscribed in the plenitude of some reason, essence, or function. Falsely, for to constitute is always to exclude; there is always emptiness around, but what emptiness? Nothing, a void, a simple way of evoking the possibility of polygons cut out differently at other historical moments, a mere metaphor.

Thus when Foucault spoke of this gesture of cutting out, or, as he put it, of rarefaction, and also of the Great Confinement under Louis XIV, when he talked about prisons and so on, he seemed to be speaking of the same thing, and of a fascinating thing, a thing that indeed fascinated Foucault the individual. But the transcendental level was in fact somewhat forgotten by many readers. However, the aim of Foucault the philosopher was not to claim that, for example, the modern state is characterized by a grand act of setting aside, of exclusion rather than of integration, which would obviously be exciting to discuss; his aim was to show that every gesture, without exception, at the level of the state or not, always fails to fulfill the universalism of a reason and always leaves emptiness outside, even if the gesture is one of inclusion and integration. Similarly, when Kant spoke of the transcendental constitution of space and time, he was not inviting us to proceed with it: the difficult point would rather be that without knowing it we have not been proceeding with it.

The other generous misunderstanding had to do with the famous void; people imagined that the finitude of every discursive practice was only empirical, to such an extent that the metaphorical void became, for some, a real space, inhabited by all the outcasts, rejects, and lepers and buzzing with all the forbidden or repressed words. The historical task was then to allow them to be heard: a rational account of the negativity of contradictories finally reestablished an encouraging philosophy that based our good feelings on reason. And yet, if there is one thing that distinguishes Foucault's thought from that of some others, it is the firm resolve not to serve a dual function, not to reduplicate our illusions, not to establish as finally true what everyone would like to believe, not to prove that what is ought to be has every reason to be. The rarest of phenomena, here is a philosophy without a happy end. Not that it ends badly: nothing can "end," since there is no end point any more than there is an origin. Foucault's originality among the great thinkers of our century lay in his refusal to convert our finitude into the basis for new certainties.

An authentic depiction of universal history, a straightforward acknowledgment of the time that erases everything; however, we shall continue to see nothing, and to reread Kant. . . . Foucault's philosophy is at the same time almost trivial and paradoxical. Foucault admits that he is incapable of justifying his own preferences; he cannot invoke human nature, or reason, or functionalism, or essence, or correspondence to an object. We are all at that point, no doubt, but if one can no longer argue over tastes and valorizations, what good does it do to have written books of history, perhaps of morality, and certainly of philosophy? Because knowledge is power: it imposes itself, and one imposes it; it does not derive form the nature of things. It has its limit, however: the present.

What is at stake here is the goal of philosophy; what does it serve? To reduplicate what men are only too ready to believe? Despite what the justificatory or self-protecting philosophers assert, the spectacle of the past brings to light no reason in history other than the struggles of men for something that is undoubtedly neither true nor false but that imposes itself as truth to be told. If this is so, a philosophy has only one possible use, which is making war: not the war of the day before yesterday, but today's war. And for this, it has to begin by proving genealogically that there is no other truth of history but this combat. Yes to war, no to patriotic brainwashing.

Here one sees a little-noticed characteristic of Foucault's work, a philosophically grounded elegance that was apparent in his private conversation, from which anger was not excluded, but indignation was. Foucault never wrote, "My political or social preferences are the true ones and the good ones" ("true" and "good" being one and the same, as we know thanks to Heidegger); nor did he write further, "My adversaries' preferences are false." All his books imply rather the following: "The reasons my adversaries give for their claim that their preferences are the truth rest genealogically on nothing." Foucault did not attack the choices

of others, but the rationalizations that they added to their choices. A genealogical criticism does not say, "I am right and the others are mistaken,"
but only, "the others are wrong to claim that they are right." A true warrior, lacking indignation, knows anger, *thumos*. Foucault did not worry
about justifying his convictions; it was enough for him to hold to them.
But to ratiocinate would have been to lower himself, with no benefit to
his cause.

People can no more prevent themselves from valorizing than from
breathing, and they do battle for their values. Foucault thus tries to impose one of his own preferences, revived from the Greeks, which he considers to be of present interest; in doing so he does not claim to be right
or wrong, but he would like to win and he hopes to be current. However,
the present limits the possible preferences. Max Weber, another
Nietzschean, exclaimed in vain, "Since there is no truth to values and
since heaven is in shreds, let each man fight for his gods and, a new
Luther, sin resolutely." But the enemy positions are not as reversible as
Weber said; the present is never indifferent. To be a philosopher is to
make a diagnosis of present possibilities and to draw up a strategic map—
with the secret hope of influencing the choice of combats. Enclosed in his
own finitude, in his own time, man cannot think just anything at any
time. Try asking the Romans to abolish slavery or to think about an international equilibrium. A memory from 1979 occurs to me. That year, Foucault began his course in roughly the following terms: "I am going to
describe certain aspects of the contemporary world and its governmentality; this course will not tell you what you should do or what you have
to fight against, but it will give you a map; thus it will tell you: if you
want to attack in such-and-such a direction, well, here there is a knot of
resistance and there a possible passage." Foucault also added something
else, the exact meaning of which I do not know: "As for me, I do not see,
at least for now, what criteria would allow one to decide what one should
fight against, except perhaps aesthetic criteria." We must not misuse these
last words, which may be only a confession of ignorance or a distance
taken with respect to the convictions of many of his listeners. At the very
most there is perhaps here a vague foreboding of what would be his major
theme the year he died: not aesthetic criteria, but the idea of a style of existence.

For in *The Use of Pleasure* and *The Care of the Self*, the diagnosis of the
present is roughly the following: in the modern world, it seems to have
become impossible to ground an ethics. There is no longer nature or
reason to conform to, no longer an origin with which to establish an authentic relation (poetry, I would say, is a special case); tradition or constraint are no longer anything but contingent facts. Still, for all that we
should not proclaim a state of crisis or decadence; the aporias of philosophical repetition have never shaken ordinary mortals. It remains the
case that ordinary men are subjects; they are mortal subjects, divided

beings who have a relation of consciousness or of self-knowledge with themselves. This is to be Foucault's playing field.

The idea of styles of existence played a major role in Foucault's conversations and doubtless in his inner life during the final months of a life that only he knew to be threatened. *Style* does not mean distinction here; the word is to be taken in the sense of the Greeks, for whom an artist was first of all an artisan and a work of art was first of all a work. Greek ethics is quite dead, and Foucault judged it as undesirable as it would be impossible to resuscitate this ethics; but he considered one of its elements, namely, the idea of a work of the self on the self, to be capable of reacquiring a contemporary meaning, in the manner of one of those pagan temple columns that one occasionally sees reutilized in more recent structures. We can guess at what might emerge from this diagnosis: the self, taking itself as a work to be accomplished, could sustain an ethics that is no longer supported by either tradition or reason; as an artist of itself, the self would enjoy that autonomy that modernity can no longer do without. "Everything has disappeared," said Medea, "but I have one thing left: myself." Finally, if the self frees us from the idea that between morality and society, or what we call by those names, there is an analytic or necessary link, then it is no longer necessary to wait for the revolution to begin to realize ourselves: the self is the new strategic possibility.

Foucault, who knew how to see things on a large scale, nonetheless did not claim to be delivering a fully armed ethics; such academic exploits seemed to him to have died along with the old philosophy. But he did suggest a way out. He took the rest of his strategy with him. But he would not have claimed in any case to have supplied a true or definitive solution, for humanity is constantly on the move, to such an extent that each current solution soon reveals that it too involves dangers; every solution is soon imperfect, and this will always be so: a philosopher is someone who, facing each new present circumstance, diagnoses the new danger and points to a new way out. With this very new conception of philosophy, classical truth is dead, yet from the modern historicist confusion the idea of the present can be disengaged.[1]

Foucault was not afraid of death; he said so occasionally to his friends, when the conversation turned to suicide, and the facts proved, although in a different way, that he was not boasting. Ancient wisdom had become personal for him in still another way; during the last eight months of his life, the writing of his two books played the role for him that philosophical writing and the personal journal played in ancient philosophy: that of a work of the self on the self, a self-stylization.

1. One night when we were talking about the truth of myth, he said that the great question, according to Heidegger, was to know what was the ground of truth; according to Wittgenstein, it was to know what one was saying when one spoke the truth; "but in my opinion," he added—and I am quoting his exact words, for I jotted them down—"the question is: how is it that there is so little truth in truth?" [*"d'où vient que la vérité soit si peu vraie?"*]

This is when an incident occurred whose memory is seared in me like a heroic feature. During those eight months, then, Foucault worked on writing and rewriting his two books to settle this long-term debt to himself. He talked to me constantly about his books and sometimes had me check one of his translations, but he complained of a stubborn cough and a continual low-grade fever that was slowing him down. As a matter of courtesy, he had me ask my wife's advice; she is a doctor, and she could not do a thing. "Your doctors are surely going to think you have AIDS," I said to him jokingly one day in February 1984 (joking with each other about the differences in our amorous tastes was one of the rituals of our friendship). "That is exactly what they think" he replied, laughing; "I've pretty well figured it out from the questions they've been asking me." Readers today will find it hard to believe that in February 1984 a fever and a cough did not yet arouse suspicion; AIDS was still such a remote and little-known scourge that it was mythical and perhaps imaginary. No one close to him suspected a thing; we only found out afterward. "You ought to rest for once," I went on, "you've done too much Greek and Latin, it's worn you out." "Yes, but afterward," he replied; "first I want to get these two books done." "By the way," I asked him out of simple curiosity (for the history of medicine is not my dominant passion), "does AIDS really exist, or is it a moralizing medical myth?" "Well," he replied calmly and after a moment's reflection, "listen. I've studied the question closely, I've read quite a bit on the subject. Yes, it exists, it's not a myth. The Americans have studied it very carefully"; and he gave me two or three sentences' worth of precise methodological details that I have forgotten.

After all, he was a historian of medicine and, as a philosopher, I thought, he is interested in the present. For tidbits from American sources on the "cancer of homosexuals" (as it was called then) appeared fairly regularly in the newspapers. In retrospect, his composure at the time of my stupid question takes my breath away; he himself must have thought at the time that one day this would be so; he must have thought over his response and counted on my memory as a tiny, bitter consolation; to give living *exempla* was another tradition of ancient philosophy. At the time I was committing my blunder, his answer left me mute and uncertain; I did not know what to say or think about an illness whose slightest symptom and whose very plausibility I knew nothing about. But the ambiguity of his reply left me with an unconscious doubt, an uneasiness, a vague embarrassment that was expressed or abreacted over months through jokes *in petto*, until it broke out in a visual hallucination[2]

2. I found myself at that time along a highway; the news available about Foucault's health was very bad; my wife had explained to me that the doctors seemed no longer to know what to do and that the treatment hardly corresponded to the official diagnosis of the illness. All at once I saw that I was being passed at a high rate of speed by a powerful car, green and joyous, that had axles wider than its chassis, and thick tires. The car, of an unusual make, had a large rectangular window in the rear, which allowed one to see inside.

the very afternoon Foucault died, a few minutes before the telephone call from Maurice Pinguet breaking the news from Tokyo where Japanese radio had just announced it.

Man is a being who bestows meaning and who also sometimes aestheticizes. A year before his death, Foucault once had occasion to speak of the ritual of solemn death as it was practiced in the Middle Ages and still in the seventeenth century; the dying man, surrounded by his loved ones, would give his lessons from his deathbed. The historian Philippe Ariès regretted that this great ritual of social integration had fallen into disuse in our era; as for Foucault, he regretted nothing and wrote this: "I prefer the gentle sadness of disappearance to that sort of ceremony. There would be something chimerical about seeking, in a burst of nostalgia, to revive practices that no longer have any meaning. Let us rather try to give meaning and beauty to death-as-effacement."

Just as it overtook me, I recognized Foucault as the driver; surprised, he turned his head quickly toward me and smiled at me in passing with his thin lips. I immediately pressed down on the accelerator in order to catch up with him, then let up just as quickly. In the first place, the strange car was going too fast; and then its appearance did not have the look of a perception but rather the scent of a hallucination. The car disappeared in the distance, or ceased to be, I don't know which (and I am not sure either that the question has any meaning). I had not even understood that the curious rear window was that of a hearse; a friend pointed this out to me, many months later. On the other hand, I knew instantly (and I stopped right away on the shoulder to make a note of this, so as to be sure later on that I had not been dreaming) that this vision meant both that Foucault's history books went much farther than mine, and that Foucault himself was going where we shall all go.

Writing the Self

Michel Foucault

Translated by Ann Hobart

These pages are part of a series of studies on the "arts of the self," that is, on the aesthetic of the existence and the government of self and others in Greco-Roman culture during the first two centuries of the empire.

Athanasius's *Vita Antonii* presents the written expression of actions and thoughts as an indispensable element of the ascetic life.

> Here is one thing to observe to ensure that one does not sin. Let us each take note of and write down the actions and movements of our souls as though to make them mutually known to one another, and let us be sure that out of shame at being known, we will cease sinning and have nothing perverse in our hearts. Who, after all, consents to be seen when he sins, and when he has sinned does not prefer to lie to hide his fault. One would not fornicate in front of witnesses. By the same token, by writing our thoughts as if we had to communicate them mutually to one another, we will better keep ourselves from impure thoughts out of shame at having them known. May writing replace the looks of our companions in asceticism; blushing to write as well as to be seen, let us keep ourselves from every bad thought. Disciplining ourselves in this way, we can reduce the body to servitude and outsmart the enemy.[1]

The "series of studies" of which Foucault speaks had been conceived initially as an introduction to *L'Usage des plaisirs (The History of Sexuality, Volume 2: The Use of Pleasure)* under the title *Le Souci de soi (The History of Sexuality, Volume 3: The Care of the Self)*. This title having been retained for a new arrangement of the parts of *L'Usage des plaisirs*, a more general series of studies on governmentality was then planned with Éditions du Seuil under the title *Le Gouvernement de soi et des autres*.

1. Athanasius, *Vie et conduite de notre Père Saint Antoine*, in *Antoine Le Grand: Père des moines*, trans. Benoit Lavaud (Paris, 1943), pp. 69–70.

Self-writing clearly appears here in its complementary relation to anchoritism; it offsets the dangers of solitude; it exposes what one has done or thought to a possible gaze; the fact of being obliged to write fills the role of companion by inciting human respect and shame. One can thus posit a primary analogy: that which others are to the ascetic in his community the notebook will be to him in his solitude. But, at the same time, a second analogy is posited that refers to the practice of asceticism as work not only on actions but more precisely on thoughts. The constraint that the presence of others exerts in the domain of behavior, writing will exert in the domain of the interior movements of the soul. In this sense, it has a role very near to that of confession to the spiritual director in the Algerian line of spirituality, which Cassien will say must reveal, without exception, all movements of the soul *(omnes cogitationes)*. Finally, the writing of interior movements also appears, according to the text of Athanasius, as a weapon of spiritual combat. Since the devil has the power to deceive and make one deceive oneself (a large portion of the *Vita Antonii* is dedicated to his ruses), writing constitutes a test and acts as a touchstone. In bringing to light the movements of thought, it dissipates the interior shadow where the snares of the enemy are laid. This text—one of the oldest that Christian literature has left us on this subject of spiritual writing—far from exhausts all the significations and forms that the latter will take later on. But one can draw from it several features that permit a retrospective analysis of the role of writing in the philosophical culture of the self just prior to Christianity: its close tie with apprenticeship; its applicability to movements of thought; its role as test of truth. These various elements are already to be found in the writing of Seneca, Plutarch, and Marcus Aurelius, but with very different values and following completely different procedures.

No technique, no professional skill can be acquired without exercise; nor can one learn the art of living, the *techne tou biou,* without an *askesis* that must be understood as a training of the self by the self. This was one of the traditional principles to which the Pythagoreans, the Socratics, and the Cynics had long attached great importance. Indeed it seems that among all the forms that this training took (and that included abstinences, memorizations, examinations of consciousness, meditations, silence, and listening to others), writing—the fact of writing for oneself and for others—came to play a considerable role rather late. In any case, the texts of the imperial period that refer to the practices of the self are devoted in large part to writing. One must read, Seneca said, but write as well.[2] And Epictetus, who however gave only oral teaching, insisted several times on the role of writing as personal exercise. One must "medi-

---

2. Seneca, lettre 84, *Lettres à Lucilius,* trans. Henri Noblot, ed. François Préchac, 5 vols. in 4 (Paris, 1945–62), 3:121; hereafter abbreviated *LL.*

tate" *[meletan]*, write *[graphein]*, train *[gumnazein]*; "may death take me while thinking, writing, reading this." Or again, "Keep these thoughts ready day and night *[prokheiron]*; write them down; read them; let them be the object of your conversations with yourself, with another . . . if one of those events that are called undesirable should happen to you, you will find yourself comforted by the thought that it was not unexpected."[3] In these texts of Epictetus, writing is regularly associated with "meditation," with that exercise of thought on itself that reactivates what it knows, that makes present a principle, a rule, or an example, reflects on them, assimilates them, and thus prepares itself to confront the real. But one sees as well that writing is associated with the exercise of thought in two different ways. One takes the form of a "linear" series; it goes from meditation to the activity of writing and from there to *gumnazein*, that is, to training in a real and taxing situation: work of thought, work through writing, work in reality. The other is circular; meditation precedes the notes that permit rereading, which in its turn revives meditation. In any case, in whatever cycle of practice it takes place, writing constitutes an essential step in the process to which all *askêsis* tends: to know the elaboration of received and recognized discourses as true in rational principles of action. As an element of the training of the self, writing has, to use an expression found in the writing of Plutarch, an *ethopoetic* function. It is an operator of transformation of truth into *êthos*.

This ethopoetic writing, such as it appears throughout the documents of the first and second centuries, seems to locate itself outside of two forms already known and used for other ends: *hupomnêmata* and *correspondence*.

Hupomnemata

Hupomnemata, in the technical sense, can be books of accounts, public registers, or personal notebooks to be used as memoranda. Their use as books of life or guides of conduct seems to have become a common thing among an entire cultivated public. They contained quotations, fragments of works, examples, and actions of which one had been the witness or had read the narrative, reflections or arguments that one had heard or that had occurred to one. They constituted a material memory of things read, heard, or thought; they would offer them thus as treasures accumulated for later rereading and meditation. They also formed the primary material for writing more systematic treatises in which one gave the arguments and methods to struggle against some fault (like anger, envy, gossiping, or flattery) or to surmount some difficult circumstance (mourning, exile, ruin, disgrace). Thus, when Fundanus asks for advice on struggling

3. Epictetus, *Entretiens*, trans. and ed. Joseph Souilhé, 4 vols. (Paris, 1963), 3:23, 109.

against agitations of the soul, Plutarch at that very moment hardly has the time to compose a treatise in proper form; he is thus going to send him without delay the *hupomnemata* that he had himself written on the theme of tranquillity of spirit. At least it is thus that he presents the text of *Peri euthumias*.[4] Feigned modesty? No doubt this was a way of making excuses for the somewhat disjointed quality of the text; but one must also see here an indication of what these notebooks were—as well as of the practice of making the treatise itself, which retained something of its form of origin.

One should not envision these *hupomnemata* as a simple prop of memory that one could consult from time to time if the opportunity presented itself. They were not destined to be substituted for the possibly failing memory. Rather, they constituted the material and a framework for exercises to be done frequently: to read, reread, meditate, converse with oneself and with others, and so on. And this in order to have them, according to a frequently appearing expression, *prokheiron, ad manum, in promptu*. "At hand," thus, not simply in the sense that one could recall them to consciousness, but rather in the sense that one must be able to use them, as soon as one has need of them, in action. It is a matter of constituting a *logos bioethikos*, a supply of helpful discourses capable—as Plutarch put it—of raising their voices themselves to quiet the passions as a master may, with one word, calm the growling of dogs.[5] And for this it is necessary that they not simply be tucked away as though in an armoire of memories but rather be deeply implanted in the soul, "driven into it," as Seneca says, and that they thus make up a part of ourselves; in short, that the soul make them not simply its own but itself. The writing of *hupomnemata* is an important relay in this subjectification of discourse.

As personal as they are, these *hupomnemata* must not, however, be understood as the intimate journals or as the narratives of spiritual experience (temptations, struggles, failures, and victories) that will be found in later Christian literature. They do not constitute a "narrative of the self"; their objective is not to bring into the light the *arcana conscientiae* for which confession—oral or written—has a purifying value. The movement that they seek to effect is the inverse of that; it is not a matter of pursuing the unsayable, nor of revealing the hidden, nor of saying the unsaid, but on the contrary of capturing the already-said, of reassembling what one could hear or read, and this for an end that is nothing less than the constitution of the self.

The *hupomnemata* must be resituated in the context of a very appreciable tension of the age. At the interior of a culture very strongly marked by traditionalism, by the recognized value of the already-said, by the re-

4. See Plutarch, *De la tranquillité de l'âme*, trans. Jean Dumortier and Jean Defradas, *Oeuvres morales*, 7 vols. (Paris, 1975), l. 464, 7:98.

5. See ibid., l. 465, 7:98.

currence of discourse, by a "citational" practice under the seal of antiquity and authority, developed an ethic very explicitly oriented by the care of the self toward definite objectives such as withdrawing into the self, getting in touch with the self, living with the self, sufficing in the self, profiting from and enjoying the self. Such indeed is the objective of *hupomnemata:* to make of this recollection of the fragmentary logos transmitted through teaching, listening, or reading a means of establishing between the self and the self as appropriate and complete a relationship as possible. There is, for us, something paradoxical in this. How can one be put in the presence of oneself through the aid of an ageless discourse that is received just about everywhere? In fact, if the writing of *hupomnemata* can contribute to the formation of the self across these scattered *logoi*, it is for three principal reasons: the effects of limitation owing to the coupling of writing and reading, the regulated practice of the disparate that determines the choices, and the appropriation that it effects.

1) Seneca insists on it: the practice of self implies reading, because one cannot draw everything from one's own funds nor arm oneself by oneself with the principles of reason that are indispensable to conduct oneself. As guide or example, the help of others is necessary. But one must not dissociate reading and writing; one must "have recourse by turns" to these two occupations and "temper one by means of the other." If writing too much exhausts (Seneca is thinking here of the work of style), an excess of reading disperses. "Abundance of books, agonizing indecision of mind."[6] Passing ceaselessly from one book to another, without ever stopping, without returning from time to time to the hive with one's provision of nectar, as a consequence, without taking notes or composing in writing a collection of reading, one exposes oneself to retaining nothing, to dispersing oneself through different thoughts, and to forgetting oneself. Writing as a way of collecting reading already done and of reflecting on it is an exercise of reason that is opposed to the great fault of *stultitia*, which infinite reading risks promoting. *Stultitia* is defined by agitation of spirit, instability of attention, changes of opinion and intention, and, consequently, by fragility before all events that can occur. It is also characterized by the fact that it turns the spirit toward the future, makes it curious about novelties and keeps it from giving itself a fixed point in the possession of an acquired truth.[7] The writing of *hupomnemata* contrasts with this dissipation in fixing the acquired elements and in constituting them, as it were, "from the past," to which it is always possible to return and retire. This practice can be linked to a very general theme of the period. In any case, it is common to the morality of the Stoics and the Epicureans: the refusal of a spiritual attitude directed toward the future (which, because of its uncertainty, provokes anxiety and agitation of

6. Seneca, lettre 2, *LL*, 1:6.
7. See Seneca, lettre 52, *LL*, 2:41–42.

spirit) and the positive value accorded to the possession of a past that one may enjoy utterly and without embarrassment. The contribution of the *hupomnemata* is one of the means by which one detaches the soul from concern for the future in order to bend it toward meditation on the past.

2) However, if it permits thwarting the dispersion of the *stultitia*, the writing of *hupomnemata* is also (and it must remain) a regulated and voluntary practice of the disparate. It is a choice of heterogeneous elements. In that way it contrasts to the work of the grammarian who seeks to know all of a work or all of the works of the professional philosophers who lay claim to the doctrinal unity of a school. "It is of little importance," says Epictetus, "that one has or has not read all of Zeno or Chrysippus; it is of little importance that one has seized exactly what they meant, and that one is capable of reconstructing the unity of their reasoning."[8] The notebook is controlled by two principles that could be called "the local truth of the maxim" and "its circumstantial, customary value." Seneca chooses what he notes for himself and for his correspondents from the work of one of the philosophers of his own sect, but from the work of Democritus and Epicurus as well.[9] The essential thing is that he can consider the sentence retained as a maxim true in what it affirms, acceptable in what it prescribes, and useful according to the circumstances in which one finds oneself. Writing as a personal exercise done by the self and for the self is an art of disparate truth; or, more precisely, a reflexive way of combining the traditional authority of the thing already said with the singularity of the truth that is affirmed there and the particularity of the circumstances that determine its use. "Thus always read," says Seneca to Lucilius,

> authors of recognized authority, and if the desire takes you to pursue a point in the writings of others, return quickly to the former. Secure yourself every day a defense against poverty, against death, without forgetting our other scourges. From all that you have skimmed, extract one thought to digest well that day. This is also what I do. Among several texts that I have just read, I set my heart on one of them. Here is my booty for today: it is in the work of Epicurus that I found it, because I also like to pass through the camps of others. As a renegade? no; as a scout *[tamquam explorator]*.[10]

3) This deliberate ill-assortment does not preclude unification. But this is not brought about in the art of making up a collection; it must develop in the writer himself as a result of *hupomnemata*, of their composition (and thus in the very act of writing), of their consultation (and thus in reading and rereading them). Two processes can be distinguished. It is a matter, on the one hand, of unifying these heterogeneous fragments

8. Epictetus, *Entretiens*, 2:65.
9. See Seneca, letters 2, 3, 4, 7, 8, *LL*, 1:6, 9, 12, 21–22, 24.
10. Seneca, lettre 2, *LL*, 1:6.

by their subjectification in the exercise of personal writing. Seneca compares this unification, according to very traditional metaphors, to either the labor of the bee, or to the digestion of food, or to the addition of figures making up a sum.

> Let us not permit anything that enters us to remain intact, for fear that it will never be assimilated. Let us digest the material, otherwise it will enter into our memory, not into our intelligence *[in memoriam . . . non in ingenium]*. Let us cordially adhere to these thoughts of others and be conscious of making them ours in order to unify one hundred different elements, just as addition makes a single number of isolated numbers.

The role of writing is to constitute, with all that reading has constituted, a "body" *[quicquid lectione collectum est, stilus redigat in corpus]*. And this body must not be understood as a body of doctrine, but rather—following the metaphor of digestion so often invoked—as the body itself of he who, in transcribing his readings, appropriates them and makes their truth his. Writing transforms the thing seen or heard "into strength and blood" *[in vires, in sanguinem]*. It becomes a principle of rational action in the writer himself.[11]

But, inversely, the writer constitutes his own identity through this recollection of things said. In this same letter 84—which is like a small treatise on the connections between reading and writing—Seneca dwells for an instant on the ethical problem of resemblance, fidelity, and originality. He explains that one must not elaborate on what one retains of an author in such a way that he may be recognized. It is not a matter of composing in the notes that one takes and in the manner that one reconstitutes in writing what one has read a series of portraits that are recognizable but "dead" (Seneca is thinking here of those portrait galleries by which one vouched for his birth; validated his status; and marked his identity with reference to others). It is his own soul that he must constitute in what he writes; but, as a man wears in his face natural resemblance to his ancestors, so it is good that one can perceive in what he writes the filiation of the thoughts that are engraved in his soul. Through the play of chosen reading and assimilative writing, one must be able to form an identity through which a complete spiritual genealogy may be read. In a choir there are high, low, and medium voices, the timbres of men and women. "No individual voice can be distinguished; only the whole imposes itself on the ear. . . . I want it to be thus with our souls, that they have a good supply of knowledge, precepts, examples borrowed from many ages, but that converge into one unity."

11. Seneca, lettre 84, *LL*, 3:123, 121–22, 123.

Correspondence

Notebooks that, in themselves, constitute exercises of personal writing, can serve as the primary material for texts that one sends to others. On the other hand, the missive, a text that by definition is destined for others, also leads to personal exercise. Seneca recalls that when one writes, one reads what one writes just as in saying something one hears what one says.[12] The letter that one sends acts, by the very act of writing, on the one who sends it, as it acts through reading and rereading on the one who receives it. In this double function, correspondence is very close to *hupomnemata,* and its form is often very close. Epicurean literature gives some examples. The text known as the "letter to Pythocles" begins by acknowledging reception of a letter in which a student testifies to his friendship for the master and in which he does his best to "recall the Epicurean arguments" that permit one to attain happiness. The author of the response gives his support. The attempt was not bad, and it in turn expedited a text—the resumé of the *Peri phuseos* of Epicurus—which was to serve Pythocles as material to memorize and as an aid to meditation.[13]

The letters of Seneca show an activity of direction, from an aged man who was already retired, aimed at another who still occupied an important public office. But in these letters, Seneca does not only inquire about Lucilius and his progress. He is not satisfied with giving him advice and giving him a commentary on some great principles of conduct. Through these written lessons, Seneca continues to exert himself according to two principles that he frequently invokes: that it is necessary to train oneself all one's life and that one always needs the help of others in the development of the soul in itself. The advice that he gives in letter 7 constitutes a description of his own relationship with Lucilius. He there characterizes well the way he spends his retirement in the dual labor that he performs simultaneously on his correspondent and on himself: withdrawing into himself as much as possible; becoming attached to those who are capable of having a beneficial effect on him; opening the door to those that one hopes oneself to make better; these are "the reciprocal duties. Whoever teaches, educates himself."[14]

The letter that one sends to help one's correspondent—to counsel him, exhort him, admonish him, console him—constitutes for the writer a manner of training. A little like soldiers in peacetime training through drills at arms, the advice that one gives others in the urgency of their situation is one way of preparing oneself for a similar eventuality. Thus, letter 99 to Lucilius. It is itself the copy of another letter that Seneca had

---

12. See ibid., 3:124.

13. See "Lettre à Pythoclès," in Lucretius, *De rerum natura,* trans. Alfred Ernout, ed. Ernout and Léon Robin, 3 vols. (Paris, 1925–28), 1:lxxxvii.

14. Seneca, lettre 7, *LL,* 1:21.

sent to Marullus, whose son had died sometime previously.[15] The text comes from the genre of "the consolation"; it offers the correspondent logical weapons with which to fight against sorrow. The intervention comes late, since Marullus, "stunned by the blow," had a moment of weakness and was "beside" himself. In this the letter therefore plays an admonishing role. But for Lucilius, to whom it is also sent, and for Seneca, who writes it, it plays the role of a principle of reactivation: reactivation of all the reasons that permit one to overcome mourning, to persuade oneself that death is not a misfortune (neither that of others nor one's own). And, thanks to what is reading for one, writing for the other, Lucilius and Seneca will thus have reinforced their preparation for the case in which an event of that kind would happen to them. The *consolatio* that was supposed to aid and correct Marullus is at the same time a useful *praemeditatio* for Lucilius and Seneca. Writing that aids the addressee arms the writer—and perhaps third persons who read it.

But it also happens that the spiritual service rendered by the writer to his correspondent is returned in the form of "advice in return"; to the extent that the one who is addressed progresses, he becomes more able in his turn to give advice, exhortations, and consolation to the one who had undertaken to help him. The correspondence does not move in one direction for long. It serves as a framework for exchanges that help it become more egalitarian. Letter 34 already signals this movement from a situation in which Seneca nonetheless could say to his correspondent "I, I claim you, you are my work"; "I have exhorted, goaded you well and, impatient with all slowness, I have pushed you relentlessly. I have remained faithful to the method, but today I exhort someone who has already clearly departed and who exhorts me in his turn."[16] And beginning with the next letter, he evokes the reward of perfect friendship, in which each of the two will be permanent help to the other, the inexhaustible aid that will be the subject of letter 109: "The fitness of the fighter is maintained by sparring; an accompanist stimulates the play of the musician. The wise man similarly needs to keep his virtues alive; thus, a stimulant himself, he also receives stimulus from another wise man."[17]

However, and despite all these points in common, correspondence must not be considered as the simple extension of the practice of *hupomnêmata*. It is something more than the training of the self by writing, through the advice and opinions that one gives to the other. It also represents a certain manner of expressing oneself to others. A letter renders the writer present to the one to whom it is addressed. And present not simply through the information that it gives him about his life, activities, successes, and failures, his luck and misfortunes; present in an immediate

15. See Seneca, lettre 99, *LL,* 4:125–34.
16. Seneca, lettre 34, *LL,* 1:148.
17. Seneca, lettre 109, *LL,* 4:190.

and quasi-physical presence.

> You often write me and I am grateful to you for it, because you thus show yourself to me through the only means at your disposal. Each time that your letter arrives, we are immediately together. If we are happy to have the portraits of our absent friends, how much more does a letter delight us, since it bears the living marks of the absent one, the authentic imprint of his person. The trace of a friend's hand, imprinted on the pages, assures that which is the most sweet about presence: rediscovery.[18]

To write is thus to "show oneself," make oneself seen, make one's face appear before the other. And, by that, it must be understood that the letter is at once a gaze that one focuses on the addressee (through the missive that he receives, he feels looked at) and a way of giving oneself over to his gaze, through what one tells him of oneself. The letter in a certain way sets up an encounter. And Demetrius, moreover, revealing in *De elocutione* what epistolary style should be, underscored that it could only be a "simple" style,[19] free in the composition, sparing in its choice of words, because each must reveal his soul there. The reciprocity that correspondence establishes is not simply that of advice and aid; it is also that of looking and testing. The letter that, as an exercise, works at the subjectification of true discourse, at its assimilation, at its elaboration as "one's own property," represents as well and at the same time an objectification of the soul. It is noteworthy that Seneca begins a letter in which he must reveal his everyday life to Lucilius by recalling the moral maxim that "we must regulate our lives as though the whole world were looking at them," and the philosophical principle that nothing of ourselves is concealed from God, who is ceaselessly present in our souls.[20] Through the missive, one opens oneself to the gaze of others and one puts the other in the place of an internal god. It is a way of giving ourselves over to this gaze that we must tell ourselves that it is plunging to the bottom of our hearts *[in pectus intimum introspicere]* at the moment that we think.

The work that the letter does on the addressee, but that is also performed on the writer through the very letter that he sends, thus involves "introspection"; but this must be understood less as a deciphering of the self by the self than as an opening onto the self that one gives to the other. It remains nevertheless that one has here a phenomenon that can appear a bit surprising but that is charged with meaning for whoever would like to write the history of the culture of the self. The first historical developments of the narrative of the self are not to be found among the "personal

---

18. Seneca, lettre 40, *LL,* 1:161.
19. See Demetrius of Phalerum, *De l'élocution,* trans. Edouard Durassier (Paris, 1875), pp. 95–99.
20. Seneca, lettre 83, *LL,* 3:110.

notebooks," the *hupomnemata*, whose role is to permit the construction of the self through the collection of the discourse of others. One can find them, on the other hand, among the correspondence with others and the exchange of spiritual service. And it is a fact that in the correspondence of Seneca with Lucilius, of Marcus Aurelius with Fronto, and in certain letters of Pliny, one sees develop a narrative of the self very different from what can in general be found in the letters of Cicero to his friends. In the latter, it was a question of the narrative of the self as subject of action (or deliberating a possible action) in relation to his friends and his enemies, of happy and unhappy events. In the writing of Seneca and Marcus Aurelius, sometimes also in the writing of Pliny, the narrative of the self is the narrative of the relation to the self; and there one sees two elements stand out, two strategic points that are going subsequently to become privileged objects of what one could call the writing of the relation to the self: intrusions of the soul and the body (impressions rather than actions), and leisure activities (rather than external events)—the body and days.

1) News about one's health is traditionally part of correspondence. But it gradually takes on the amplitude of a detailed description of corporal sensations, of feelings of malaise, of the various troubles that one can experience. Sometimes, one seeks only to introject advice about diet that one considers useful for one's correspondent.[21] Sometimes it is a matter of recalling the effects of the body on the soul, the action of the latter in return, or the healing of the former by the care taken of the latter. Thus the long and important letter 78 to Lucilius. It is in large part devoted to the problem of the "good use" of illnesses and suffering; but it opens with the memory of a serious childhood illness from which Seneca suffered and that was accompanied by a moral crisis. The "catarrh," the "small bouts of fever" of which Lucilius complains, Seneca recounts that he, too, experienced, many years before.

> At first I wasn't worried about them; my youth still had the strength to resist the attacks and to bravely keep its head under various forms of malady. Subsequently I succumbed to the point that my whole person was melted away by the catarrh, and I was reduced to extreme thinness. Many times I abruptly made up my mind to make an end of my existence, but one consideration held me back: the great age of my father.

And what healed him were remedies of the soul. Among these the most important were "the friends that encouraged him, watched over him, spoke with him and thus brought him comfort."[22] It also happens that the letters reproduce the movement that led from a subjective impression

---

21. See Pliny the Younger, lettre 1, *Lettres*, trans. and ed. Anne-Marie Guillemin, 4 vols. (Paris, 1927), 1:97–100.

22. Seneca, lettre 78, *LL*, 3:71–72.

to an exercise of thought. Witness this excursion-meditation recounted by Seneca:

> It was indispensable to me to shake up the organism, whether, if bile were caught in my throat, to make it recede, or whether, if by some means the air was too dense [in my lungs], to rarefy it by a knocking about that restored me. It was thus that I prolonged an outing to which the shore itself invited me. Between Cumae and the villa of Servilius Vatia it curved, and the sea to one side and the lake to the other hugged it like a narrow shoe. A recent tempest had strengthened the shore. . . . However, according to my habit, I started to look at the surroundings if I could not find something from which to benefit, and my eyes fixed on the house that had formerly been Vatia's.

And Seneca relates to Lucilius his meditations on retirement, solitude, and friendship.[23]

2) The letter is also a means of presenting oneself to one's correspondent in the course of one's everyday life. Recounting his day—not because of the importance of events that could have marked it, but precisely when nothing has happened to distinguish it from all others, thus testifying not to the importance of an activity but to the quality of a mode·of being—is a part of epistolary practice. Lucilius finds it natural to ask Seneca to "give him an account of each of my days, and hour by hour"; and Seneca accepts that obligation all the more willingly in that it commits him to live under the gaze of others without concealing anything. "I will thus do what you require: the nature, the order of my occupations, I will willingly communicate all this to you. I will examine myself from this very instant and, according to one of the most salutary practices, I will make the review of my day." In effect, Seneca evokes the precise day that has just passed and that is at the same time the most common of all. Its value stems precisely from the fact that nothing happened that could have diverted him from the only thing that was important to him: to attend to himself. "This day is wholly mine; no one robbed me of anything." A bit of physical training, racing with a young slave, a bath in barely tepid water, a simple meal of bread, a very brief nap. But the essential part of the day— and it is that which occupies the longest part of the letter—had been devoted to meditation on a theme suggested by a sophisticated syllogism of Zeno apropos of drunkenness.[24]

When the missive makes itself a narrative of an ordinary day, of one day in itself, one sees that it comes close to a practice to which Seneca elsewhere makes a discrete allusion, at the beginning of letter 83. There he evokes the very useful habit of "reviewing his day." It is the examination of consciousness whose form he had described in a passage of *De*

---

23. Seneca, lettre 55, *LL*, 2:56–57. See letter 57 as well, *LL*, 2:67.
24. Seneca, lettre 83, *LL*, 3:110–11.

ira.[25] This practice—it was customary in different philosophical movements: Pythagorean, Epicurean, Stoic—seems to have been above all a
mental exercise tied to memorization. It was a matter both of constituting
oneself as an "inspector of oneself" and thus of gauging common faults,
and of reactivating the rules of behavior that must always be present to
the mind. Nothing indicates that this "review of the day" took the form
of a written text. It thus seems that it was in the epistolary relationship—
and consequently in order to put oneself beneath the gaze of the other—
that the examination of consciousness was formulated as a written narrative of the self: narrative of daily banality; narrative of actions, correct or
not; of diet followed; of mental or physical exercises that one has engaged
in. Of this conjunction of epistolary practice with the examination of the
self, one can find a remarkable example in a letter from Marcus Aurelius
to Fronto. It was written in the course of one of those sojourns in the
country that were strongly recommended as moments of detachment in
comparison with public activities, as cures of health and as moments to
take care of oneself. One finds joined in this text the two themes of peas-
ant life, healthy because natural, and of the life of leisure dedicated to
conversation, reading, and meditation. At the same time, an entire set of
notations kept on the body, health, physical sensations, diet, and feelings
show the extreme vigilance of an attention that is intensely focused on
oneself.

> I am feeling well. I slept little because of a slight tremor, which ap-
> pears to have been calmed, however. I thus spent the time, from the
> early hours of the evening until three in the morning, in part reading
> Cato's *Agriculture* and in part writing successfully, but to tell the truth,
> less than yesterday. Then, after having greeted my father, I took
> some honeyed water in my throat, and in spitting it out I soothed
> my throat more than if I had "gargled," for I can use that word,
> following Novius and others. My throat restored, I went to my father
> and joined him at his sacrifice. Then we went to eat. On what do
> you think I dined? On a bit of bread, while I watched many others
> devouring oysters, onions, and very fat sardines. Afterwards, we set
> ourselves to harvesting the grapes; we sweated a lot, shouted a lot.
> At six o'clock we came back to the house. I studied some, without
> results; then I conversed a long time with my little mother, who was
> seated on the bed. . . . As we spoke that way, and as we argued about
> which of the two one of us loved best . . . the gong sounded and it
> was announced that my father had gone to bathe. Thus we had sup-
> per after we had bathed in the wine press; not that we bathed in the
> wine press, but after we bathed, we had supper and heard with plea-
> sure the joyous talk of the villagers. Having returned home, before
> turning on my side to sleep, I go through my task *[meum pensum ex-*

25. Seneca, *De la colère*, in *Dialogues*, trans. Abel Bourgery, 4 vols. (Paris, 1922–27),
1:102–3.

plico]; I make an account of my day to my sweetest of masters *[diei rationem meo suavissimo magistro reddo],* whom, were I to be consumed by it, I would love still more.[26]

The last lines of the letter show well how it is articulated with the practice of the examination of consciousness. The day ends, just before sleep, with a kind of reading of the day gone by. There one unfurls in thought the roll on which the activities of the day are inscribed, and it is this imaginary book of memory that is reproduced the next day in the letter addressed to the one who is at the same time master and friend. The letter to Fronto in a way transcribes the examination performed the evening before through the reading of the mental book of consciousness.

It is clear that one is still very far from that book of spiritual combat to which Athanasius, in his *Vita Antonii,* alludes some two centuries later. But one may also measure how much this process of the narration of the self in the dailiness of life, with very meticulous attention to what happens in the body and in the soul, is different from Ciceronian correspondence as well as from the practice of the *hupomnêmata,* a collection of things read and heard, and a prop for exercises of thought. In this case—that of the *hupomnêmata*—it is a matter of constituting oneself as the subject of rational action through the appropriation, unification, and subjectification of a fragmentary and carefully chosen already-said. In the case of monastic notation of spiritual experiences, it will be a matter of flushing out from the interior of the soul the most hidden movements so as to be able to free oneself from them. In the case of the epistolary narrative of oneself, it is a matter of coincidentally summoning the gaze of the other and that which one trains on oneself when one measures one's daily actions according to the rules of a technique of living.

26. Marcus Aurelius, lettre 6, in *Lettres inédites de Marc Aurele et de Fronton,* trans. André Cassan, 2 vols. (Paris, 1830), 2:249–51.

Contributors

Pascale-Anne Brault is assistant professor of French at DePaul University. She has written articles on contemporary French literature and drama and is currently working on a book on the revisioning of female identity in classical Greek literature.

Georges Canguilhem (1904–1996) was the director of the Institut d'Histoire des Sciences et des Techniques and professor at the University of Paris (Sorbonne). His works include *A Vital Rationalist: Selected Writings from Georges Canguilhem* (1994), *Ideology and Rationality in the History of the Life Sciences* (1988), and *The Normal and the Pathological* (1978).

Noam Chomsky is Institute Professor at the Massachusetts Institute of Technology. His many books include *Power and Prospects: Reflections on Human Nature and the Social Order* (1996), *The Minimalist Program* (1995), and *Aspects of the Theory of Syntax* (1965).

Arnold I. Davidson is professor of philosophy, divinity, and a member of the Committee on the Conceptual Foundations of Science at the University of Chicago. He has been a fellow of the Wissenschaftskolleg in Berlin and in 1997–1998 will hold a visiting professorship, *chaire d'État*, at the Collège de France. His forthcoming book is entitled *The Emergence of Sexuality: Historical Epistemology and the Formation of Concepts*. He is the executive editor of *Critical Inquiry*.

Gilles Deleuze (1925–1995) was professor of philosophy at the University of Paris VIII (Vincennes-St. Denis). His books include *Essays Critical and Clinical* (1997), with Félix Guattari, *Capitalism and Schizophrenia* (1987, 1983), and *Difference and Repetition* (1968).

Jacques Derrida is Directeur d'Études at the École des Hautes Études en Sciences Sociales in Paris and professor of French at the University of California, Irvine. Some of his most recent books include *Le Monolin-*

guisme de l'autre, ou, la prothèse d'origine (1996), *Specters of Marx* (1994), and *Memoirs of the Blind: The Self-Portrait and Other Ruins* (1993).

Michel Foucault (1926–1984) was professor of the History of Systems of Thought at the Collège de France. *Dits et écrits,* a four-volume collection of his writings, was published in 1994.

Pierre Hadot is professor emeritus of the History of Hellenistic and Roman Thought at the Collège de France. Among his works are *Philosophy as a Way of Life: Spiritual Exercises from Socrates to Foucault* (1995), *Qu'est-ce que la philosophie antique?* (1995), and *Plotinus, or the Simplicity of Vision* (1993).

Ann Hobart is a law student at the University of Arizona and a freelance translator. She has published essays on nineteenth-century British fiction and social criticism.

Felicia McCarren is assistant professor in the department of French and Italian at Tulane University. She is the author of articles on Mallarmé and Céline and is currently writing a book on dance and hysteria.

Michael Naas is associate professor of philosophy at DePaul University and the author of *Turning: From Persuasion to Philosophy* (1995). Along with Pascale-Anne Brault, he has translated, among other works, Jacques Derrida's *Memoirs of the Blind* (1993).

Catherine Porter, professor of French at State University of New York College at Cortland, has translated numerous authors, including Luce Irigaray, Tzvetan Todorov, and Shoshana Felman. Among her most recent translations is of Bruno Latour's *Aramis, or the Love of Technology* (1996).

Deniz Şengel is a Ph.D. candidate in comparative literature at New York University and a reader in cultural studies at Bosphorus University.

Michel Serres is professor of the history of science at the University of Paris (Sorbonne) and professor of French at Stanford University. A member of the Académie Française, he is the author of many books, including *The Natural Contract* (1995), *Rome: The Book of Foundations* (1991), and *Hermes: Literature, Science, Philosophy* (1982).

Daniel W. Smith recently received his Ph.D. in philosophy from the University of Chicago. He has translated Gilles Deleuze's *Francis Bacon: Logic of Translation* (1991) and Pierre Klossowski's *Nietzsche and the Vicious Circle* (forthcoming).

Peter Stastny is associate professor of psychiatry at Albert Einstein College of Medicine. He is currently editing a book on social relationships and recovery.

Paul Veyne is professor of the history of Rome at the Collège de France. His many works include *René Char en ses poèms* (1990), *Bread and Circuses: Historical Sociology and Political Pluralism* (1990), and *Did the Greeks Believe in Their Myths?* (1988). He is an editor of and contributor to volume 1 of *A History of Private Life* (1987).

Paula Wissing is a freelance translator and editor. She has translated Marcel Detienne and Jean-Pierre Vernant's *The Cuisine of Sacrifice among the Greeks* (1989).

Index